JOSEPH O'CONNOR

The Irish Male
at Home
and Abroad

Minerva

Grateful acknowledgement is made to the following for
permission to reproduce copyright material: from *The Female
Eunuch* by Germaine Greer, reproduced by permission of
HarperCollins on behalf of Germaine Greer, copyright ©
Germaine Greer, 1971; from 'Banana Republic: Recollections of
a Suburban Irish Childhood' by Joseph O'Connor, which first
appeared in *Idle Worship*, edited by Chris Roberts, reproduced
by permission of HarperCollins; from *Getting Married* by
George Bernard Shaw, reproduced by permission of the Society
of Authors on behalf of the Bernard Shaw estate; from *Matters of
Fact and Fiction*, reproduced by permission of Curtis Brown Ltd,
London on behalf of Gore Vidal, copyright © Gore Vidal, 1977;
from *Vile Bodies* by Evelyn Waugh, reproduced by permission of
Peters, Fraser and Dunlop; from 'Looking After Number One',
'Joey' and 'Banana Republic' by the Boomtown Rats, reproduced
by permission of Sherlock Holmes Music Ltd – Promostrat B. V.
The author and publishers have taken all possible care to trace
the copyright holders of the materials used in this book, and to
make acknowledgement of their use.

A Minerva Paperback
THE IRISH MALE AT HOME AND ABROAD

First published in Ireland 1996
by New Island Books
This Minerva edition published 1996
by Mandarin Paperbacks
an imprint of Reed International Books Limited
Michelin House, 81 Fulham Road, London SW3 6RB
and Auckland, Melbourne, Singapore and Toronto

Copyright © 1996 by Joseph O'Connor
The author has asserted his moral rights

www.minervabooks.com

A CIP catalogue record for this title
is available from the British Library
ISBN 0 7493 8688 6

Typeset in 10 on 13.5 point Trump Medieval
by CentraCet Limited, Cambridge
Printed and bound in Great Britain
by Cox & Wyman Ltd, Reading, Berkshire

The Irish Male
at Home and Abroad

Joseph O'Connor was born in Dublin in
1963. His début novel, *Cowboys and
Indians*, was short-listed for the Whitbread
Prize. His second novel, *Desperadoes*, his
collection of stories, *True Believers*, and his
non-fiction works, *The Secret World of the
Irish Male* and *Sweet Liberty: Travels in
Irish America*, have all received widespread
acclaim, as has his smash hit 1995 stage
play, *Red Roses and Petrol*.

Also by Joseph O'Connor

Fiction
Cowboys and Indians
True Believers
Desperadoes

Non-Fiction
The Secret World of the Irish Male
Sweet Liberty: Travels in Irish America

Drama
Red Roses and Petrol

Screenplays
A Stone of the Heart
The Long Way Home
Ailsa

For Aodghán Feeley,
with admiration

Probably the only place where a man can feel really secure is in a maximum security prison, except for the imminent threat of release.

The Female Eunuch, Germaine Greer

Contents

Introduction

MOST OF THE STUFF IN THIS BOOK WAS WRITTEN because somebody was either sufficiently kind or insane enough to ask me to write it. I'm grateful to the editors at such fine publications as *D'Side Magazine*, the *Observer*, the *Guardian*, *Elle*, *Cosmopolitan*, *Cara*, *Esquire*, the *Melbourne Age*, *Time Out*, the *Termonfeckin Picayune* and *Swedish Bikers Monthly* for picking up the telephone and persuading me to take a brief respite from researching my next novel – i.e. staring dolefully out the window and scratching my neck for hours at a time – in order to write something for them. Thanks must also be expressed to the good ladies and gentlemen at HarperCollins publishers for permission to reproduce the long article that concludes this tome from their own anthology *Idle Worship*, where it was first published in a slightly different form. The majority of pieces here appeared in shorter and considerably less offensive versions in the *Sunday Tribune*, Ireland's quality Sunday newspaper, it says here. So I guess there are one or two things I should explain.

There are several interesting aspects to writing a column for a weekly newspaper. The regular heartless beatings from the editor, for instance. Another interesting thing about writing a weekly column is that your column has to be written several days before the newspaper is actually published. My *Tribune* column, for example, is written on a Wednesday afternoon. It's supposed to be written on a Monday morning, but this is a simply ludicrous idea. It is all I can do to get out of the bed and give myself a bit of a wash on a Monday morning, never mind write anything. Thus, I have managed by stealth and begging to extend my *Tribune* deadline to Wednesday. It's still not great. Having to write on a Wednesday what will not be read until the following Sunday can make life difficult. I am the kind of person who changes his mind the way others change their Calvin Kleins. Five days is a long time for one such as myself to believe anything consistently. Or is it? I don't know. Yes, it is. Well, maybe not. (See what I mean?)

Newspapers presume an odd suspension of disbelief, wherein readers are invited to think that everything in the paper was written ten minutes before said paper was purchased. This is absolutely not the case. When, three years ago, I was first plucked from the hapless nostril of obscurity by the finger of fate and flicked to the almost laughable greatness of weekly *Tribune* journalism, I used to write my column on a Friday. This was a fine day for the penning of a column. A relaxed, speculative time of the week, good for the assembling of profound insights, dazzling perceptions and puerile double entendres. But now my deadline has changed. Now, every seven days, I arrive at Wednesday afternoon, that grey Athlone in the Midlands of the week, and I am often at a loss for where to turn next.

Take last year's divorce referendum, for example. It took place on a Thursday. My column on the subject had to be written the day before the vote, to be published three days after it. This is what is known in the jargon of the trade as a pain in the ass. I mean, consider my position. Imagine, if you will, it's the morning before the vote. There I am at the desk. I do not know if tomorrow a great blow will be struck for progress or whether the citizens of our poor windswept rock will have opted to spend another few decades in the late 1300s. The result will be announced on Saturday. Following this, I have no idea whether there will be a tremendous outpouring of either grief or beer *chez moi*. Whatever the outcome, my beloved readers will have their cherished personal views. If they are anti-divorce, and the vote was passed, no doubt they will already be deafened by the sound of the very fabric of society being reefed asunder, and they will have got hardly any sleep last night because the fornicating forces of evil will have been capering through the streets until dawn, led by the Whore of Babylon and Alan Shatter TD. If they are anti-divorce and the referendum was lost, they will be happy, and, in a spirit of reconciliation and Catholic charity, they will be offering rosaries for the eternal damnation of Mervyn Taylor. If they voted yes, and divorce was defeated, they will be pondering the effectiveness of that age-old Irish political strategy – a ballot paper in one hand and a Carmelite in the other. If they are pro-divorce and the referendum went their way, I don't know what they'll be doing. Booting out the husband before installing a member of the Chippendales, I suppose. Whatever. The point is, I don't know the result! And this is bad. Because I'm supposed to have a view on all this, as a columnist.

3

What am I supposed to do? Next week is too late. All the interest in divorce will have faded by then. Next week we will have moved on to something the media considers really important, such as the Beatles reforming. (And as Henry VIII once said, now that's what I call a *reformation*.)

So how am I supposed to do my job properly? How will I avoid being wrong and out-of-date with my column in future? One solution is for me to do books like this where I can go back and silently correct my mistakes and make myself look a lot more clever and perceptive than I actually was at the time. The only other solution is for me to start coming around to your house on a Sunday morning to discuss the news with you personally. Admittedly, the number of readers I could actually visit might be limited. But then, if Santa can get to all the boys and girls in one night, I'm sure I can get to all the *Sunday Tribune* readers in one morning. Yes. That's agreed then. Next Sunday, I'll be round to your gaff just after half-eleven Mass. So do remember to get the kettle on. Or not. Because, of course, by the time you read this, I'll probably have changed my mind.

In the meantime, I would like to thank the editor of the *Sunday Tribune*, Peter Murtagh, and all the staff at the paper for their unfailing kindness and help, particularly those in the magazine department. I know calling it 'the magazine department' makes it sound like the kind of mammoth and smoke-filled open-plan office alive with the stuttering of a hundred typewriters which you see in the Alan J. Pakula film *All the President's Men*, whereas, in point of fact, it is two relatively quiet and calm rooms at the end of a narrow corridor. But still. Many thanks to the magazine department, for giving me ideas, for giving

4

me cigarettes and for allowing me come into the office sometimes and look through the mail and peer at the computer screen like I understand it and loudly say newspaper stuff like 'deadline' and 'colour piece' and 'sub-editor' and, indeed, 'magazine department' and fantasise that I am a real journalist called 'Scoop'. (Look, I don't get out of the house much, OK?) A special obsequious crawl of gratitude must go to magazine editor Ros Dea for her ineffable wonderfulness in the face of my persistent lateness with copy, my shameless recycling of jokes used two years ago and my quite laughably lame excuses for demanding weeks off at the very last minute.

Many thanks are also due to Anne-Marie Casey, to my family and friends for ideas, to Edwin Higel, Bairbre Drury Byrne and Billy Doran at New Island Books for their constant help, friendliness and professionalism, to Tony Glavin, a most thoughtful and scrupulous editor, and to everyone at Reed Books in London for their commitment and support, which I truly appreciate. Finally I would like to thank my bank manager and all the helpful people in the Overdue Accounts Departments at Visa Card, American Express, the ESB, Bord Telecom, Bord Gais, Cablelink and my car insurance company for their many letters over the years, encouraging me to keep right on working. Couldn't have done it without you, guys.

Chapter 1

Getting to Know the Lord

'*The Peerage* is one book a young man about town should know thoroughly. It is the best thing in fiction the English have ever done.'

A Woman of No Importance, Oscar Wilde

IT IS JUST AFTER THREE-THIRTY ON A RAINY LONDON Monday afternoon and the moment is fast approaching for which God put me on the earth and made me a journalist. After all the years of suffering and loneliness and poverty, all the relentless hackery, all the unappreciated experimental theatre reviews and the failed feature article ideas, I am here. It's the big time. I am in Lord Jeffrey Archer's bathroom! *LOOK AT ME, MA. I'M ON TOPPA DA WOILD!!* Not the bathroom of his country residence, the old vicarage, Grantham, once inhabited by the poet Rupert Brooke. No, I am in one of Lord Archer's other bathrooms, the one so elegantly surrounded by his luxury penthouse flat on the banks of the River Thames. It is, it must be said, a very nice bathroom indeed. And my proudest moment is coming soon. But I am not enjoying myself.

I am so nervous at the prospect of meeting my hero. I close my eyes and take deep breaths. I open my eyes again. I pace the floor. I try to whistle. I notice suddenly, for some reason, that there is hardly any bog roll. But

7

that's OK. Nothing to worry about there. I do, after all, have a copy of Lord Archer's latest book, *Twelve Red Herrings*, in my holdall. If the worst comes to the worst. Not that you would actually use *Twelve Red Herrings* for that particular purpose. And I really do mean that sincerely, folks.

I pace the floor again, relentless anxiety flickering through my nerve endings. I am so thirsty. There is no glass. I turn on the cold tap and try to get my mouth underneath it. I accidentally splash water all down my front. It is all a disaster. I try again. I actually have to crane my neck and pucker my lips and put them around the end of the tap and suck. Good God in heaven, I am sucking the cold tap of the most popular novelist in Britain! It just doesn't get very much better than this.

Getting in to see Lord Archer was a bit of a big deal. I turned up five minutes early and explained myself to the laconic concierge, who showed me into the lift and pressed the button. 'When the lift stops,' he intoned, gravely, 'just push the door. And you will be in Lord Archer's apartment.' Hey, the man has his own lift door. That's how rich he is. His own lift door! I don't even have my own ironing board.

'Good afternoon,' one assistant said, as the door opened.

'Welcome,' the other said.

'Can I use the bathroom?' I said.

But I am so nervous now that I cannot actually pee. The knowledge that there is nothing but wall space between an author of Lord Archer's godlike magnitude and my own lowly self is making me so tense that my urethra is practically prehensile. Lord Archer's soap! My God, Lord Archer's towels!

Look, this man is really famous. He is the cultural

8

wing of the Conservative Party. He is to the modern Tories what Jean-Jacques Rousseau was to Abraham Lincoln. And then there's all his famous mates to consider, too. I mean, Lord Archer has some pretty glitzy and influential friends, you know. And he's well known for the posh society parties he throws here in his luxurious gaff. So who knows what noses have been briskly powdered within these walls? Who knows who has slugged down the champers and popped in here to Jeffrey's jacks for a spot of quick relief over the years? Perhaps John Major himself has pointed the Prime Ministerial percy at this particular porcelain? And which of that shower of Tory bastards, to use Mr Major's affectionate term for his colleagues, have had a satisfying tinkle in here? Perhaps Cecil Parkinson has gingerly lifted this very seat? Perhaps Michael 'Tarzan' Heseltine has rearranged his Little Richard hairstyle in that very mirror? Perhaps, oh my God, perhaps even Mrs (now of course Lady) Thatcher has . . . no, no, I'd better stop. The excitement really is getting too much for me. And anyway, I am now ready to meet The Lord.

I complete my ablutions and venture out, down a long corridor hung with framed political cartoons and into Lord Archer's living room. I stop in my tracks. The living room is bigger than my entire flat. If you were to fart now, perchance, no matter how discreetly, there would be a resounding echo. There are white armchairs and big fat sofas, two huge glass coffee tables piled high with art books. There are paintings on the walls, a large English classical scene and a couple of L. S. Lowry oils. Through a half-open door I can see a bedroom containing an enormous canopied four-poster bed of the type I feel sure Madonna must own.

An efficient young woman comes in and asks if there is anything I would like. What a question. An immediate and rather totalitarian communist revolution, I am thinking, but all I say, cringing moral coward that I am, is 'A glass of water, please.'

'Fizzy?' she enquires.

'Yeah,' I say. 'Fizzy.' (I don't want to appear unsophisticated. I am in with the literary set now, after all.)

From somewhere above me I hear Lord Archer's booming voice. I look up and see that the apartment is designed in what I believe is called in polite society the 'split-level' manner. He is up above me, where he belongs, on the telephone, discussing, no doubt, some contract or another. 'Right,' he keeps saying. 'Yes. Right. Now look, this is too important to get wrong, OK?'

I chew my nails. With a sudden and terrible start I realise that I want to go to the toilet again. I wonder if the bathroom is vacant, or if it's being cleaned by the butler. But it's too late. Lord Archer descends the stairs with the proud grace and swanlike majesty of Scarlett O'Hara in a Savile Row suit. I proudly shake the very hand that wrote *Kane and Abel* and *Not a Penny More, Not a Penny Less*.

Lord Archer is surprisingly small. He is well preserved and lightly tanned and a little chubby around the midriff. He looks a bit tired today. Perhaps he has been counting his money. I wonder, just for a moment, whether this is the correct moment to ask him if his toilet is vacant. Perhaps not. But even if his toilet is not vacant, his oleaginous smile certainly is. Hey, it's a swings and roundabouts thing.

I sit on one of the big sofas and Lord Archer sinks into an armchair, putting his feet up on the coffee table. He puts on his glasses and reads over the letter he has received from the *Sunday Tribune*, requesting this interview. The letter mentions in passing that I know his editor at HarperCollins, the London publishing house that has just signed him up for a multi-million-pound three-book deal.

'How d'you know Stuart?' he says. 'Were you at college with him?'

'No,' I simper. 'I used to be published by him.'

'What do you write then?' he says.

'Novels,' I say.

He looks at me, beaming, his eyebrows raised. 'Do you?' he says. 'Do you really? Well, well, well.' He regards me the way senior members of the British Royal Family regard Rastafarians from the inner city whom they occasionally have to meet at charity functions. 'Do you? Really. How marvellous. Well, well. How marvellous for you.'

Lord Archer is wearing a beautifully cut two-piece tin of fruit, an immaculate shirt, a red-cream-and-blue striped tie and glittering gold cufflinks shaped like the House of Commons portcullis. He is nicely turned out, but his black shoes are in need of a good polish. For some odd reason, this does not surprise me at all.

I take a deep breath and kick off by asking his Lordship to tell me about an average day's writing.

'I rise,' he says, 'at about five in the morning.' (You see? Greatness already. You and me, being peasants, get up. But Lord Archer 'rises'. What a marvellous sight it must be, Lord Archer rising at five in the morning.) 'I work from six until eight. Ten until twelve. Two until four. Six until eight. Go to bed about nine-thirty, ten. Get up at five the next morning. I will do that for a first draft, which takes about six weeks, every word handwritten, and then I will do probably, oh, the last book was fifteen drafts, every one handwritten, and took two years. So it's a long, tough process. Anyone who imagines' – suddenly stops and beams at me – 'I am not saying this to *you*, Joe, I am saying it to your readers – anyone who imagines that you can knock a novel off is living in a dream world.'

But people do imagine that, I point out. People often say, 'God, I'm so broke, I think I'll knock off a crap bestseller and make lots of money.' And then they usually say, 'Look at that Jeffrey Archer. He makes millions out of his books and they're a load of atrocious auld blather.'

Lord Archer casts his eyes towards the heavens and smiles tolerantly at the pure idiocy of these poor imbecilic creatures, before shrugging manfully and shooting me an all-boys-together glance of artistic solidarity.

'Ah well,' he says. '*You* know only too well, Joe, eh?'

'Oh yes,' I say. 'Yes, Lord Archer. I do.'

He joins his fingertips and chortles again, at the ludicrous idea that anybody might think he actually spends all year long in his four-poster scratcher and then writes his books in a weekend. 'I think the easier it looks, the more convinced they are they can do it. And if they realised how much work went into making it look easy, they wouldn't say those things. To be fair, Joe, there are several of my friends who have tried. They say' – His Lordship affects devastatingly hilarious 'cockney' accent at this point – '"Oi've known Jeffery all me life. Oi'll 'ave a go." And they had the courtesy, in some cases, and the good manners to say, "It is not as easy as it looks."' (Snorts with laughter.) 'Otherwise everyone would be doing it!'

He has the most amazing laugh. HAHAHAHAHA. If you crossed a burst of machine-gun fire with the sound of a steroid-stuffed woodpecker attacking a tree, you would come up with something not unlike Lord Archer's laugh.

'I don't enjoy writing,' he confides. 'I find it very hard work.' Now, I must say that this surprises me greatly. I have been keenly studying his ample *oeuvre* in preparation for meeting him, and, God, now, I would have sworn that any author who could actually pen the immortal sentence 'Only a blind man could have missed what was likely to happen next, and although I might not have been blind, I certainly turned a blind eye' was utterly in love with the myriad possibilities of the English language.

Other people – knockers, has-beens, philistines and left-wing lesbian-loving begrudgers – seem to think his books are a steaming pile of fetid guano. But not me. I love them. Lord Archer is quite rightly celebrated for all his famous charity work, but nothing to me is quite as charitable as his writing. There is, for instance, no clapped-out and unfortunate old cliché so hackneyed that Lord Archer will not find a good home for it. Consider the story 'Trial and Error', the opening salvo of *Twelve Red Herrings*. 'The hours turned into days, the days into weeks, the weeks into...'? You guessed it. 'Months.' What is the hero's friend as good as? 'His word.' What hours did the hero work? 'All the hours God sent.' What are Yorkshire men well known for? 'For being blunt.' What do crime reporters turn up to court in? 'Their hordes.' (Not their taxis.) What do they follow every word of the trial with? 'With relish', of course. And with mustard and mayonnaise, too, I suppose.

For me, the playfully ironic use of language is what is ultimately most impressive about the maestro's style. 'I devoured them hungrily,' the hero tells us, of his fish and chips. (Like, how else would you devour something?) 'I was put in a cell with a petty criminal called Fingers Jenkins. Can you believe, as we approach the twenty-first century, that anyone could still be called Fingers?' Well, the answer to that is a very firm, 'No, I couldn't, Lord Archer, we stopped giving fictitious criminals names like Fingers very shortly after Charles Dickens departed the corporeal realm.' You see, a thing like that would give a lesser author cause for mild concern, yet it didn't stop Lord Archer. Oh, no. He is truly an artist who blazes, as he would say himself, his own trail. He paddles his own canoe, he has his nose to the grindstone, his back to the wheel, his head on the ground and his feet in the clouds. Not only does he bring his literary horse to water, but he also makes it, in a very real sense, drink. And every word handwritten, too.

'I can't type,' he explains. 'I don't know how to use any machinery.' It is a very long time indeed since I have heard a typewriter described as 'machinery'. Again, again, the revolutionary use of language. 'Also, I have a feeling at the end of a six-week session, it's ... it's ... it's a bit puritanical, but I have the feeling that I have done it. It is my work. It doesn't belong to anyone else.' He pauses and nods and beams at me. 'I like that,' he says. I reflect that if there's one thing Lord Archer shouldn't worry his fluffy little head about, it's the possibility of other authors anywhere in the whole wide world claiming that his work belongs to them, and not him.

Lord Archer in conversation has two expressions. There is the smile, of course. He smiles like a man who has had emergency corrective facial surgery in a Third World country. And then there is the serious, concerned look. This means not smiling, basically, and knotting up his eyebrows, and sometimes removing his spectacles and sucking on the bit that goes over the ear. When I ask him to tell me some of his views on the short story form, he flips into serious mode. The eyebrows are so knotted they are practically Gordian. The spectacles are so thoroughly sucked they are nearly hyperventilating.

'Well, I think I am a storyteller first and foremost. I mean, lots of people write short stories. And they're not short stories at all. They're described in the press as, you know, so-and-so-and-so-and-so, the world-famous author, has written twelve short stories. Often they're twelve essays. Or twelve very well-written pieces. But short stories are . . .'

I lean forward, waiting for enlightenment.

'Short stories . . . they have to be stories. H. H. Monroe wrote stories. Maupassant wrote stories. Ummmm, Somerset Maugham wrote stories. Graham Greene even. Fitzgerald even.'

Gosh. As I listen to Lord Archer, I am practically overcome with gratitude for his revealing so kindly and incisively to me that Scott Fitzgerald wrote stories. I pick up my copy of *Twelve Red Herrings* and flick through it while he expounds. Actually, I just want to take my eyes off his spectacles, which by now are so moist they are practically orgasmic. I must confess, it is a tad difficult to detect the influence of Scott Fitzgerald and Guy de Maupassant on such delicate examples of the Archerian prose style as the following:

> Under the terms of the flotation, fifty-one per cent of the shares would be retained by Rosemary and myself. Jeremy explained to me that for tax reasons they should be divided equally between us. My accountants agreed, and at the time I didn't give it a second thought. The

> remaining 4,900,000 one pound shares were quickly
> taken up by institutions and the general public, and
> within days of the company being listed on the stock
> exchange their value had risen to £2.80.

This, again, is from 'Trial and Error'. As is the following little gem: 'Funny, it wasn't the fact that Jeremy had been sleeping with my wife that caused me to snap, but that he had the arrogance to think he could take over my company as well.' Cracking stuff, huh? *Tender is the Night*, roll over and die. When I place the book with reverence back down on the coffee table and look at Lord Archer again, the spectacles too are on the table (smoking a cigarette and asking how was it for you?) and their owner is still wittering on about stories. 'Stories. Stories. Yes, other people write . . . ummm . . . essays. And write very erudite important pieces. And they're not stories. I tell a story, you see. So they're certainly stories . . . You see, a story, to me . . .'

(Sheesh, I guess what the guy's saying here is, he writes *stories*, OK?) I ask whether people ever come up to him and tell him anecdotes as raw material for his . . . er . . . stories.

'Yes.' He shakes his head and closes his eyes and does his tolerant smile again. 'But I'm afraid ninety-nine out of a hundred are useless. I was just on a tour of Australia and New Zealand. And I foolishly said in one speech, "I'm always searching for a good short story." And three people came up to me afterwards and told me three of the most pathetic stories I've ever heard in my life. And I had to smile and be polite.'

I convey my sympathies. It must be awful, I imagine, having to deal with a whole room full of over-excited Jeffrey Archer fans, particularly in an Antipodean climate. 'But sometimes someone gives you an absolute gem,' he says, 'like "Cheap at Half the Price".' (This shattering masterpiece is about a woman who tricks her husband and her lover into each forking out half a million pounds to buy her a necklace. I felt it was very reminiscent of early Kafka, with faint echoes of late Enid Blyton.)

'I mean,' Lord Archer continues, 'a girl stopped me in the street just straight after lunch.' ('Girls' seem to stop Lord Archer in the street quite often, the lucky old bounder.) 'And she said, "The whole of New York is talking about 'Cheap at Half the Price'. And everybody wants to know who the girl is." And I said, "Well, that's very flattering." She said, "We're all asking each other 'Who is this amazing Consuela Rosenheim?'"'

Funny, that. I had just been lying awake in a lather of sweat every night for six weeks asking myself the same question.

All this stuff is so extraordinary that it is almost impressive. Lord Archer really does expect you to swallow that in the week in which we are having this conversation, the week of the beginning of the O. J. Simpson trial and Gerry Adams' first visit to America, 'the whole of New York' is discussing his book. It is a quite remarkable and utterly convincing pantomime of self-belief. 'But why do you write, Lord Archer?' I say, in a heartfelt manner. 'I mean, *why*? Do you ever ask yourself that?'

He ponders for a moment. He gives the specs another good lick. 'It's certainly not for the money,' he assures me, fervently. 'I don't need any more. I could live out of this country, of course, and not pay my tax. Or I could have yachts and dancing girls . . . But I don't.'

'Oh, no,' I say. 'As if.'

'So,' he says, 'I don't write for money. I have enough to last me the rest of my life. And more than I need. Far more than I need. I don't want that printed, because then I'll have a thousand begging letters the next day, but as you can see looking here' (he gestures around the digs with a faintly regal flick of the wrist), 'as you can see, I don't need any more. So it's not the money.'

So what is it? He purses his lips and shrugs and attempts a kind of aw-shucks-little-boy-lost grin.

'I do enjoy people stopping me in the street in every country. In every country on earth. That is thrilling, Joe. And anyone who says it isn't is a nut. And in your country in particular, if I walk down O'Connell Street, I mean, I can't get from one end of O'Connell Street, you know, to the other in under two hours. In under two hours!! Without them coming up to me and going' (closes eyes and grits his teeth), '"Wah wah wah wah wah wah wah wah wah." And they all go at you. And I love it.'

This is actually the noise Lord Archer makes. Wah wah wah wah wah wah wah wah. He sounds like either a runaway police car or a former member of The Supremes. I am very concerned about this. I mean, I actually *live* in Dublin and nobody has ever come up to me in O'Connell Street and gone 'wah wah wah wah wah wah', for even five minutes, never mind two whole hours. A terrible thought strikes me. These people coming up to Lord Archer in O'Connell Street and going 'wah wah wah wah wah wah' for several hours at a time, thereby preventing the poor man from going about his proper business – are they really his fans, or are they in point of fact deranged and potentially violent smackheads prematurely released from custody?

But he loves it, he says. There is nothing in life really better than being stopped in the street by his fans and listening to them go 'wah wah wah wah wah wah' at him. It makes all the hard work worthwhile. He seems to have a huge need to be liked, I say. Does he have any idea why this is?

'It's just human, isn't it?'

Well, yes, I concede, it may be just a human need, but Lord Archer does seem to have it big time, with extra mayo and fries to go.

'Yes, well, if you take the trouble to write, you want people to enjoy it. Aren't you the same, Joe?'

'Well, I suppose so.'

'HAHAHA,' he laughs. 'Yes. You see. HAHAHA. HAHAHA.'

When I take my fingers out of my ears, and the dull ringing sound eventually recedes, I suggest that surely there's more to it than this. Perhaps, I suggest, Lord Archer is trying to compensate for something. Did he have a happy childhood?

'Yes. Very. In Weston-Super-Mare.'

And what about this chap who keeps popping up in the papers these days, claiming to be Lord Archer's long-lost brother?

'What about him?'

'Well, is he? Your brother?'

'I don't know. He might be. He might not. I haven't met him.'

'He says he met you at a cricket match a few years ago.'

Lord Archer shrugs. 'I meet a lot of people. People come up to me, Joe, every day, you know, and they say all sorts of things to me.'

'Things like, I'm your long-lost brother?' (Or things, I ponder, like wah wah wah wah wah wah wah?)

He shrugs, and gazes in silence at his fingernails.

'So you don't really know whether or not you're an only child.'

'I am,' he says. 'I think I am.'

I point out to him that the mystery of the disappearing brother is symptomatic of a problem I encountered often while researching this interview. The facts of Lord Archer's early life tend to get shifted more often than an attractive junior researcher at the Tory Party annual conference. Did he, for example, attend Brazenose College, Oxford?

For the first time during our conversation, the smile fades. Lord Archer looks a trifle miffed. The handsome face is attempting to work its muscles back into grin mode, but it's not quite succeeding. It's all coming out instead as a rather disquieting leer. Lord Archer looks like an irritated Muppet. 'Call them,' he says. 'You just ring them up later and ask them.'

'Why can't you just tell me?' I ask.

'No, no, no,' he says, still attempting to grin. 'You just ring them. It will only cost twenty pence. You ring them and see what they say.'

He fiddles with his wedding ring, twisting, twisting. He takes it off and pops it from palm to palm as though it is suddenly very hot to the touch.

'Call them,' he says.

'Alright, I will,' I say.

'Good,' he says. 'You do that. You ring them.'

It seems like a good moment to stop. I have taken enough of the great man's time. There are stories to be written, after all, and begging letters to be answered. I

20

hang around for a few minutes, wondering if there is something I could steal and watching the photographer arrange Lord Archer by the window so that we can see the House of Commons and the Thames in the background. His Lordship looks very comfortable indeed in this pose. You even begin to suspect that he might have done it a few times before. What a guy. What an old pro. (Not that Lord Archer would know anything about old pros, of course. Old prose, maybe. But old pros, no.)

And we are just leaving, the photographer and I, when a funny thing happens. There is a big white statue out in the hall, by the lift, and the photographer asks very politely if he can take a picture of Lord Archer beside this statue.

'No, no,' Lord Archer snaps. 'You can't photograph that. That's my wife's. Not mine. You can't photograph it!!'

I am halfway down in the lift before it occurs to me. What a genuinely strange thing that was to say. But then, I guess that's The Lord for you, ain't it? They do say he moves in mysterious ways.

Chapter 2

Live and Let Diet

NOW LOOK HERE, I'M A NEW MAN. I AM. SWEAR TO GOD. I can express my feelings. I am in touch with my feminine side, my inner child, my personal karma. I cry at films. I iron my socks. I hug trees so hard there's been a bit of talk in the neighbourhood. You name it, I do it. And yet, and yet, here I am walking into Brown Thomas to get my first-ever facial massage feeling every bit as calm as a condemned criminal about to ascend the scaffold.

What the hell is wrong with me? I am sweating. I am nervous. I have chewed my fingernails down to the knuckles. If the cheeks of my bum were clamped together any more tightly I'd be able to crack walnuts with them. Why?

Yes, yes, yes, I know Irish men are uneasy about looking after their skin. Of course they are. This, of course, is because of our historical role models. Would Patrick Pearse have had a facial massage? Would Eamon De Valera? Would they heck. Yet the truth is, we've all had a surreptitious little dab in the mott's cold-cream when she hasn't been looking. So it isn't a macho thing with me, oh, no. I think I'm uneasy because I'm putting myself into the hands of experts. Like most Irish people, I'm uneasy about experts. This is because I don't know what they're going to find out about me. Plumbers, doctors, washing-machine repair guys, it's always the same. They always make me feel embarrassed. Is the woman who's going to massage my face going to take one look, throw up her hands in horror, shriek piercingly and accuse me of treating my epidermis the way my mechanic says I treat my car? I've assumed, of course, that it's going to be a woman. In fact, my masseur turns out to be a bloke called Dave, who is from Manchester. As I shake hands with Dave, the full import of this descends on me. My God Almighty. In a few minutes' time, a Mancunian is going to be stroking my face. I cannot tell you how calm this makes me feel.

We go into a little white room which has the soft redolence of a dentist's surgery. Good God Almighty, is this guy gonna massage my face or do a bit of emergency root-canal work? I take off my jacket and lie down on the table. Dave puts a towel around my neck and tells me to relax. I whinny with high-pitched laughter. I'm now so relaxed I'm speaking in a soprano voice so striking that Dame Kiri Te Kanawa would be emerald green with envy.

He starts by telling me he's going to wash my face. Fine. I've even been known to do that myself sometimes, I tell him. He produces a bar of soap which costs nine pounds. Nine pounds?! I wouldn't spend nine pounds on a shirt! Dave grins beatifically. It costs nine pounds but it lasts you nine months, he says. He himself has a bar that has lasted a year. I can't help hoping that it ain't the one he's going to use on me.

I close my eyes and wait. I feel the lather being smeared

23

all over my kisser. It's not too bad. Damn it all, it's quite nice actually. Dave's dextrous fingers knead and pummel my puss until it tingles. Then he washes off the soap and smears on this gel-like substance which exfoliates the skin. Exfoliation is a polite word for scraping. If any of you guys have ever snogged somebody without having shaved yourself properly beforehand, 'exfoliated' is the correct scientific term for the way they look afterwards.

The exfoliating jelly is then removed from my boat race, which is now tingling so exquisitely that it feels like it's got pins and needles. A new lather is efficiently prepared and thickly plastered onto me. Dave explains that this is a revolutionary and special kind of shaving foam that moisturises your skin while softening your stubble. It's an absolutely vital product, Dave says. Indeed, you think, how in the name of God above did our grandfathers manage without it? While he is massaging this into me, he enquires whether there's anything I'd like to ask him about my face. I wonder where to start. Why couldn't it have been Alec Baldwin's, for instance. Dave titters dutifully.

Off comes the shaving foam. At this stage my mug feels pink and naked as a baby's bum. But we are not finished yet. Dave purses his lips in a disconcertingly thoughtful manner. He feels that I need a bit of anti-ageing treatment. I have one or two tension wrinkles, he tells me. I didn't when I woke up this morning, I reply. They must have burst splendidly forth the minute I walked into BT's. He produces a bottle of lotion and briskly uncaps it. This is the business, he says. If you use this stuff for three days it makes your skin look forty-five per cent younger. I am thirty-two years old now, so forty-five per cent younger, in my case, would make me look about seventeen and a half. I am not so sure I want to look seventeen and a half again. When I actually *was* seventeen and a half, I had acne so bad that my face looked like the surface of the moon. Still, Dave is not to be discouraged. On goes the anti-ageing cream, like icing onto a Christmas cake. I lie back and feel it seeping into my cells. When it comes off, I don't really look forty-five per cent younger, but I have to say, I feel it.

The whole process takes about forty minutes and I'd warmly recommend it. It is every bit as relaxing, calming, soothing and pleasurable as being touched by a Mancunian can be. And as forms of exfoliation go, it's definitely the second best in the world.

But then you can't help wondering: what is the point of having a face as soft as a new dishcloth if the rest of you is not up to scratch? Look at me, for God's sake. I am out of shape, out of kilter, out of energy and almost out of time. When I was young I loved displaying my body to the world. These days I am afraid to lie on a beach in case I get hit on the head with a bottle of champagne and launched by President Robinson. In college I was thin and lithe and svelte. These days I could wear my stomach as a very attractive kilt.

This is the reason why I have been on a strict diet since the start of this year, and I must say it's been going quite well. I did have a weak moment recently when I read an article about liposuction, a revolutionary new technique where you pay to have a small incision made in your body through which your fat is sucked out. I was initially very excited about this, and, indeed, had managed to make contact with Elle MacPherson's agent. But then, on further research, I discovered that you have no control whatsoever over who does the sucking, and, indeed, where they make the incision. So I decided to abandon that thought and continue with more traditional methods of weight loss.

And it's been tough, I have to say. For breakfast I am allowed an egg. That's it. One egg – as in hen, not ostrich – and a cup of tea or coffee. An egg might sound healthy to you, but I feel sure it is not. I feel sure that an egg just lies around in your stomach all day, fervently attracting dangerous corkscrew-shaped microbes and wicked intestinal parasites which would look under a microscope the way Noel Gallagher of Oasis looks in real life.

Anyway, egg consumed, I get down to the day's work. Boy, am I in a good mood? I mean, who needs a big plate of sausages, bacon, beans, mushrooms, and black and white pudding (swoon) when you can have a whole egg?! My energy levels are so gasp-makingly high at this stage that I can work for a full twenty-five minutes before having to go back to bed in a darkened room with the duvet over my head and a bottle of gin.

When I get up again, my 'mid-morning snack' is 'one cup of coffee'. Phew! I am so bloated by now that I have to tickle my tonsils with a peacock feather and make myself throw up.

For lunch I am allowed a crispbread and a tomato. Great, huh? I explained to my ferociously expensive dietician that a tomato might make a very agreeable lunch for a rabbit, but not for a fully grown adult male human. She smiled the smile of a woman around whose waist a small bracelet could be comfortably accommodated, and explained that, of course, I would sometimes be allowed to deviate from this dietary purgatory. If it is my birthday, I am allowed to masturbate briefly over a

26

photograph of a bowl of tiramisu. If it is a Sunday, or a big family occasion, I am permitted to be lightly spanked on the arse with a piece of steak. On big family occasions I am also allowed to smear myself with mayonnaise or sink my fingers into a bowl of custard and wiggle them about for two minutes.

Mid-afternoon comes around then. Now, I don't know about you, but what I feel like around three o'clock is a smoked cod and chips with a side order of onion rings, a large slice of chocolate cake and several pints of Guinness. What I am allowed to have, however, is 'a piece of fruit'. For the first week of my diet I took 'a piece of fruit' to mean an entire melon, or perhaps a pineapple, including the skin and the leaves and a good chunk of the bark. But no, my patient dietary adviser advised. 'A piece of fruit' means a small piece of fruit. 'Like a kiwi fruit or a piece of mango or something simple like that.' Good God. Any woman who considers a piece of mango something simple has a very bizarre notion indeed of simplicity and clearly does not live in a neighbourhood where the local supermarket is a Dunnes Stores. (Mind you, for the money she's charging to put me through this misery the woman could buy her own mango plantation.) An apple or an orange is what something simple means to me. It takes, oh, a whole fifteen seconds to delicately wolf this down and a further two minutes to masticate the fuck out of the pips.

After this, the hours between mid-afternoon and dinner do tend to drag, I must say. However, I have discovered a good way of quelling hunger pangs, which is to smoke lots and lots of cigarettes. Thus, in the name of fitness, I shall probably die of lung cancer or coronary thrombosis at the age of forty. The fact that at least my coffin will not have to be carried by the former East German shot-put team is, of course, some consolation.

Dinner, when it arrives, is a veritable banquet. A bowl of clear soup or Bovril (yeah, Bovril!), followed by six ounces of meat or fish and either a salad or 'a portion of vegetables'. Now, my feeling about Bovril is that there is only one circumstance wherein it makes an attractive meal, and that is if you are halfway up Mount Everest and so fucking cold that you are seriously contemplating sliding into a sleeping bag with Chris Bonnington. And as for six ounces of meat or fish, well, six ounces might sound like a lot to you, but let me just put that in perspective. This book weighs about six ounces. The salad, needless to say, must be as undressed as a newborn infant. The portion of vegetables has to be small enough to fit in a leprechaun's condom. Dessert is a heaped spoonful of natural yoghurt. Yum, yum. I am told by some of my women friends that a heaped spoonful of natural yoghurt makes a very effective treatment for certain vaginal infections, and I am indeed glad to hear this, because it certainly doesn't make a very effective dessert.

My lithe dietician has recommended all sorts of ways of getting used to hunger, such as not thinking about food, drinking lots of water and going to bed early. But I find that rolling around on the floor and crying hysterically for several hours at a time helps, too. For supper – I ask you, *supper*, how can the skinny cow sleep at night? – I am allowed a crispbread with a slice of cucumber. All this for six months so far, and I have lost half a stone. Off my bloody wallet.

But people are very supportive when you are on a diet. They stop you in the street and offer you diets of their own for consideration. A sweet thought, but I need a new diet right now like a moose needs a hat stand. I am on the Saddam Hussein of all diets. My daily calorific intake is equivalent to that of a fully grown adult gnat, but I think it is working. I have lost seven pounds, and believe me, I have suffered a staggering purgatory for every single measly ounce. And while it is not yet quite true that you would see more meat on a butcher's bike on a Friday afternoon than you would on my detumescent midriff, I am making progress, and for this I must be thankful.

Yet the thing is, a diet will only take you so far. My dietary adviser told me recently that the time had now come for exercise. I had to 'give my metabolism something to really think about', she said. I assured her that my metabolism had plenty to think about, large plates of steak and chips in particular. But she didn't even laugh. This woman has actually studied the molecular composition of cellulite, and I guess that does peculiar things to your sense of humour. But anyway, I took her advice, and thus it was that I found myself recently signing up for the 'Bums'N'Tums' aerobics class in the gymnasium frequented by my sister.

Now, to say that the aerobics instructor was not exactly a rocket scientist would be something of an understatement. He was, in fact, thick as shite in a bucket. For some reason or another the women in the class seemed to have taken to him, but I really couldn't figure this out. The fact that he had the face of Gabriel Byrne, and that his body looked like it had been chiselled by the late Michelangelo Buonarroti out of a large block of granite, made absolutely no difference to my assessment of him. I mean, there's so much more to sexual attractiveness than pretty cheek-bones, rippling thighs, outstandingly defined buttocks, stunningly perfect triceps, enviable pectorals, etc., etc. Personality and a good sense of humour are so much more important in the long run, myself and the only other male member of the class agreed afterwards, as we soaped down our spare tyres in the communal shower. But we weren't too critical of our instructor, because, poor man, the prominent bulge in his lycra trousers had almost certainly been caused by a distressing sporting injury of some sort.

Let me tell you, I was glad the aerobics session was over. There is something disconcerting about hopping maniacally around a dimly lit hall, hyperventilating to the strains of 2 Live Crew while trying not to let your track-suit bottoms fall down. 'Work that body,' the instructor kept bawling, 'come on, girls, let's funky things up here!' Now, you can credibly say things like that if (a) you come from South Central Los Angeles, or (b) you are a member of Spinal Tap. But this chap sounded like he came from South Central Stillorgan. He strutted about the hall like a peacock on steroids barking 'yeah' and 'I loik it' and 'yeah, yeah, dew it to me, baby!' in his Dortland accent, while we bounced around the walls like sweat-soaked little steel ball bearings in a broken-down pinball machine. Then, as I lepped about wishing fervently that I was dead, he sauntered over and glared at me with his hands on his scrawny hips. He let out a hollow sardonic laugh. 'Kick thews legs,' he said. If I had kicked them any higher I could have been taken for one of the Tiller Girls with a bad case of rabies. But he was not happy. I noticed that he shook his head sadly from side to side as he chortled at my efforts. Then he opened his mouth and screamed, 'Come ON! You're not troying! I said go for the burn, Joe!' If only he had said, 'Go for a pint of Guinness and a kebab,' I would have been so happy to concur.

When the class was over I lay on the floor of the changing room and thought about my life. How had any of this happened. One day you are young, trim, hopeful, the next you are being bawled out by a suburban troglodyte who thinks he's one of The Temptations. I staggered to my feet and weighed myself. I had lost two ounces. Two whole ounces! I put my clothes on and went straight to the pub, where I had a pint of lager and a packet of crisps. And that, I feel sure, gave my metabolism something to bloody think about.

Jogging was the next thing I tried. Readers who have tried this themselves will know full well that there is one truly important thing about jogging, which is, make sure you get the correct equipment. I am not talking about the pricey runners, the baggy knickerbockers, the attractive sweatband in imitation 'towelling' material and the lurid garment proudly announcing: 'My girlfriend went to New York and all I got was this lousy T-shirt.' I am talking, of course, about the Sony Walkman. I mean, I live very near the UCD campus at Belfield, and I have thus observed joggers for many years, cantering past at all hours, sweating and spewking, and quite simply, a person cannot go jogging without a Sony Walkman, or similar device. My dears, it is simply not done.

So I purchased one of these annoying little machines and took it home to experiment. But to what do you listen while running? Should I go for an explicitly athletic theme? Something that would fill me with resolve? 'Chariots of Fire', perhaps? Or would that just fill me with resolve to learn to play the synthesiser, not resolve to jog? What else? Barry White? No good for jogging. Not vertical jogging anyway, fnaar, fnaar. The Cranberries? Nah, you couldn't jog to that shower. I don't know what exactly you could do to The Cranberries, but I do hope somebody will get around to doing it bloody soon. Blur? Perhaps. I mean, yes, Blur have often given me a good dose of the runs, but whether I would actually want to run to them, I wasn't sure.

I found a tape by a well-known and very hirsute Irish folk group. It featured such daarlin songs as 'Molly Malone', 'Dublin in the Rare Auld Times', 'Rinketty-Dinketty-Wanketty-Woo-Pass-the-Porter-Mother', and other searing accounts of real life as it used to be lived by the poor of Dublin. It also included 'A Nation Once Again', which our beloved leader of the opposition, Mr Bertie Ahern, is on the record as suggesting as the new national anthem for the tolerant, pluralist Ireland, into which Northern Unionists will want to gallop at the speed of lemmings over a cliff. (Oranges and lemmings?) But anyway. Out I trot into the rain, Walkman clamped to my lugs. I had not heard 'A Nation Once Again' for some years, and I looked forward to doing so now, as I hauled myself around the Belfield track.

Now, I sort of liked Bertie Ahern before, but I utterly adore him now. I never knew he had such a profoundly Pythonesque sense of the absurd. 'A Nation Once Again'?! Do you know the words? Does Bertie Ahern?!

> When boyhood's fire was in my blood
> I dreamt of ancient freemen
> Of Greece and Rome where bravely stood
> Three hundred men and three men
> And yet I pray to see the day
> Our fetters rent in twain
> And Ireland, long a province
> Be a nation once again

A nation once again (up yeh boy yeh)
A nation once again (go on yeh good ting)
That Ireland long a province be a nation once again,
   TIOCFAIDH AR LA!!!!

Now, tell me honestly, what is the very first word that comes into your mind reading that? Yes. It's 'pluralism', isn't it?

Let us engage in a little close textual analysis. Problem One here is the toe-curling rhyming of 'freemen' with 'three men'. This would create difficulties for some of our international footballers, whose Cockney, Geordie, Scouse and Brummie accents would make 'freemen' and 'three men' come out exactly the same! Problem Two is that if you substituted 'Deutschland' for 'Ireland' in the verse quoted above you would arrive at something that would have gone down a storm over the schnapps in late-thirties Berlin. And if you were to insert 'England' where 'Ireland' is now, you would get a piece of vacuous supremacist shite the like of which could very acceptably be chanted at the annual general meeting of the South London Chapter of the National Front. Can I just say, Bertie, that I would sincerely prefer to have 'Don't Love Me for Fun, Girl' by Boyzone as our new anthem rather than 'A Nation Once Again'? I jogged around that track in shock as I listened. And it occurred to me then, as I broke into a sweat: you could buy one mighty Walkman with the salary Bertie Ahern is paid to come up with ideas as clever as that. So I'm giving up health and going into politics. It mightn't do much for your waistline, but it sure as hell slims down your IQ.

But it doesn't work like that. Oh, no. You might be full of resolve to forget about the bits of your body you exercise, but then what happens? Yes. The bits you can't exercise start acting up. Your toenails start ingrowing. Your eyesight begins to fade. Your hair starts greying, or begins to grow in your nostrils at the same rate at which it falls out of your scalp. I was over beyond in New York on business earlier this year, a fine city full of lovely avenues, fantastic nightlife and organised gang warfare involving nasty sharp implements. As regular television viewers will know, the buildings in New York are tall, slim and graceful, in inverse proportion to the citizens, who tend to be short, fat and clumsy. But still, New York is a great town, so rightfully celebrated in story and song. How many of us have heard Francis Albert Sinatra croon those immortal lyrics 'Da Da Deedle-Dum, Da Da Deedle-Dum, Da Da Deedle-Dum' and felt our very souls thrill to the thought of the place where, if you can 'make it', you can 'make it' anywhere? Where else could he be singing about? Yes, alright, possibly Cootehill, County Cavan. (It's up to you! Coote! Hill! Coote! Hill-Da-Da-Deedle-Dum, etc.) Or perhaps Dundalk? (It's up to you! Dun-Dork. Dun-Dork.) But no, New York is the subject of Ole Red Eyes' affectionate paean. And anyway, there I was that Saturday night, cruising down Fifth Avenue in a yellow cab, feeling full of life and strange mischief and tequila sunrise, when something awful happened to me.

The ache began right at the back of the left side of my top gum. I immediately did the responsible thing. I ignored it and lit a cigarette. But by the time the cab had got to my destination and the laconic taxi driver had extracted a half-inch-thick wad of dollar bills from me, the pain felt like Satan himself and all his unholy minions were prodding the left side of my bonce with a red-hot ice-pick.

34

Well, in a way I was lucky. Because if you are going to get a toothache outside of office hours, New York is the place to get one. It is a twenty-four hour city. Whatever you want, you can get it in New York at any time of the day or night, with perhaps the sole exception of intelligent conversation, for which you have to book several weeks in advance and pay cash. Like sadomasochistic prostitution or sushi, however, after-hours dentistry is no problem if you have the readies, and so I located a dentist's surgery and conveyed myself there without delay.

It was some years since I had been to see a dentist, and so I was feeling more than a little apprehensive. I hate to admit it, but I had neglected my teeth. I don't know why, because one's teeth are among one's best butties. Think of what they go through with you. Think of all you make them chew, all that which gets stuck between them, think of the abuse you give them, think of their lonely and unfulfilled lives, yellowing prisoners in that malodorous hot wet cave, your beak, without even a video machine or a pack of cards. Yes, yes, you give them the occasional brush, the odd sporadic lick if it's Christmas. Big deal. But do you floss? No, you do not. The only floss that ever gets near your mouth is the pink kind that comes on sticks by the seaside. That, in a way, is the problem.

Anyway, I sat in the reception room practically hyperventilating with pain and weeping openly. The open weeping was not caused by the pain itself, but by the thought of the bill, which the charming assistant had kindly gone through with me, explaining that they would take cash, credit cards, travellers' cheques, or, failing that, my first-born child.

The dentist, when she appeared in the room, was dressed like one of the NASA scientists from the film *Close Encounters of the Third Kind*, in a white zip-up bodysuit, face mask, heavy boots and thick plastic gloves. She lurched over to me and said hello. 'May the force be with you,' I replied, and she asked what seemed to be the problem. The problem, I made clear, was that the pain in my shagging kisser was enough to make the Pope blaspheme. She clamped my mouth open and began to prod my teeth with a long thin metal implement that looked for all the world like something you would use to eat a lobster or perform a circumcision, or, perhaps, both. 'Wow,' she kept saying, 'wow,' in a tone that simultaneously conveyed both bloodcurdling horror and an odd kind of wonderment. 'I'm guessin' here ya havvin bin to a dennist for a whoile, huh?' she asked. 'Unnnghgh,' I agreed. 'How many yeeze?' she enquired. 'Aragahangh,' I told her. 'Hmmmm,' she said, 's'what I tawt.' Every so often she would helpfully jab her skewer into one of my molars with the delicacy of a mountaineer hammering a crampon into a granite rock. Sometimes this would reduce me to a helplessly screaming wretch, whereas other times it would make me want to spring from the chair and hurl myself through the window and down into the busy streets of Greenwich Village. 'Does dat hoyt?' she would ask, after scraping me down from the ceiling and pouring me back into the seat. 'FunghinESSSSewefunghinooopidwarghonnn,' I would reply. She was either very well trained or just naturally perceptive, I reflected, as she got out her hose-pipe and whacked it into my mouth.

The next five minutes were like something out of the worst moments of the Counter-Reformation. Old Princess Leia produced a syringe and needle and stuck it into my gum, repeatedly, all the time telling my yelping and ululating body that this 'would help deal with the pain'. She then flicked a few switches on her bleeping console, cracked her knuckles and reached for her drill, selecting for my tooth the same drill-bit a navvy would use to bisect a paving slab. The bit sank into my poor misfortunate molar and the unmistakable aroma of rapidly powdering tooth-matter began to fill the air, along with a high-pitched whine (myself). Indeed, I felt like a bottle of wine in the process of being uncorked.

Only God and His Holy Mother really know what she did to me, but for the amount of money it cost I could have flown home to Dublin first class, put up in the Shelbourne bloody Hotel for the weekend and bought Irish passports for myself and the whole family. Even after all this time, I am still not convinced that this would not have been the better option. 'At least you'll have a nice smile now,' The Brother quipped. Yes, indeed. I certainly feel like smiling alright.

The week I got back from the Big Bagel I got the flu. It was Christmas week, too. (Thank you very much indeed, God, for giving me the flu the very week before your only son's birthday. Junior needn't think he'll be getting a present from me in future!) Everyone else in the country seemed to have it, too; but me, I had it big. I've had some very nasty diseases in my time, as regular readers of the *Sunday Tribune* will know (I've now broken it off with that Ban Garda from Ringaskiddy, however, and the penicillin is beginning to take effect at last), but I do not think I had ever had this strange ailment before.

This germ was so virulent that I felt I could actually see it. The vile little creature doing the hokey-cokey through my bloodstream had, I felt, loud clothes, long pointed teeth and a hairstyle broadly reminiscent of a rugby player's armpit.

Just in case you have never had this flu yourself – and if you haven't, poor reader, you will have it very soon, because it's so contagious that you can get it from reading this book – let me explain some of the main symptoms to you. A number of things happen when you have this flu. Your nose, of course, ebbs and flows like the broad majestic Shannon. Substances come out of your nostrils that you have not seen since that nasty Dilophosaurus spat all over that poor little man in the film *Jurassic Park*. Your mouth is as dry as a downtown Tehran disco-bar. Your throat and eyes ache. You shiver and shake and shudder like the early Elvis Presley. You cough and splutter and wheeze. You wake up every morning with the inexplicable yet certain feeling that Good Rockin Dopsie and The Cajun Twisters are playing an extended boogie-woogie session in your head, and they ain't unplugged. And the main symptom, of course, is that you desperately, profoundly, wish to die.

Another symptom is that you stagger around your house or flat stark naked all day. This is because it actually hurts you to put on clothes. Your skin actually aches when you have this flu. A sheet or a shirt, it makes no difference, your flesh actually feels like several layers of it have been removed with a red-hot spatula. There are other odd feelings. If you try to comb your hair, your scalp feels like it is being pricked by a million deranged acupuncturists very much the worse for strong drink. Your energy level completely collapses. If you manage to raise your head long enough to hawk feebly into a crumpled hanky, you feel that you have swum the English Channel on your back.

Pills, potions, serums and lotions: none of them work at all. In the course of my perennial dealings with the bug I have swallowed, imbibed, inhaled, sucked and inserted more chemical substances than Keith Richards did while he was working on 'Sympathy for the Devil', and every year it's the same. I end up feeling not so much like Death-Warmed-Up as Death-In-A-Bloody-Cranky-Humour- First-Thing-Of-A-Monday-Morning-When-The-Telephone-Bill-Has-Just-Arrived.

This year when I got the flu I slept like a baby. That is to say, I woke up every three hours screaming, crying and wetting the bed. The bathroom department, do you say? Do not talk to me about the bathroom department. The bathroom, now, I will not go into, while the flu bug is exploring my innards. This is because when I do go into it, after a lonely half-hour trek across the landing floor, punctuated only by extended spells of curling up on the carpet and gibbering, I find it very hard to get back out. I don't think you want the details. I think you know what I am saying here. Some days, as Voltaire (or was it Locke?) once put it so cogently, the bottom falls out of your world. Whereas other days the world falls out of your bottom. Suffice it to say, I have suffered over the years.

Anyway, enough of this disgusting stuff. Let us talk more of health, grooming and beauty. In the search for manly deportment, a good haircut can go a long way. Look at President Clinton. Who can forget that great scandal last year when he delayed the take-off of Air Force One because he was having a haircut? The haircut cost $300 and was done by a man who trades under the name of 'Paulo'. Jesus. The most powerful man in the world, and he's getting his hair cut by a bloke with only one name.

Ah, the memories that came flooding back as I read the story of Slick Willie's appointment with the tricky trichologist. It was on my fifteenth birthday that I truly became a man. My mother let me get my hair cut in Herman's Klipjoint in Dun Laoghaire. This was a watershed, because to my friends and myself – shorn monthly like miserable ewes in what we regarded as the torture chamber of the old barber's shop in Glasthule – Herman's Klipjoint was the paragon of taste. Herman's Klipjoint did not sell haircuts. It sold a lifestyle. You could tell this because of the 'K' in the word 'Klipjoint'. It was modern. It was post-Vatican Two. It had pictures of Kevin Keegan on the walls. It had an eight-track cartridge player – remember those? – and a full set of Steely Dan eight-track cartridges. Damn it all, it had blow-driers, for God's sake, and far from blow-driers was I reared.

I belong to a generation that saw washing its hair once a week in the bath as the height of personal hygiene. And yet, as I sat in the swivel chair that day in Herman's Klipjoint and had my hair blow-dried to within an inch of its life, I thought that I had arrived. The barnet was sprayed and lacquered and back-combed and frizzed. It was crimped and ironed and sculpted. Several of the fundamental laws of science were broken by my hair that day, including the law of gravity. I looked, when I emerged from Herman's Klipjoint, like a chrysanthemum in a tank top. And I felt that I was riding a wave. A permanent wave. In school on Monday morning the teacher took one look at me and said he wanted to help me out, which I thought was nice of him. 'Which way did you come in?' he added, however.

In the years that followed, my love of such establishments faded. Even that oh-so-cool post-modern 'K' began to bother me. It was trying too hard, I soon came to feel. I remember noticing as a teenager, on annual holidays in rural Ireland, that nightclubs which had neon signs outside flashing the words 'Nite Klub' were always dreadful places, whereas establishments that used standard English spelling were not.

I thought about all this the other day when I went into town to get my hair cut. These days I usually go to a barber's shop, a civilised place where the barber does not talk to you. But it was closed, and so, feeling hirsute and raggedy, I was forced into one of those modern gaffs, the nineties equivalent of Herman's Klipjoint.

No sooner was I in the place, than I began to suffer a strange and uneasy feeling. I have since checked with colleagues, and I now know that what I was experiencing was the clearly definable psychological phenomenon known as Trendy Hairdresser Anxiety (THA). Take this, for example: I am sitting by the sink waiting for 'Blake' to come and wash my hair. After ten minutes there is no sign. After twenty, still nothing. I begin to feel: They Have Forgotten Me. Now, apparently, this is a major symptom of THA. Lots of people suffer this in fashionable hairdressing establishments. Pretty soon afterwards, I start thinking: They Are Deliberately Ignoring Me. This, too, is a common phobia.

Finally 'Blake' comes and washes my hair. While he does so, we have a chat. For some reason, 'Blake' wants to know two things about me: (a) am I not working today, no? and (b) did I manage to 'get away anywhere' this year? He is quite persistent about this. He really does want to know. I try to change the subject. It seems that 'Blake' is not his real name, but his 'professional name'. Did he name himself after the great Romantic poet, William Blake? I enquire. No, he says, as a youth he was a fan of the TV programme *Blake's Seven*. His real name is Morris, he finally confides, and Morris is not a good name for a hairdresser.

After a time, 'Blake' leaves me, sodden hair dripping down my neck. I am anxious. I am chewing my nails. But there is worse to come. I am only just recovering from Hairdresser Conversation Terror when I start mumbling to myself: That Person Over There Came In After Me And Yet He Is Having His Hair Cut First. Another paranoid delusion, I have since been told, much suffered by those who patronise such establishments. (Sigmund Freud wrote about it in his seminal work, *Curl Up and Dye: The Oedipus Complex and the Bad Hair Day*.)

Finally, 'Marco' arrives to give me a short back and sides. He stares at me for a while before asking what I 'would like done with it'. I wonder about this. He fingers my hair. 'I mean,' he sneers, 'would you like them both cut or just the one of them?' Oh my God, he's saying I'm bald! I look at 'Marco'. He looks at me. 'Blake' comes over and looks at both of us. 'Are you cutting today, Marco?' he asks. 'Is he cutting,' I think to myself.

The man is a complete bitch.

Chapter 3

Give Me a Home
Where the Cockroaches Roam

> 'Home life as I understand it is no more natural to
> us than a cage is to a cockatoo.'
>
> *Getting Married*, George Bernard Shaw

I   Sharing a Bedroom with Dick

IT IS VERY IMPORTANT IN LIFE TO HAVE A PLEASANT
home. This is something I have myself. I live in a really
lovely apartment, overlooking the rent, and this year
I decided to do myself a big favour and get the digs
done up. I should tell you that I now live in the very
flat that I inhabited throughout most of my college
career, if career is the word you would use for that
collection of lost and disconnected years. Here I am, a
decade later, after all that time away in pagan London,
back living in my old gaff, surrounded by the ghosts of
my youth. I do like the flat, I must say, even though the
general visual impression is of suddenly waking up in a
cave inhabited by some class of deranged and savage
carnivore. The unusual decorative effect in my living
room was achieved by a good deal of beer chucking,
cigarette burning and drunken staggering into the walls.
It was completed by the ancient and sacred student ritual
known as bouncing a tennis ball against the ceiling for

43

many hours, sometimes, indeed, for several days at a time.

Back in those days myself and my various flatmates didn't worry too much about interior decor. We had other things on our minds. I can't remember what just now, but take it from me, things were on our minds. Forget your deep-pile shag carpet, your rush matting, your press-ure-washed pine floorboards. For floor covering we pre-ferred a tasteful tapestry of pizza boxes, unlaundered underclothing and textbooks about the metaphysical poets long overdue at the UCD library. In addition, I had a bus stop, of course, which somebody had hilariously nicked from the Stillorgan dual carriageway one night and presented to me as a token of comradely affection. I also had a traffic cone, something which every student flat I've ever been in seems to have, for some strange reason. (Do they give them out free with the Leaving Cert or something?) I had a sofa so battered that by the time it was thrown out it looked like it had been attacked by a Rottweiler on steroids. I had a rug that looked like the same Rottweiler, six months deceased. And, of course, I also had the obligatory poster of a First World War soldier being shot, with the word 'WHY?' printed below in big black meaningful letters. Why, indeed?

But I had other decorative features also. My auld butty John McDermott reminded me recently of a college event we had once helped to organise called 'Poets Against Apartheid'. I had the 'Poets Against Apartheid' poster on my kitchen wall for a long time. It featured two memor-able images: (a) a black trade unionist being batoned by a South African policeman; (b) a scrawny young man with a quiff and a quill pen staring into the distance as though he had just been stricken by a sudden attack of hiccups.

If ever there was a poignant signifier of the almost transcendental uselessness, and yet the idealism, of college politics, perhaps it is the very idea of an event called 'Poets Against Apartheid'. (Kiss your Fascist ass goodbye, Eugene Terreblanche, I feel an iambic pentameter coming on, you sucker!)

There were two posters on my bedroom wall. One was a poster of the late Herr Beethoven. The other, pardon my blushes, was an election poster of Dick Spring, with the memorable slogan 'Labour: A Voice That Will Be Heard' printed thereupon. (I was young, OK?) Let me tell you, it is quite a memorable experience waking up every morning for some years with Dick Spring gazing speculatively across the pillow at you. But anyway, you don't want to know about my problems of practically sharing a bed with Dick, unless, of course, your name happens to be John Bruton, whereupon you probably do. But I liked these posters. I thought they were fine. I also thought that in the unlikely event that I would ever manage to persuade some poor moll to enter the confines of my boudoir, these two posters would strike just the correct balance between intimations of profound intellectualism on the one hand and passionately held social conviction on the other. (Sort of Jeremy Paxman crossed with Mother Teresa.) The effect was slightly spoilt, however, when another friend got to work on the posters with a scissors one night while I was out. ('Out' as in unconscious from drink, I mean, not as in absent from the premises.) When I woke up, the great oracularly challenged genius's head had been transposed onto Dick Spring's body, with the result that the heart-stopping and previously mass-inspiring slogan 'Labour: A Voice That Will Be Heard' was suddenly rendered devastatingly ironic.

My flat had an odour all its own in those days. Instead of ever opening a window we sprayed the place regularly with Right Guard, cheap aftershave, air freshener, fly-spray and just about anything else that came in an aerosol can. (This was, of course, before the days of eco-friendliness.) But the aroma had other interesting contributors also. Old sock, antique hamburger, pint of milk so putrid that you could have cut it into slices: melt these down and spread them on toast, they all played their part. There was one occasion after a party when somebody heaved into a soup bowl – my, how we laughed – and the bowl remained unemptied on the jacks floor for a period of at least nine months. This added a certain *je ne sais quoi*. Even now, on a windy day, the memories come flooding back. Ah, sure, God be with the days. Maybe I shouldn't have bothered decorating. Maybe I should have just left my auld flat the way it was. It is a terrible thing, after all, to try to paint over your past. And anyway, the painters would need to get danger money.

A hideous living area is one thing, but a bad bathroom can really be depressing. So this year I also had my bathroom replaced. It wasn't really my idea, I have to admit. Personally, I was quite happy with the grotesque assemblage of hideousness which comprised my bathroom, but the new wife, when she moved in, made it clear that certain changes would have to be expedited forthwith or she would ship straight back out and home to The Mammy. Jennifer is usually a very tolerant woman. Hell, she can listen to three whole Chris de Burgh numbers without coming out in a rash. But my bathroom proved to be her Waterloo. She is a very clean person, you see. Every morning she puts a sheet of newspaper under the cuckoo clock.

It was the fact that things were actually growing in the bath that made her get a tad fractious, along with the fact that the sink perpetually looked as though it had recently puked. During the tempestuous years of our courtship, she gave me many potted plants as presents whenever we would have a little row. These were sturdy plants which had survived unattended in the deepest jungles of the Southern Americas. Three weeks in my flat and they would keel over, take on the colour of Mayo muck and die roaring. You could grow nothing in my flat. But now, however, my bathroom resembles the hothouse at the Botanical Gardens. There are things in that sink that would give David Bellamy a coronary.

Then there is the bath. I mean, I do actually clean out the bath, at least once a year, but for some reason that's not enough for the whinging virago. Anyway, she wouldn't get into it, unless she had spread four large black plastic rubbish sacks (empty of course) across the enamel in advance of the hot water being poured in. I say 'hot' water, because for some reason the water in my bath is hot enough to remove paint, whereas the trickle that emanates from the cold tap is reminiscent of a sparrow pissing. The only way to have a bath which will not roast you alive is to run the hot water when you are going out in the morning and get into the bath when you come home after work that night. The spouse was not happy about any of this, and as, I think, Yeats once put it, an unhappy spouse is an awful pain in the bollocks.

So off we went to the bathroom showroom one Sunday to evaluate and admire the assembled enamel. Everything in the gaff was so gleaming and white that I started to get a headache. Herself was in raptures, however, as she flitted from jacks to Jacuzzi like some sort of deranged

47

Connaught butterfly. Then it happened. Over in the corner of the barn-like structure I heard a frantic cry of ecstasy which I (somehow) recognised as emanating from the lips of my own little sugarplum. When I found her she was standing there, hands clutched together, practically swooning with excitement. 'Look, poodle,' she gibbered. I looked.

The object of Snuggly-Wuggly's affection was something called a 'bidet'. Readers who have been to the Continent for the hollyers may have come across (if I may use the phrase) such an item, but for those of you who have not, let me just explain that a 'bidet' is a bathroom appliance of very dubious moral character indeed. It is a small and quite innocent-looking cousin of our old friend, the humble water closet, yet when you press various infernal controls, a jet of pressurised liquid is ejaculated upwards into the air like some kind of miniature Old Faithful. Let me tell you, I have been around a bit. I have lived in London, for example, and I have visited Paris, and yet I never saw the like of it, not in the worst Soho sex shop or Pigalle flophouse. It is difficult for a person possessed of even a relatively normal erotic sensibility to imagine the true purpose of a 'bidet', and yet here it was, openly on sale in our capital city one Sunday afternoon.

The assistant wandered over, a young man with the face of a stressed cherub. He had a good head on his shoulders, and in the course of the ensuing conversation I found myself wondering whose it was. 'We want to buy a bathroom,' I began.

'Oh,' he nodded, 'well, this would be the place for you, so,' the witty fucking bastard. He enquired delicately about how much dough we had in mind to spend.

48

'About a grand,' I said. When he had stopped laughing, he assured us that he had some very nice toilet roll holders in that general price range.

'How much would we be talking, so?' enquired Cup Cakes. The assistant noted down the dimensions of our bathroom and took a calculator from his pocket.

'About two and a half grand,' he said.

'How much?' gasped Treacle Chops.

'Two and a half,' he said, 'but that's only an estimate. Of course, it will cost more than that.'

I woke up a few moments later to feel a hot moist tongue enthusiastically waggling around in my mouth. I was only slightly disappointed to find that it belonged not to the present Mrs O'Connor, but to the assistant, a former boy scout, who had once won a merit badge in life-saving and was briskly giving me the kiss of life to get me over the shock of the price. Two and a half grand for a bathroom! Good God Almighty, I wouldn't spend that for a seat in the Dáil! He and Bunnikins got me to my feet, slapped me in the face a few times and shoved a handful of smelling salts under my uncontrollably twitching nostrils.

'Would that include the bidet?' enquired the Missus. Yer man shook his head dolefully and explained that the bidet would be five hundred smackers extra. The room swum again, but somehow I managed to retain my consciousness if not my composure.

'How do you use it anyway?' the War Department asked.

'Well,' said *mo dhuine*, 'you sit on it.'

She sighed, 'I know that, Sherlock, but how? I mean, which way around?'

Your man put down his clipboard and mounted the

thing, legs akimbo, facing the wall!! This was how they all did it 'in Europe', he said. Well, I don't know about this. I mean, I attended a Roman Catholic boarding school for boys, as you may know, but never in my whole life have I seen such a display of unapologetic depravity. Nothing would do my nabs, bar straddling the thing and riding it like it was some sort of rodeo stallion. The dirty fecker was practically roaring 'yippie-aye-bleedin-yay'. I grabbed the Better Half and made for the door. I don't know. If this sort of thing is what European integration means for Ireland, it's time we thought seriously about washing our hands – and the rest of us, indeed – of the whole damn thing.

Back we went to the flat, the War Department and myself, to do a bit of spring cleaning. Now, I hate this kind of thing. I mean, you hoover the floor, you clean the toilet, you scrape out the grill and three years later you have to start all over again! And then there's your possessions. You start cohabiting, they have to be organised. This means nothing but trouble. It is not right.

Take the following: for about two years, back when I was a student, there was a crumpled white ball gown in the wardrobe of my flat. Now, given the general lack of sexual success, not to mention the committed socialism of those who inhabited my flat (i.e. myself), I cannot now recall just why there would have been a crumpled white ball gown in my flat, but take it from me, there was. And one night anyway, I was sitting in what we might euphemistically call the living room – although 'hangover and dying room' would have been a better description – when the door opened and my friend John Bourke strolled silently in wearing this ball gown. John was a chap who weighed in at about fourteen stone. He had a chubby face, a full beard, many earrings and a particularly severe skinhead haircut. His usual form of sartorial style involved a lot of military-style clothing, chunky Doc Martens and a malodorous black overcoat, so it was quite a surprise to see him strolling into my room wearing a flimsy white ball gown and, I think, stilettos. John sat down on the sofa and said nothing at all. After a few moments he began to laugh. Indeed, he laughed so hard that he actually broke the arm off my sofa. That's all that happened. Harmless fun. Well, arm-less fun, at any rate.

I tell you this story not to amuse you – although I myself find the recollection of it amusing – but to give you an insight into the truly transcendental sadness of my life. Because that week, while doing our bit of early spring cleaning, I found in the back of my current ward-robe the arm of that very sofa, which I had kept for about ten years. I stared at it for five whole minutes trying to figure out what it was, and then, why in the name of God I had kept it. I mean, I have moved address seven times since that night twelve years ago. I spent many of those years coming and going, travelling to America and many other pagan lands. Yet here it was, in the bottom of a suitcase. The arm of a sofa. (I'm not making this up.)

This instinct to hoard has blighted my life. I have a pathological inability to throw out anything that has no practical use whatsoever. Useful things I chuck away immediately. In my time I have lost, accidentally destroyed or put into the washing machine, two Irish passports, several cheque books, huge quantities of cur-rency both foreign and domestic, important personal letters, my MA degree, every single family photograph I've ever possessed and enough credit cards to keep

Michael Jackson's cosmetic surgeon in plastic for several decades. But the front page of the *Irish Times* the day after Nelson Mandela was released? Got it. My lecture timetable for 1984? Yup. The stub of my entry ticket to Elvis Presley's Graceland? Like, you have to ask?

Mr Yeats ended his days believing that all important things came from 'the foul rag-and-bone shop of the heart'. Forget the heart, Billy Boy, just see my attic if it's rag-and-bone you want. A psychiatrist friend has explained to me that this hoarding instinct represents an immature view of my past. So I've decided to do something about it. In the coming weeks I'm going to go through my stuff and bin every last thing I don't need to actually maintain life. Perhaps, reader dear, you too have an unhealthy relationship with the useless objects of your past? Well, perhaps we could swop? You could have my past, and I yours. If you write to me I could drop all my stuff out to you without delay.

There is for a start my collection of records. 'Records', for the benefit of younger readers, are things we used to have back in the early 1300s. Twelve-inch discs of black plastic, they went all sorts of funny shapes when you applied cigarette lighters to them. They also played music. What joys are contained in my collection. There is my copy of The Communards' 'Don't Leave Me This Way' shaped like a red star. There is my complete collection of Bay City Rollers albums, including the early breakthrough record 'Shakey Shakey Shake', the seminal collection 'Shang A Lang' and that tartantastic culmination of lyrical loveliness, 'Shimmy Shammy Shit', featuring Stuart 'Woody' Wood. Other relics from my past include a walking stick purchased in revolutionary Nicaragua, a salt cellar shaped like Boy George, a Yield Right

Of Way sign liberated from the Bray Road one night in 1981 and a not inconsiderable number of cappuccino-flavoured condoms (unused).

What I would like in return are a few nice tasteful bits and pieces that would help me conjure up a new set of memories. A blue glass vase bought in Venice, perhaps, with a crack down the side where, I could say, an early significant other chucked it at me one night when I came home scuttered from a secret Cabinet meeting. A rug from Afghanistan, which I could pretend I bought when I was undercover with the Mooja Hadeen. The battered Rickenbacker guitar kept from my early days with U2. You know the kind of thing I want. Any of the above. Or, of course, a sofa missing an arm.

II   Cowboys and Engines

READER, THERE ARE SOME WEEKS YOU WILL NEVER forget in your life and late last year I had one of those. I am talking about the week I finally did my driving test! Although I had attained the age of thirty-two, I had never attempted the test before, even though I did have some lessons once as a student, in an establishment that I seem to recall was called the Saddam Hussein School of Motoring ('Death Before Yielding').

This time around I went to a better school. My teacher, Eamon from ISM in Ranelagh, was a pleasant man with the patience of Sisyphus, the courage of Hercules and the wisdom of Solomon. Through many hours together we studied the intricacies of the three-point turn, the hill start and the smooth right-lane manoeuvre, all of which, three months ago, I would have thought were line-dancing steps. The man's persistence in the face of utter

53

frustration was nothing short of heroic. Again and again, he would repeat the order 'mirror, signal, manoeuvre', like a maharishi chanting a mantra, until even I got the message. Mirror, signal, manoeuvre. I am starting to say it in my sleep.

Another problem was keeping my distance. I don't know why, but this was a problem for me. Youarenotsupposedtodrivelikethis. You are supposed to drive in a nicely spaced-out manner. That's nicely spaced out in terms of your proximity to the next vehicle, by the way, not nicely spaced out on drugs or cheap drink, for the benefit of younger readers.

Despite Eamon's many valiant efforts, the Friday before the test I was still in serious need of improvement. So The Brother, who has been driving since he was a gossoon, admirably stepped into the breach and gave me a few last-minute lessons. He is feeling much better now the blood pressure has returned to normal and the waking up in the middle of the night screaming in abject terror has subsided a little. His last piece of advice to me, as he stepped gibbering out of the car the day before the test, was the following: 'Would you not get out the clippers and do your nasal hair, no? You don't want Yer Man the tester to punt his lunch all over yeh.'

Thus, fully prepared, I turned up to take my test on Monday afternoon. Part One was an oral exam on the rules of the road.

'How would you know a zebra crossing at night?' the instructor enquired. At first I thought this was a joke. I frantically search my subconscious for the punch line. Is it: because he wanted to get to the other side? No. What is it again? Oh, yes. Flashing amber lights. A few more easy-peasy questions followed to which I knew most of the answers. Himself then produced a list of road signs and invited me to identify them. No problem.

Out to the car park, where we leapt into the motor and off we went. The first thing that happened was a pothole so big I got a large number of air miles for successfully negotiating it. Then onwards. A deft right, a couple of lively lefts, the gear changes as smooth as politician's lies. So far, so good, as the optimist said plummeting past the fifteenth-storey of a sixteen-storey building.

The most disconcerting thing about the driving test, as many readers will know, is not the actual driving itself, but the fact that the tester does not talk to you, except to tell you what to do. There is no chitchat, no light laughter, no commenting on the Keatsian beauty of passing Churchtown or the desirability of the indigenous peoples of that parish, no re-hashing of the Oasis/Blur debate. Nothing. Zilch. Your tester, actually, is not *allowed* to talk to you. You are thus driving along for over half an hour with a person who is staring intensely at you without ever uttering one single social syllable. It is like being married, I suppose.

Anyway, twenty minutes in and things were going fine. I had reversed around the corner with the grace of ... something very graceful. I had demonstrated the hand signals you use to other motorists – or, at least, the polite ones. Everything was groovy and I was definitely in with a fighting chance of passing this test. And then ... we were just about to turn off the main road and into an estate when, suddenly, I saw this drunken hairy-looking gom come bounding and staggering out into the road, where, having reached the exact centre, he stopped and gawped at me. Just stopped. He started to beckon. Sheer terror wrapped its cold hand around my heart. I ignored him. He stared at me and beckoned harder. After some moments he sashayed to the side of the road where he stood and watched as I completed my right-hand turn. I couldn't help feeling he was an actor employed by the Department of the Environment for this purpose.

Back to the test centre toot sweet, where I was invited to park the car. Then, I was requested to follow the tester into the building, where he would tell me the result of my examination. I felt like Danton about to keep an appointment with Madame La Guillotine. I was so nervous I would cheerfully take a chomp out of a teacup. He sat at a desk. He scribbled a note. He turned. He looked up at me. He didn't smile. Then he said I passed! I couldn't believe it. I sprang out into the crisp winter evening, a new man, a grown-up, a driver, waving my certificate of competency in the air, a banner of self-fulfilment! Mirror, signal, manoeuvre. Mirror, signal, manoeuvre. I will never be the same again.

But passing my test put me into a bit of a quandary. The thing is, up until then I had never owned a car. I do not know why this is, because I have owned lots of other useless rubbish in my time, including the complete works of Rod Stewart, the keys to the *Sunday Tribune* executive washroom (i.e. the alleyway beside the office) and a television that only gets RTE 2. But anyway, the week I passed the test I finally became a whole person. I went out and bought myself a car!

The Brother came along with me to do the actual negotiating, and I must say, he is a good auld scout to have about you in a situation like this. The thing is, The Brother objects to paying the asking price for anything, as a simple matter of principle. He is the only person I know who haggles about bus fare. If The Brother was employed by Brinks-Mat, he would persuade villains and robbers by sheer logic to take only a million or two during heists and leave the rest behind and persuade them, too, that this was a considerable bargain. The Brother used to be a salesman himself, and despite – or perhaps because of – this, he tends to regard salespeople the way Eric Cantona tends to regard football supporters. (Eric Cantona: the first case in modern football of the shit hitting the fan?) But anyway, he is quite merciless about it.

'We want a car,' said he to the salesman.

'How does a BMW sound?' said the salesman.

'Vroom fuckin' vroom,' replied The Brother, 'now, be serious.'

We selected a car and made an offer. It was a fascinating spectacle, the salesman elucidating the basic principles of profit and loss upon which the entire free market system is predicated, The Brother responding with his hollow sardonic laugh and his repeatedly mumbled observation, 'Ah, you're a tight-fisted mowldy auld bollocks. You'd hire your auld wan out be the hour.'

He tried, the unfortunate salesman, but when he was reduced to getting out the deeds of incorporation of the company to demonstrate that it was not, in fact, a registered charity, I felt he had lost the argument. By the time we left the premises we had chopped a quarter off the original price and the poor custodian was slumped over his desk, gibbering about his difficult childhood and his elderly widowed mother who, apparently, needed a complicated and expensive eye operation.

The next step was to get insurance. We went to an insurance company and the nice man explained the details. Now, I had heard that car insurance was expensive, but I was not fully prepared for the discussion which ensued. After I had finished cackling maniacally, the insurance broker talked me in off the ledge and got out the forms. The gist was that the insurance company would need an amount of money large enough to pay off the foreign debt of a good-sized Third World country, along with my credit card, my watch, my television, my typewriter, my late grandmother's gold teeth, my trousers ... You know, the usual. They would also require my first child to be handed over to them upon the occasion of its birth, along with regular *droit de seigneur* rights concerning its mother. I listened, quaking with shock. The broker then took the pair of tights off his face and I signed the forms. He put my cheque into a large sack marked 'swag', adjusted his striped jersey and informed me that I was now 'fully covered'. I reflected silently on my fervent wish for the broker to be fully covered also, preferably with lukewarm panther piss.

'You nearly had the shirt off my back,' I quipped.

He licked his lips and glared at me. 'Oh yes,' he said, 'I forgot about that.'

I emerged from the office, naked from the waist up, and got into the car. The Brother was in a bit of a sulk, because car insurance seems to be one thing you really cannot haggle about. I had to bring him into Moore Street and let him loose with two pounds in order to restore his good humour. He came back an hour later with an enormous sack of bananas, three crates of cigarette lighters and a shopping bag full of white socks. And since then, my existence has been pink and rosy. Having a car has really changed my life, I have to tell you. I think having a car is a very healthy thing, in that it does get you out and about a lot more. Now I can drive across to the shops every day to buy cigarettes and ice cream. Now

I can drive down to Abrakebabra for dinner every night. It is terrific! I feel better already. If any of you need a lift anywhere, please do let me know.

But the thing is, the happiness does not last. You purchase a car, thinking that this will improve your life. As soon as you do this, you start to have second thoughts. My own first second thought, if you know what I mean, happened about a fortnight after I had got the car. I had just left the *Sunday Tribune* office where I had presented myself for my weekly heartless caning from the editor, and I was wandering down Baggot Street at a leisurely pace, safe in the knowledge that my parking meter had at least a full half-hour left to tick away. Suddenly I saw her: about a hundred yards down the street, this little middle-aged brown-uniformed woman, standing by my car and writing me a ticket! I'll tell you, the bould Sonia O'Sullivan had nothing on yours truly when it came to cantering that hundred yards.

Breathless I stood by her side and asked what my offence was. 'Expired meter,' she said, in the voice of a Midlands dalek. I said the meter must have been broken. She smiled the patient smile of a woman who has heard it all before. She said there was nothing she could do. Even if she wanted to. My fate was sealed. Once she had stared to write a ticket, she said, she couldn't stop. She 'wasn't allowed' to stop; she had to continue to the bitter end. She would 'get into trouble' if she did not write me a ticket now. Once that biro had made contact with that paper, pleas for mercy were quite useless and I was wasting my sweetness on the desert air. I took a deep breath and began to explain a few of the more basic concepts of existentialism: for example, the notion that in the absence of any divine ordering force we as rational human beings can and, indeed, must take responsibility for our own moral and ethical actions. But to no avail. 'You're gettin' a bloody ticket and that's that,' she confirmed. She was obviously a member of the Socratic school.

Next weekend I went down to Galway for a few days, and came back to Dublin on the Sunday night. There I was, cruising merrily eastwards across our green and lovely country in what one of my friends has insisted on christening The Babe Magnet (it is actually a Subaru Signet, which looks a little like a biscuit tin on wheels), happy as Larry and listening to the radio. There was a song playing by The Artiste Formerly Known as Prince (that is, The Artiste Presently Known as Pretentious Wanker – by myself at any rate), and I was happy to hear that he would soon be playing in Dublin because I was looking for an excuse to stay in one of these nights and wash my hair. Anyway. There I am, ridin' along in my automobile, when suddenly, quite out of the blue, the damn car begins to gibber and shake like a person with an unpleasant medieval disease. It is very difficult to render in print the noise that my car is now making, but it is something like 'hung achock achock achocka thunka'. Before very long, it simply stopped. I got out and made a great show of opening the bonnet and looking underneath, but as I am actually the kind of person who cannot understand how a can opener works, this display was purely theatrical.

Thus it was that I found myself alone and lost and on the outskirts of Mullingar! (If that sentence was the opening of a horror novel, you'd know you were in for a bloody scary read.) Mullingar is not a town I know at all well, and like most towns in Ireland, it is not a great place to try to find a mechanic at seven o'clock on a Sunday night. I suppose, to be frank, in fact, that Mullingar is the kind of town about which people from Dublin sometimes laugh quietly and tell cruel jokes. But I will not hear a word against it. No, no!

A fine young Mullingarian fellow called Paul came to my rescue. He located the problem – a dicky fuel pump – patched it up and sent me on my way, advising that this was strictly a temporary repair. Next morning, back in the smoke, I took the car to the garage where I had bought it. I parked it outside, ambled in and explained my problem to a mechanic who was energetically leaning against a wall and scratching his armpits. 'Leave her out there and ring me Chewsdeh,' the mechanic yawned, when I had finished my tale of woe. I handed him the keys and strolled out to the car. There, on the windscreen, was another parking ticket!! I ranted, I raged, I cursed. If things go on at this rate I intend to push it over a cliff and spend the money I save on parking tickets employing a full-time chauffeur. Having a car seems to be a full-time job. There is really a lot to be said for walking.

III   Drastic Plastic

THE OTHER AFTERNOON I WENT INTO TOWN TO BUY myself a new suit. This is not something I do very often. The last new suit I purchased was such a sartorial wonder that I held onto it for many years. The jacket had velveteen pocket flaps, vast triangular lapels, buttons the size of dinner plates. The trousers had a zip designed exclusively for the trapping and removal of pubic hair, turn-ups in which you could have hidden a small orchestra and flares which flapped in the breeze like the wings of a gigantic and deranged and almost certainly flightless bat. When I say this suit was tasteless, what I mean is that even the Pope would not have worn it in public. But it had a certain magic, that suit. It always got me noticed at parties, for example. Whenever I wore it I used to attract women like flies. I would have preferred to attract women without four legs and a diet of decomposing flesh, of course, but never mind that for the moment. You don't want to know about my problems.

Anyway, there I am in the changing room, trying on jackets, trousers, waistcoats, tottering out to the mirror and then back in behind the curtain, stripping off again with the alacrity, grace and erotic appeal of a Broadway showgirl trying to suck in her stomach. I am enjoying myself immensely, but the assistant is not much help. His name is Gervaise, according to the badge so firmly attached to his left mammary, and perhaps it is this aristocratic moniker which suggests dealing with the public is some sort of profoundly unpleasant necessity. Either that, or the fact that every time I ask for another suit, he sighs deeply and looks at his fingernails before going to get it. Gervaise is silently thinking, 'Ten thousand suits in the shop and this fucking pleb is going to try on every one.' And I am silently thinking, 'Ten thousand sperm in every ejaculation and Gervaise had to get through.'

In the end I choose a tasteful and subtle number in deep cerise. Gervaise immediately cheers up. He smiles with the enthusiasm of a man who is being paid on commission. He congratulates me warmly on the excellence of my choice and assures me fervently that 'it will ride up'. He peers at my tumescent midriff. The trousers will need to be let out just a tad, he says, but that's OK. As luck would have it, they've just got in a shipment of bungee-jump elastic that morning.

He marches to the counter, my beautiful new suit folded over his arm. Moments later I emerge from the changing room and present myself, wallet at the ready. I hand over my credit card and Gervaise swipes it through the machine that lurks so threateningly beside the cash register, bleeping every few seconds. The machine, that is. Not Gervaise. Gervaise is not bleeping every few seconds. Yawning and staring at his fingernails, yes, but bleeping, no.

A little time passes. We stare at each other, Gervaise and myself. I notice that his eyes are just a smidgen too close together. Gervaise should be employed by the Department of Education, I feel. He should be taken around schools and displayed to hormonally overactive teenagers as a poignant example of what will happen if they fuck their first cousins without using contraception. He drums his fingers on the cash register drawer. The radio is playing 'Love Is All Around Us' by Wet, Wet, Wet. Gervaise begins to sing quietly along. 'You know ah love ya and ah always weel. Ma mand's made up by the way that I feel.' I ponder silently that T. S. Eliot really better look out, Marty Pello is on the case. 'There's no beginning,' croons Gervaise, 'and there's no end. Coz on ma love . . . Yew can deep end.' Thanks be to God Almighty and His Holy Mother in Heaven, the credit card machine interrupts this display of lyrical incontinence. It begins to bleep wildly as it rattles, bursts into life and spits out a piece of paper. Gervaise takes the paper and peers at it. His eyes widen. He stares at me accusingly.

'Your credit card has been declined,' he says.

63

'What?' I say. (Can't beat a brilliant rejoinder, huh?)

'YOUR CREDIT CARD HAS BEEN DECLINED,' Gervaise repeats, slowly, loudly, emphasising every syllable, in the manner of Basil Fawlty addressing a Teutonic tourist.

'Oh my God,' I ejaculate, 'what? You can't be serious,' as though he has just confided that he would give the opportunity of having sexual intercourse with the late Shergar serious consideration.

'Oh, no,' Gervaise cackles crazily, 'I'm serious alright. YOUR CREDIT CARD HAS BEEN DECLINED, SIR.'

Every single person in the shop turns to look at me now. I feel strangely naked. I simper and shrug and grin. 'DECLINED,' Gervaise bawls, thrusting the piece of paper into my quivering hand. 'YES. LOOK. DECLINED!! D.E.C.L.I...'

'Would you like a fucking megaphone, Gervaise?' I beam. 'There's a very deaf little old lady about half a mile down the shagging road who didn't quite catch what you said?' Well, I made that bit up. I don't say that.

What I actually say, for quite some time really, is nothing at all. Rather I stand by the counter, head hung low in shame. When I look up pitifully, Gervaise regards me as though I am a globule of snot that he has just found on the sleeve of his jacket. (I do not mean that he enthusiastically rolls me up and eats me.) I am dumbstruck. I am nervous. I can feel the sweat moistening the small of my back. 'I don't know how this could have happened,' I stammer.

'Huh,' he says.

'No, really, Gervaise,' I plead. 'I checked my account yesterday and everything was hunky-dory in the balance department.'

He stares up at the ceiling, then folds his arms and closes his malevolent eyes. 'I don't suppose you have another credit card?' he sighs, wearily.

Now, I know I don't have another credit card. I do actually know this, but I get out my wallet and open it and peer into its cavernous depths. All I can find in its vast echoing spaces is a crumpled fiver and a photograph of the dog. I wonder if I can offer him that. I decide not to. I tell him I've forgotten all my other credit cards. He makes an unkind guttural scoffing noise. I offer to go and get cash from my bank machine. Gervaise's eyebrows practically disappear into his hairline. He almost levitates, he laughs so insanely. 'Cash?' he chortles. 'Cash? I can't take cash now. I've put it through as a credit card sale.'

'Well,' I blurt, 'I'll come back tomorrow then. Thanks.'

'Yes, sir,' he says. 'Why don't you do that, sir. Thank you very much, sir.' It is extraordinarily difficult to convey in print the pure withering sarcasm with which Gervaise manages to invest the word 'sir'. I slink from the shop feeling like a major criminal.

It was a terrible defining moment, as though a large white hand had come bursting through the ceiling with its long finger pointing accusingly at me. In the old days, life played horrible tricks on you by making you want to grow up to be Noddy Holder out of Slade, or making you feel you might one day get off with Valerie Singleton, or making you doubt the existence of God. Now it just declines your credit card, a disaster both plastic and drastic, which ruins your whole day in the process. There is nothing really worse, while walking the tightrope of fate, than getting your balance wrong.

65

IV The New Man

THIS WEEK I GOT A LETTER FROM A WOMAN FRIEND WHO
lives in a nasty part of downtown Boston, a suburb so bad
that the muggers are practically unionised. There was a
new man in her life, her epistle informed me. His name
was Safe-T-Guy.

Safe-T-Guy is a rubber man who can be purchased
through the mail for about $100. He comes in Caucasian,
Black, Native American, Oriental or Latino, and is available in three sizes: large, extra-large and Peter Clohessy.
(Well, OK, I'm kidding. There's no extra-large.) Anyway,
the idea is that you send off your cheque, get your Safe-
T-Guy back from the company in the mail (male order,
ho ho ho) and blow him up – the nozzle is located in the
left armpit, just in case you were wondering. Before too
long, Safe-T-Guy is in a happily inflated state. And let's
face it, who wouldn't be?

Anyway, tumescence having been successfully achieved,
you then put Safe-T-Guy in your passenger seat when
driving about the city, from which mobile vantage point
he acts as an effective deterrent to would-be muggers,
vagabonds, roaming cutpurses and other ne'er-do-wells.
One glance at this towering slab of testosterone in the
seat beside you and off they canter, eyes wide with
abject terror, streams of widdle meandering down their
inner thighs. So the argument goes. Safe-T-Guy is useful in the home also. According to the instruction
brochure he can be placed 'seated in a lighted window' or
'arranged horizontally in your bed'. (Horizontally! What
a lack of imagination.) He can be put sitting in an
armchair just inside your doorway in such a position that
he will frighten seven shades of Shinola out of intending

66

burglars, kidnappers or peripatetic representatives of the Church of Jesus Christ and the Latter Day Saints. Yes, Safe-T-Guy, in short, is a useful guy to have about the gaff.

Much is made in the accompanying literature of Safe-T-Guy's 'high degree of anatomical accuracy'. He has a 'realistic' smile – whatever that is – as well as 'movable hands' and 'a fully swivelling head'. (I mean, Jesus Christ Almighty, I'm a real human being and I don't have a 'fully swivelling head'. What the hell is he? Something out of *The Exorcist*?!) At this stage of the brochure, a discreet veil is drawn over the full extent of Safe-T-Guy's reality. Hmmmm.

'A high degree of anatomical accuracy', eh? The phrase began to taunt me. I rang up my friend in America and asked her the obvious question. Sadly, it turns out that Safe-T-Guy's degree of anatomical accuracy is not quite *that* high after all. In fact all Safe-T-Guy products are a little like the Eamon Dunphy fan club. No significant members. *Quel dommage.*

But what he lacked in some areas, he made up for in others. For example, he didn't answer back, she said. He was not moody, self-obsessed or argumentative. He didn't shave himself and leave little bits of beard in the sink. He had no problem with commitment. He did not bite his toenails. He was always available when you needed him. His feet didn't smell. OK, yes, so he wasn't so great at communication, but compared to her previous boyfriend he was a distinct improvement. A little unfair, I felt. I mean, yes, it has always struck me that her boyfriend hadn't got much to say. But then, at least he didn't try to say anything else.

In many ways, my friend seemed to feel, Safe-T-Guy

was the ideal partner. Loyal, dependable, oddly predictable. But the absolutely best thing about him was that when he arrived in his box, he was buck naked. The instruction brochure suggested that you go out immediately to your local store and buy a wardrobe of clothes for Safe-T-Guy, 'the kind of clothes you – and only you – feel he should wear'. This was not just heaven, she told me. This was Nirvana. The previous boyfriend was the type of chap who regarded a decade-old leather-elbowed jumper as the height of sartorial sophistication. My friend had been out every morning to the men's shops. Whatever she purchased – lilac shirts, paisley socks, Nehru jackets, silken posing pouches and pastel ties – Safe-T-Guy accepted her suggestions with a grateful (not to mention 'realistic') smile. Her credit card was beginning to melt into twisted and distended Dali-esque shapes, she told me. But she didn't care. She had bought him aftershave, deodorant, posh soap and flavoursome antiperspirant, and it was worth every scent, she opined.

Safe-T-Guy was sweeping America, she told me. But, she wanted to know, did I think that he would catch on here? What would the women of Ireland make of Safe-T-Guy? I laughed hollowly. No, I said, I didn't think he would ever catch on here. A brainless, expressionless, compliant clotheshorse with no personality whatsoever? I mean, come on, it's not as if we have an election coming up.

V The Emerald Fleece

WHEN I WAS A CHILD GROWING UP IN DUBLIN, THERE was a popular playground chant that went as follows: 'Georgie Best, Superstar, wears frilly knickers and a see-through bra.' The reason the chant was so widespread is very simple. Georgie Best was the only Irish person we knew who was famous and successful and skilled and rich. As such, he was so ineffably weird that he deserved to be pilloried, which he was, at every available opportunity. Attributing transvestism to its sporting heroes is perhaps not the mark of an emotionally healthy society. But that's what happened in Ireland.

What I remember most about growing up in Dublin is the sheer, unadulterated, mind-numbing boredom of the place. Dublin was the world capital of tedium. There was quite simply nothing to do, and nowhere to go, unless you happened to be a nun. I cannot overemphasise the dullness of growing up in Dublin. The highlight of your week would be getting the bus into town on a Saturday afternoon, slouching up and down Grafton Street like some clapped-out hooker touting for business, and then, perhaps, if you were lucky indeed, gathering with some of your friends to watch paint dry and, of course, to deride Georgie Best.

The other thing I remember about Dublin was the feeling, as constant as the rain that seemed to come down horizontally, of wishing you were somewhere else. Anywhere else. London, Paris, New York, Mars. We would have sold our grannies to get out of Dublin; and our grannies, being understanding old dears, would have understood and gone along compliantly with the plan. But in a very bored way.

Now, it seems, all this has changed. Something odd has happened here. Dublin has become the new European capital of style, culture, hipness, all the very things which it so demonstrably lacked when I was a kid. English and European style magazines are doing cover stories on the place. Pop stars and supermodels are attracted to Dublin the way toddlers are attracted to dog turds. So many films are being shot here that you can't walk down the street without tripping on a mega-star. The mega-stars, meanwhile, arc tripping on a mixture of Guinness and nose candy. And all these famous types want to come and live in Dublin. Julia Roberts, Tom Cruise, Sean Penn, Johnny Depp, Def Leppard and various members of Status Quo are just *some* – phew – of the major international talent who want to grace our shores. They want to do this for a variety of reasons. 'Liking the Irish scenery' seems to be one reason. Other stars 'love the Irish people', apparently. (The fact that artists and musicians pay no income tax in Ireland, has, of course, nothing at all to do with it. No, no. Just a coincidence. Honest. It's the scenery, you see. And the people. So pure. So ... innocent. So ... so ... gullible.) And then there's all that literary heritage. Sharon Stone wants to live in Dublin, she said in a recent memorable interview, because she 'really admires the great Irish writers, such as Dylan Thomas'. Our government encourage such enlightened cultural influx because it feels that we Irish need exposure to the outside world. And hey, let's face it, if there's one person who really knows a lot about exposure to the outside world, it's Sharon Stone.

More disturbing than all this is the fact that ordinary folk from all over Europe also want to come to Ireland now. This is probably fair enough, seeing as ordinary folk from all over Europe contribute a very great deal to Ireland through our very favourite charity, the EEC. (Germany, for example, is currently responsible for contributing six per cent of Irish GNP.) Our countryside is thus speckled with English New Age travellers with emerald-green hair, pipe-smoking German hippies in Aran sweaters, French performance artists who have learnt to speak fluent Gaelic, Seamus Heaney experts from minor British universities, leprechaun-hunting Lithuanians, emaciated Swedish bagpipe players in tricolour polo-necks, all trying to discover that most elusive of subterranean plants, Irish roots. The whole country is beginning to look like one of Shane McGowan's songs. The Irish meanwhile are discovering the gentle art of fleecing tourists instead of sheep. Posters of Beckett and Yeats and Flann O'Brien are cranked out like banknotes in Weimar Germany. There are Brendan Behan boxer shorts, Oscar Wilde eiderdowns, Sean O'Casey sweatshirts, Patrick Kavanagh key rings, Bernard Shaw shopping bags. And as for poor old James Joyce: a law has recently been passed to make it illegal to rent, own or frequent a Dublin pub that is not named after a James Joyce character. His face has been out on the five-punt note, but his books, needless to say, have still not been put on the Irish school curriculum. That would be going a tad too far. Yes, yes. You show us an Irish writer and for a small fee we'll slap his face on a shaving mug for you. We're good at that. We Irish really know a mug when we see one.

All this is very good for our economy, which is currently the healthiest in Europe. So, foreign readers, come on over and have a look at how successful and authentic and unspoilt we are. After all, you paid for it. And by the way, please try to remember that here in Ireland we don't like being stereotyped, which is why you will see so many T-shirts on sale in Dublin stores featuring leprechauns, shillelaghs, red-haired colleens plucking harps and really authentic Irish sayings such as 'My Boyfriend

Visited Ireland And All He Brought Me Back Was This Begorrah Shirt'. Happy Saint Patrick's Day. Top o' the mornin'. Pass the Deutschmarks and altogether now . . . 'Oh Danny Boy . . .'

Chapter 4

The Happiest Daze of Your Life

I   Peig Sayers is Dead!

'Education is a wonderful thing, but it is well
to remember from time to time that nothing
that is worth knowing can be taught.'

The Critic as Artist, Oscar Wilde

LET US START, MY DEARS, BY LOOKING BACK ACROSS THE
burning bridge at the distant past and remembering the
joy of going to school in Ireland. Wasn't it fun? Wasn't it
grand? I miss it still. Really. Truly. Yes, I do. Serio. And
monkeys regularly fly out of my butt.

You know, sometimes, particularly in the long lone-
some dawns before the spring has finally sprung, I find it
a tad hard to get out of the bed in the mornings. But then
there are the other times! The mornings when I waken
with a song in my heart and I rocket out of the scratcher
singing 'Who, Ray? Who, Ray? It's a Holly Holly Day' by
those late lamented lyricists, Boney M. I had one such
morning recently. There I was, feeling glum as I coughed
feebly, lit up a fag, extended a trembling hand from

73

beneath the duvet and switched on the radio. And all of a sudden, I heard the glorious news! Peig Sayers' days were numbered!!

There was a man on the radio called Maidhc Dainín Ó Sé speaking about a book he has written called *A Thig, Na Tit Orm* (*House, Do Not Fall on Me*). This accomplished and very funny work is to replace that steaming pile of putrid compost, *Peig*, which eponymous drudge-fest used to be the required Irish text for secondary school students in our beloved country. Maidhc Dainín Ó Sé, I thought to myself, since the happy day I finished my Leaving Cert a dozen long years ago, I have been waiting to hear this news.

I am, as regular readers may recall, a bit of a lapsed Catholic. But I am not ashamed to say that on that morning last week when I heard of Peig's demise I got out of the *leaba* and went down on my knees and thanked the Lord above for his mercies. Peig Sayers, in the dustbin of history! Bliss it was to be alive in this dawn. Peig bloody Sayers, the pox be upon her, may she be broiled over the hobs of Hades and then made to listen to the Kilfenora Ceilidh Band for all eternity.

You remember what it was like, don't you, readers? You'd go into your Irish class feeling relatively content with your little self, but then the *moon tore* would open the book and begin to read aloud and next thing you knew, down would come the misery. *Thit an lug ar an lag ort!* Oh, alas, and *ochón*, affliction, agony, distress, pain, sorrow and woe peppered with a light smattering of depression, despondency and heartache. Peig Sayers, the woman who lived to be eight hundred and seven without ever being happy once.

By coincidence I have recently been reading the English

translation of Myles Na Gopaleen's satirical novel *An Beal Bocht*, which parodies *Peig*, Séamas Ó Grianna and the only one of that whole shower worth reading, Tomás Ó Criomhthain. Now, I am really a very big fan of yer man Myles, but in writing this book he had an almost insurmountable problem. *Peig* was simply too absurd to satirise. You don't believe me? Open *The Poor Mouth* and read any sentence. Here's one: 'And is it the way, said I, that new hardships and new calamities are in store for the Gaels and a new overthrow is destined for the small green country which is the native land of both of us?' Could you really swear that's not from *Peig*? Be honest now. You could not.

Peig was a celebration of gombeen passivity, written in a language that for all its remarkable beauty records in its very structure the psychology of victimhood. How do you say 'I am sad' in Irish? *Ta brón órm*, which means literally, 'sadness is upon me'; that is, I am the passive recipient of an emotion which is outside me. The other way to say 'I am sad' is *Taim go brónach*, which might be translated as 'I exist sadly'. Thus, as the Irish-American historian Kerby Miller has written, 'the Irish language categorises experience as either active or stative, and by making the distinction between the categories overt in the structure of sentences, forces an awareness of that distinction upon the Irish-speaker in a much stronger way than does a nominative language such as English'. In other words, Irish features categories of passivity which other languages don't even dream about.

Still, what a beautiful and precise language. ('Twenty-seven different words for seaweed', as one Irish poet reminds us.) But if there is one person at whose feet we might lay the near-death of modern Irish, surely it is Peig,

mawkish, cringing, miserable, forelock-tugging, acquies-
cent, superstitious, auld baggage that she was. What a
great idea it was to make us all read her. How relevant
she was to our lives! What a great way to murder a
language. Peig Sayers was the droning voice of Irish
failure, the kind of literary character that only a truly
colonised society could produce. Her long overdue demise
is cause for celebration. *Na beidh a leithidi aris ann!*
Well, boo-hoo-hoo, *ochón ochón, agus Dia idir sinn agus
an tOlc.*

Now that we've got that out of the way, let me go on
to say this: my university education was severely dis-
rupted by the outbreak of World War Two. This had
actually happened forty-two years earlier, but I was still
very upset about it. Nah, seriously. I went to college
myself some years ago and I must say I had a fine old
time. College, just in case you are wondering, is basically
like school, only there are bar extensions. That's at night,
of course. During the day, there are many demands on
students' time, such as sitting about the canteen in funny
clothes, languidly drinking coffee and discussing controversial books which you haven't read. This last student
activity is really a lot of fun! In fact, some people are so
good at it that they are never allowed to leave college and
end up having to become professors!

But college, of course, is not just about enjoying yourself. It is also about enjoying other people. No, seriously,
the main point of college is to pursue learning. Such
learning can be divided into two kinds; namely, the kind
that will be of some remotely practical use to you when
you leave college and then, on the other hand, philosophy. I studied philosophy in first year. This involved a
lot of sitting in a stuffy little room just off the Stillorgan

dual carriageway discussing the meaning of reality. I don't think I will ever quite forget the philosophy tutorial where myself and my friend John McDermott were asked by our tutor to define reality. 'This,' John said confidently. 'What?' smiled the tutor. 'This,' said John once again, expansively gesturing around him. 'You know, this.' The tutor began to roar, 'What? What?' And John continued saying, quite sensibly I thought, 'Well, this. I mean, this is reality, isn't it?' It went on like that for some time before the poor tutor finally cantered screaming from the room and launched himself into the Belfield lake, loudly chanting epigrams from the writings of Heraclitus, an ancient Greek bloke who believed everything in the world was made out of fire. PAYE taxpayers will, I imagine, be very happy in the knowledge that there are publicly funded institutions in our country where our young people can devote as much time as they need to studying everything in the world being made out of fire. Phew, I can hear them saying, what a relief. There was also an ancient Greek bloke who believed that everything in the world was made out of water. Doubtless, there was also an ancient Greek bloke who believed everything in the world was made out of jelly, but I think I must have been out sick that day.

One of my other subjects in first year was English literature. This is a fascinating subject to study, particularly if you are quite stupid and don't like reading much. The point about English literature is, of course, that there is no point, and no correct answer. You can say whatever the hell you like in an English tutorial and you will always be right. Take the play *Hamlet*, for instance. Everybody who has ever seen it in a theatre knows that *Hamlet* is about a Danish guy who is haunted by the ghost of his father and smacks the head off everyone in sight as a result. But no. In college, *Hamlet* is symbolic. In college, English literature, generally, is a load of symbolics. *Hamlet* can actually be about anything from whaling rights in the Antarctic to the Leinster Senior Hurling Finals. Scott Fitzgerald's novel *The Great Gatsby* is about how all rich American people are appalling and deserve to be murdered. It's that simple. But if you write, in your essay on said work, that *The Great Gatsby* is really about the fact that Scott Fitzgerald was a repressed bisexual compulsive overeater who regularly contemplated cunnilingus with his own grandmother, you will get an A-plus. If you don't believe me, just try it.

In addition to English and philosophy, when I was in college I also studied history, in the vain hope that it would one day repeat itself and I'd make a killing the second time around. I was wrong about this, but still it was a pretty interesting subject. Another interesting subject is psychology. This is all about sex and experimenting on rats. If you like either one of these activities, you will do very well at psychology. If you like both, preferably simultaneously, you will make many friends and probably be offered a lectureship in your first week. Yes, indeed, all aspiring psychology students would do well to remember that beloved old joke: what's the difference between a psychologist and a conjuror? One pulls rabbits out of a hat, while the other pulls habits out of a rat. Then there are all the interesting subject combinations you can do in universities these days. Maths and origami. Physics and pole-vaulting. Art history and golf. One institution I know is offering a combined media studies-Irish history course about the important links between the great Irish potato famine and the English

78

comedy film. (Lecture One is intriguingly entitled 'Carry On Starving'.) So, something for everyone there!

To be serious for a moment, I get a lot of letters from readers who are students, and it is important to remember that, every summer when the rest of us are sunning ourselves and leaping around the beach in our pelts, many of these poor feckers are studying for their repeat examinations, which they would have got first time around if they hadn't been taking drugs and fornicating. So now, as a fully qualified and trained novelist, I give as a service my own personal notes and important insights into some of the classic works of world literature that are likely to come up in all exam papers on the subject of English lit. (Intending candidates may want to cut out and keep this page.) To begin with, poetry!

'Show me a poet,' wrote the critic A. J. Liebling, 'and I will show you a shit.' That's a quote that might be worth remembering, not just for education, but for life. But anyway, all English poetry begins with *Beowulf*, a long liver-meltingly dull poem which proves that Old English people either had a terrific boredom tolerance level or else took serious drugs. Another Old English poem is 'The Dream of the Rood', which is about a talking tree. Seriously. Then there is Geoffrey Chaucer's *Canterbury Tales*. This is quite a good poem, but Chaucer, unfortunately could not spell very well. Take the following couplet, selected at random: 'In thatte Apprile morne whenn I gotte outt of ye bed/ I had a fiers payne in me ballockse and lykewise in me hayde.'

After Chaucer, nothing much happened until John Donne came along. Donne was a master of the metaphysical conceit, a kind of complicated and very sophisticated metaphor, an example of which (from 'A Nocturnal upon

79

Saint Lucie's Day') is 'You know, I've always thought believing in Godde is a bit like having a Daihatsu Charade, yeah?' (Father Brian D'Arcy, like John Donne, is a great man for the metaphysics.)

Next stop on the whistle-stop tour of English poetry is, of course, the Romantics. The most important Romantics were Keats, Shelley, Byron, Blake and Duran Duran. The Romantics were famous for believing in the essential divinity of nature, positing a radical and subversive view of politics, having sex with their sisters and other female relations and dying young in bizarre drowning accidents. They wore long capes, took a lot of drugs and often went for walks down the pier while stoned, which may well explain the drowning accidents.

After this, the most important English poet is T. S. Eliot, whose very name will always be celebrated in the annals of literary history for being an anagram of TOILETS. When not being a rude anagram, Eliot wrote very long and famous poems such as *The Waste Land*; summary: Bloody foreigners, bloody English, bloody Ezra Pound, I wish I was a professional footballer or ANYTHING instead of a poet.

It may be helpful at this point to include similar concise summaries of the work of some of our home-grown Irish poets. For example, Oliver St John Gogarty's *Complete Poems*: I am nice, James Joyce is a shit. Patrick Kavanagh's *Complete Poems*: Canals are nice, Monaghan is shit. Samuel Beckett's *Complete Poems*: Everything is shit.

William Butler Yeats will need special study. He is an important Anglo-Irish writer. It is difficult to give a precise and non-academic description of this term, but basically, an Anglo-Irish writer was a person who owned a big castle and wrote admiring poems about peasants, but who wouldn't have wanted his daughter to marry one. Yeats's work can, of course, be split into three quite distinct periods. Period One (the early stuff): Fairies are nice, aren't swans weird, when you think? Period Two (the middle bit): I wish to God Maud Gonne would either snog me or shag off. Period Three (the monkey-gland operation and after): I am a saddo.

And now, drama! Let us begin with a key quote from *The Importance of Being Earnest* by Oscar Wilde: 'The world is divided into two kinds of people, Algy. The kind of people who divide the world into two kinds of people and the kind of people who do not. HAHAHA, pass the cucumber sandwiches. You know the world is divided into two kinds of cucumber sandwich, Algy, the kind . . .'

Then there is the significant and very blind playwright, Sean O'Casey. It is vital to mention in your answer that O'Casey was, of course, 'a Dublin writer', which means, as the examiner will know, that he hightailed it out of Ireland as soon as he possibly could and went to live in the English suburbs for the rest of his life. Blindness, you will be aware by now, is an important tradition in Irish writers. James Joyce was blind as a bat, Samuel Beckett was more than a little myopic and Brendan Behan, if not actually blind, was at least blind drunk quite often. Readers who entertain ambitions to be talented Irish writers – and, hey, who doesn't these days?! – must go and at the very least get themselves spectacles or, even better, pluck out their eyes immediately. Which brings us neatly to Shakespeare.

Shakespeare is famous for being a notable quotable. His plays are full of stuff which everybody half-remembers, such as his great soliloquy on the Seven Ages of Man.

This was shortened and put into limerick form by the late Sir Kingsley Amis, and as a learning aid to all students of the bard, I reproduce it here:

> Seven ages, first puking then mewling
> Then very pissed off with one's schooling.
> Then fucks and then fights,
> Then judging chaps' rights.
> Then shuffling in slippers, then drooling.

Here is another fine Shakespeare limerick which neatly sums up the plot of *Hamlet*:

> Prince Hamlet thought Uncle a traitor
> For having it off with his mater;
> Revenge Dad or not?
> That's the gist of the plot,
> And he did – nine soliloquies later.

Like Sir Kingsley Amis, Shakespeare, too, was English, but despite this wrote thirty-seven plays, including a large number of 'comedies' which are about as funny as a dose of the galloping piyakers. They contain the kind of jokes that English teachers always cack themselves laughing at, such as, 'Prithee, sweet wench, I shall un-cuckle thy cockles or a pox upon my knackers for a loutish knave.' Thematically, his three most important tragedies may be usefully summarised as follows. *Hamlet*: Well, blow me, life, it's a funny old game, eh? *King Lear*: Well, blow me, kids these days, what can you do? *Romeo and Juliet*: Please. Blow me.

Then, of course, there is Joyce. That's James Joyce, by the way, not Joyce who used to go out with dashing Captain Frank Furrilo in *Hill Street Blues*. Joyce is a very important writer. You can tell this because so many Dublin pubs are named after his characters. You will do well to memorise the following summaries of his books. *Dubliners*: Dublin is a pile of shit. I wish I lived in Trieste. *Portrait of the Artist as a Young Man*: Nobody will get off with me. I wish I lived in Trieste. *Ulysses*: And he said, will we go and live in Trieste, and I said, yes, we will, yes, we will, yes, yes. *Finnegans Wake*. Stumbly-bumbly-un-doublin-fear-silly-wear-da-gurls-are-so-proddy, Daddy.

So I hope that will be of some help to you. If not, halfway through your exam, simply go through your wallet, select a banknote that has a picture of a famous Irish writer on it and attach it firmly to the paper with a staple or paperclip. It certainly worked for me.

Apart from passing exams, I have often been asked for advice on other aspects of student life. And my main piece of advice is: shag off asking me silly questions and go get a job! Having a student job is a very important thing, because, in the absence of the Vietnam War, it gives students something oppressive to complain about.

I do not have very many regrets about the five years I spent in University College Dublin. One or two, perhaps. I suppose the main one is that halfway through second year myself and my friend John McDermott, for some bizarre reason, got into the habit of hedge-jumping. This was a game we actually invented and developed ourselves – they say university is there to extend the young mind – involving the consumption of a lot of strong drink in the Belfield Bar and the subsequent jumping into a hedge. There wasn't really much more to it than that, but we considered hedge-jumping a lot of fun. I guess you had to be there. Useful and educational as this activity undoubtedly was, I do sometimes think that if John and I had devoted as much time to, say, medieval European history or the dialogues of Plato as we did to hedge-jumping, we might now have more things to talk about at dinner parties. So, that is one regret.

But my other main regret is that in all those years I never once went abroad to work during the holidays. Nearly all my friends did this every year, including John McDermott. Summer would come, exams would be undergone and then almost immediately afterwards everyone would disappear en masse, off to France or England or Spain to teach or work in factories or, presumably, to jump into the hedges of the new and developing Europe. The really adventurous ones went to America, from which distant land they would return with fistfuls of dollars and tales of living in unusual places, such as houseboats and Manhattan squats. They were exotic creatures, these students who had been to America. The thought of getting off with one of them was wildly exciting. We felt that they had learnt a thing or two about life.

I can't remember now why I never went abroad, but one reason was love. My first two summers in college were spent in a relationship that was, shall we say, a little tense. So tense, indeed, that there were times when it felt like it was being directed by Alfred Hitchcock. Looking back now, I think travel would have been very good for the relationship, preferably one-way travel by one or the other of us to Mars. But at the time, we believed that togetherness would help us. (I should point out that at the time we also believed worldwide democratic socialist revolution was inevitable in the next few years, led by the Irish Labour Party.) Another reason for my lack of peripatetic activity was that I wanted to be a journalist, and I thought that if I got a summer job on a newspaper or magazine this would help my chances. Ah, the sweet innocence of youth. I still remember with crawling horror the letter I typed and circulated to every single editor in Dublin, explaining that, while I had absolutely no experience whatsoever in the field of journalism and no ideas to speak of, I was an asset whose potential was right up there with Woodward's and Bernstein's. Amazingly, I got no replies, and so, that summer, while my friends frolicked on the banks of the Rhine and the Seine, I ended up working for a company that manufactured rubbish bags in Dundrum. (At the time I was living in Ranelagh. They do say that travel broadens the mind.)

My job was to sell rubbish bags over the phone. This, in case you are tempted to give up your current occupation and make an exciting career change, is not quite as satisfying as it sounds. There are some products people do not mind being sold over the phone – indeed, there are some products that people actually *expect* to be sold over the phone. Take it from me, rubbish bags are not one of them. After a while, the routine became distressingly predictable. I would ring up and ask if the person wanted to buy some rubbish bags. They would then cackle maniacally, or say something astoundingly offensive, or hang up. Sometimes they would do all three. But I worked and worked, staying on that telephone, dialling and re-dialling until my index finger looked like ET's. In a month I think I sold six orders of rubbish bags, and to this day I am convinced that at least two of them were to barking lunatics who just wanted somebody to talk to on the phone.

Another job I had that summer was waiter in a very up-market restaurant in Dublin. I knew it was up-market

85

because the rats in the kitchen frequently wore tuxedos and addressed each other as 'Serge'. On the menu of this restaurant was a dish called 'Orange Surprise'. This was an orange, scooped out, filled with ice cream and then bunged into the semi-banjaxed freezer, where the ice cream would acquire the consistency of wallpaper paste. One night, a young attractive couple arrived for a meal. The woman was wearing a low-cut dress. (This becomes important later in the story.) Anyway, this couple ordered their grub, ate it, and sat giving each other the hairy eyeball for a few romantic moments before deciding they wanted to order dessert, one orange surprise. I got it from the kitchen, brought it out to the dining room and, at a crucial moment, tripped over the carpet. The orange surprise flew out of its glass, sailed through the air describing a perfect arc and landed right in this young woman's cleavage, splattering semi-molten ice cream all over what I believe is known in polite society as her *embonpoint*. A split second passed before she looked up at me, grinned and said, 'Well, I suppose that's the surprise.' Now there's presence of mind for you.

That summer went bloody slowly, I can tell you. After a while, myself and my boss came to the mutual conclusion that the good Lord had not put me on the earth to sell refuse sacks, and I got another job, selling double glazing door to door. I was just as successful at this. I tramped the doorways of Dublin, wearing a suit and tie I had borrowed from my father, my eyes a good deal more glazed than the windows I was offering to sell. Next, I got a job collecting information for the census. To borrow a joke from Mr Sean Mac Reamoinn, it was not long before I, like the census form, was broken down by sex, age and religion. From time to time colourful postcards would arrive from Europe written in the spidery script of the drunken, the sexually exhausted and the utterly happy. 'Wish you were here,' my friends would write. 'Hope the journalism job is working out well.' Boy, did they know how to hurt, or what?

And then, in October, they all returned for the new college year. They were full of mad stories and wild adventures. One or two of them had beards. They had money to spend and tall tales to tell. While I had been hawking double glazing to the desperately single-glazed people of Dublin, my friends had been living it up, getting into rows, having the time of their lives. One memorable story involved a friend who had got drunk and insulted a large US Marine at a rock festival in Germany. This Marine had been going on ad nauseam about how his father was Irish, and my friend had explained that we in Ireland were sick and tired of Irish-Americans and all their auld guff. The Marine did not like this one bit. 'If my father was here, he'd kick your ass,' the Marine said. 'If your father ever saw my ass, he'd want to fuck it,' my friend said. The result was mayhem. What I believe is called, in diplomatic circles, 'an incident' almost took place. In the coming year this story and other stories were endlessly re-told with the wink-and-elbow language of delight, the conspiratorial giggles of those who have shared important experiences. All I could do was listen and grin mirthlessly and silently recall my own summer in Dublin, selling rubbish bags and talking rubbish to loonies over the phone. Take it from me, if I were you, I wouldn't let that happen.

But anyway, one great thing about college is the friends you make while you are there. In the ensuing years you never lose your closeness or intimacy. The friends you make in college are the friends to whom you can talk about anything at all. They have seen you dancing, remember. They know just how bad you can get.

A good friend of mine has just recently started attending college over in England, as a mature student. She rang me for a bit of chin-wag recently, and it was good to hear from her. Student life was wonderful these days, she said, although things had changed just a tad since what she rather depressingly insisted on calling 'our day'. Her student union was about to call a lecture boycott demanding a new coffee machine be immediately installed in the common room, she told me. *Hasta La Victoria Siempre!* It was so good to see that the spirit of Paris '68 is alive and well. But she was also saying to me that she had a problem. 'This young bloke's after falling for me,' she said. 'He keeps ogling me in the canteen.'

'Ogling you?' I said.

'You know,' she said, 'giving me the hairy eyeball and the thousand-yard stare.'

'Is that a bad thing?' I enquired. (I should say that this friend of mine is single and currently looking for a partner. That's not putting it strongly enough, really. She is looking for a partner the way Captain Scott looked for the South Pole. Interested male readers with all their own teeth, a sense of humour and no wives may write to me for further information.)

'So what's the problem with this one?' I said.

'I'm twenty-nine,' she sighed, 'he's twenty-three.'

'So what,' I said. 'Is that his age or his IQ?'

'He was still in short trousers in 1977,' she said. 'It would never work. He doesn't remember John Noakes being on *Blue Peter*.'

'Poor creature,' I said. 'My heart bleeds.'

'Maybe,' she said, 'but he's just different to me. YOUNGER!! See, I don't actually know anything about Take That.'

'You could learn,' I said. '"Don't Love Me for Fun, Girl" isn't too bad, you know, if you really listen to the words.'

There was a silence for a moment. The telephone line crackled and bleeped.

'Well, there's another problem,' she said. 'He's ugly.'

'How ugly is he?' I said.

'He's a bit of a hound,' she said. 'I'm sorry, but he is.'

'A hound?' I said.

'Look, Joe,' she said, 'the man is a furry domesticated carnivorous quadruped. I'm not fussy, you know, but the chap is a shagging *madra*. He has a face only a mother could love, and I'm talking a mother with sunglasses, an Alsatian and a white stick. We're talking Rover here. He is canine city Alabama. You would need a licence for him. He has only recently learnt to walk on his hind legs and not pee against lampposts. Pedigree Chum on toast is his favourite snack. He runs around in a circle trying to bite off his own balls. He is man's best friend. The fact that his surname is Barker, shall we say, is not a coincidence. He is . . .'

'Why don't you say what you really mean,' I said. 'You really should try to coax yourself out of that shell of yours.'

'He's a nice enough chap, I suppose, and I know I'm not God's gift or anything and my bloody brother is forever telling me I look like an astronaut's wife and I know some of the frights I've gone out with have mugs that'd curdle milk. But this guy is different. It would be like wearing the face off Lassie.'

'Hmmmm,' I said. 'You could always turn the lights out.'

'Wouldn't work,' she said. 'His acne would glow.'

'You could always put paper bags over two of his heads.'

'No, listen, Joe,' she said, 'you remember that Dana song "Everything Is Beautiful (In Its Own Way)"?'

'How could I ever forget it?' I said. 'The sway of the violins, the roar of . . .'

'Yes,' she said. 'Well, that song should have been called "Everything Except This Bloke Is Beautiful (In Its Own Way)".'

'Wow,' I said.

'And that's how ugly he is,' she told me.

I was astonished to hear this. In my whole life, I don't think I have ever met anybody truly ugly. I mean, yes, there are degrees of physical attractiveness. We cannot all be Mel Gibson or Claudia Schiffer, but then again, they cannot be us, either, which, I'm sure, keeps them both awake at night. But what I'm saying is that I'd always denied ugliness. I'd always believed few people have no redeeming features whatsoever. So I put the phone down in a haze of depression.

Of course, I should have known what would happen. My friend rang back a few days later. She's going to the pictures with Mr Oil Painting on Friday. 'I bumped into him last night and we had a drink,' she said, 'and he made me laugh, so we had another few, and I mean he's still ugly as bloody sin, but he can kiss like there's no tomorrow and when he held my hand on the way home, it made the soles of my feet tingle.'

'Buy him a balaclava,' I told her. 'It sounds like love to me.'

Now *that's* a conversation you could only have with a college friend.

II Travels in Hyper-Hackery

> 'The majority of journalists are ignoramuses and
> not a few of them are also bounders. All the
> knowledge that they pack into their brains is, in
> every reasonable cultural sense, useless . . . It is a
> mass of trivialities and puerilities; to recite it
> would be to make even a bartender or a barber beg
> for mercy.'
>
> *Letters*, Leo Nikolayevich Tolstoy

IT'S A FUNNY THING, BUT YOUNG PEOPLE OFTEN ASK ME for advice on what they should study if they want to grow up and work for a newspaper, and how should they go about becoming journalists. My main piece of advice, of course, is try to get the kind of journalistic job I have myself, that is, the kind of journalistic job where you never have to go outside the door, the kind of journalistic job where you have to write an amusing, yet incisive newspaper column once a week. Writing an amusing, yet incisive newspaper column is a relatively straightforward activity. You just sit down at your computer once a week and wait for the droplets of blood to appear on your forehead. There are three unbreakable rules for writing a newspaper column such as this, but unfortunately nobody knows what they are. Personally I just write whenever I am inspired, and, like I told you before, I make damn sure I'm inspired at nine o'clock every Wednesday morning, which is four hours before my column has to be delivered.

One bad thing about writing an amusing, yet incisive

newspaper column is that it tends to be full of your opinions about things, and as such, you tend to get a lot of letters from angry readers about *their* opinions. Many of these letters are written in green ink, I have noticed, and just like in politics, the deeper the green, the madder the person. A lot of people who are completely insane read newspapers, and in between rattling their chains and barking at the moon, they're all keen letter writers. Another difficult thing about writing a column is that you tend to get noticed by other journalists who can't wait to criticise you. For example, a prominent part-time gossip columnist and full-time shithead recently wrote about me that I was effeminate. I didn't mind that so much, because beside her, I am.

But anyway, at some point during my childhood I decided that I wanted to be a journalist. My parents greeted this news with excitement and enthusiasm. It's a sign of the innocence of the times that they seemed to regard journalists as being somehow above other people, as being like teachers or doctors, people with a sacred vocation in life. They had clearly never met one. They would sometimes concede, in hushed and regretful tones, that they had heard that many journalists occasionally drank a bit. What they did not know is that many journalists would suck the alcohol out of a dishcloth.

By this stage, I had become a fan of the great Australian investigative journalist John Pilger. And so I thought that being a journalist would involve rampaging around the war zones of the world, standing up for the oppressed while getting myself a good suntan and meeting lots of girls. This, by the way, is not the case. The early years of being a journalist involve a good deal of reporting on the local dog show and not a lot of dangerous distant travel, unless of course you get to report on the local dog show in Limerick city, in which case, God help you.

As you know, I went to college in UCD and studied English, philosophy and history, thinking that this would be a good combination of subjects for an aspiring journalist, particularly because UCD was not at that time offering the really useful interdisciplinary combination for journalists: drunkenness, gossip and malice. At some point during my first year in college I somehow came across and read a book called *The New Journalism*. This was an anthology that featured the writing of a group of American journalists who emerged in the 1960s and 1970s such as Norman Mailer, Hunter S. Thompson, Joan Didion, Tom Wolfe, Gay Talese, Truman Capote, P. J. O'Rourke and many others. The book was a revelation to me. The thing about these writers was that they were not just interested in the story, but in how it was told. They were actually interested in the craft of writing. They didn't just tell you the facts, they used their skill as writers to go to the emotional heart of a story. Often they used the techniques of fiction. (I don't mean that they made things up, though, in the case of Hunter S. Thompson's description of how he had once bought a gorilla while smacked out of his bonce in a Las Vegas casino, I did have my doubts.) They tended to use a lot of dialogue, a good deal of description of place and landscape. Sometimes they told you what smell you would get as you walked down a certain street. Sometimes they put in details that at first glance seemed unnecessary – there is a famous article by Tom Wolfe about a Hell's Angel murder, where he includes lyrics from songs that he heard on the radio while writing the story – and individually these details would mean nothing, but taken together they would tell you a hell of a lot about the heart of the story.

In college, anyway, I began to write for a variety of left-wing student publications. I'm sure you know the type of thing. Badly typeset with appalling photographs and stolen cartoons and Letraset headlines and graphics in the shape of hammers or clenched fists and lots and lots of articles about oppressed minorities of one kind or another, usually in faraway places. Anyway, having surprisingly failed to bring the apartheid state to its knees with my prose style, I continued my journalistic career by reviewing books and films, usually books that I had not read, and films that I had not seen. But I always wanted to do a real story. My breakthrough finally came when I was allowed to write a piece about the disgraceful state of the toilets in the Belfield Bar. With true undergraduate modesty and understatement, I insisted to my editor – a Foxrock Trotskyist who is now a member of the Progressive Democrats, and who back then was drunk most of the time, and a good deal less coherent when he was sober – that my article should have the headline 'Power, Corruption and Lies'. There are investigative journalists in this town who have been working on exposing scandals for three or four decades, and who have never gotten to write an article headed 'Power, Corruption and Lies', but I did, at the age of nineteen, and I have to admit that I was hooked.

I began to read more Irish journalism around that time, and was attracted to the writing in *Magill* magazine, which had been founded in the late 1970s by Vincent Browne. Vincent was exactly the kind of figure who appealed to aspiring young left-wing journalists, in that he was combative and bright and was often asked to appear on the *Late Late Show*, where he would look as though he had just been savaged by a lion and dragged through a hedge backwards, as he merrily ripped politicians to pieces without bothering to pause for breath. There were lots of exotic rumours about Vincent, for example, that in order to illustrate to his former editor how easy it was for a person to buy an illegal firearm, he had bought a sub-machine-gun in a Belfast pub and brought it into his editor's office. Recently I asked a journalist who had once worked for Vincent whether this rumour about the machine-gun was true, and he said he wasn't so sure. He didn't really think it *could* have been that easy to buy a machine-gun, because if it was, Vincent would have bought one and shot him.

Vincent gave me my first proper journalistic job, as a part-time researcher, and he even allowed me to write a few articles. From then on I made it my business to bombard *Magill* magazine with ideas for more articles. I camped outside the office waiting to assail the staff on the way in. I followed them into pubs up and down Baggot Street. I would have happily paid the editor Colm Tóibín for permission to make the tea in the *Magill* office, so you can imagine how delighted I was when in the summer of second year I finally wore him down and managed to get a part-time job with the magazine. The job I got – theatre critic – was not quite as John Pilger-esque as I had once hoped it would be. While Pilger was kicking in doors and dodging bullets and smuggling spools of illegal film out of Cambodia up his bottom, I was sitting in the Abbey Theatre marvelling at the latest Hugh Leonard play. Sometimes I wondered which of us truly knew the most about human suffering.

Anyway, ten years after my first summer job with

Magill magazine I was in New York when Vincent Browne rang me up and asked me to write a column in the *Tribune* for six weeks. I did this. It seemed to go down OK. Well, nobody sued anyway. When I came back from New York, Vincent asked me to keep it going, and so I did, and I also began to write longer pieces for the paper. After a few months Vincent gave me a booklet he had written about the *Sunday Tribune* house style and suggested I should read it. My favourite passage was headed 'Obscenity', and it listed the words that could never be mentioned in the *Sunday Tribune*. At the end of this sentence I'm going to tell you what they are, so those of you who went to nice schools or voted 'No' in the divorce referendum should skip a few lines now. The words that you could never use in the *Sunday Tribune* were: fuck, cunt, piss, shit and cocksucker. The funny thing was, you would hear some of these words in the *Sunday Tribune* newsroom any day of the week, particularly if Vincent was in it at the time. I was amazed to find that the *Tribune* operated such a scheme of censorship. I mean, yes, it probably didn't affect the journalists too directly, in that you would only very rarely feel the need to use the word 'cocksucker' in, for example, a restaurant review. But still, the prohibition was there and we all had to live with it. (I myself sometimes feel that the list of words not to be mentioned in the paper should be amended to read: fuck, cunt, piss, shit, cocksucker and Aodghán Feeley.)

So the contemporary scene is not always encouraging. And yet people still want to be journalists. Nowadays you can even study journalism, no less, and acquire a professional qualification in it. Perhaps you might expect me to be cynical about that, but I'm actually not. In truth, an odd kind of anachronistic snobbery sometimes operates in the world of the hack. The idea is common that studying journalism is somehow dangerous and woolly, that in the good old days you cut your journalistic teeth pounding the streets in a raincoat and jamming your foot into doors and meeting mysterious informants in underground car parks. It's an image of the life of a journalist that has far more to do with Hollywood *film noir* than it does with real life, and perhaps that's why some hacks are so fond of pushing it. They all want to be Woodward and Bernstein.

But the truth is, some of them are Beavis and Butthead.

Chapter 5

Wife-Swopping Sodomites

'All this fuss about sleeping together.
For physical pleasure I'd rather go
to the dentist any day.'

Vile Bodies, Evelyn Waugh

I   The Bank That Likes to Say 'Yesss!'

IT IS A TRUTH UNIVERSALLY ACKNOWLEDGED THAT POV-
erty, like adolescence, drugs and Roman Catholicism,
can do funny things to the mind. This has occurred to me
many times in my life, but perhaps never so forcefully as
it did when I ran up against poverty myself for the first
time, in the summer of 1985. I had spent the summer
immediately after my graduation from University College Dublin working in London as a furniture remover.
The way it turned out, my flat-mate was a little more
well suited to the profession of furniture removing than
myself, in that one night, while I was down the pub, he
had removed a good deal of it from our flat, along with
my wallet, which contained all of my summer's savings.
Thus it was that I found myself alone, almost friendless
and broke in London. I reacted the way any red-blooded
and stout-hearted Irishman would. I broke down crying
hysterically for my mama. When I had finished doing
this, I considered my position. It wasn't good. How in the

name of God would I ever get back to Dublin? Eventually, driven to distraction by the sound of my protracted sobbing, the poor old blind widow who lived upstairs offered me some money that she had been saving for a complicated hip-replacement operation. Even after I took it, however, I was still ten whole pounds short of my ferry fare home to Ireland. I was absolutely desperate. There was only one thing for it. I would have to go to a sperm bank. Not only would this course of action provide me with the means to get home, I told myself, but it would be contributing something lasting to humanity. The way it turns out, however, an ambition to contribute something lasting to humanity can be a bit of a heavy burden.

I knew several people who had made deposits at said sperm bank from time to time, when the cold winds of penury had really begun to howl and bite. I consulted these friends and colleagues, who expressed tender sympathy for my plight by laughing until they fell off their bar stools. One mate, a young man who was studying to become a Catholic priest at the time, had serious moral doubts about my plan, I have to admit. But ultimately my own view was that you may as well get properly paid for something you'd be doing for nothing anyway, so I rang up the clinic and they told me the score. You turned up, signed a few forms. Then, a quick indulgence in a bit of a J. Arthur Rank, and hey presto, there you were, fresh, relaxed, glowing with satisfaction, ten quid richer, sharing a post-coital cigarette with yourself.

I arrived at the clinic on the appointed morning and was welcomed by two nice middle-aged ladies in white coats, Dora and Lillian. They handed me a glass jar the size of a pill bottle. I stared at it in disbelief. To have

99

filled it efficiently would have required the aim of William Tell combined with the well-honed muscular control of a Tibetan guru. I was told to 'just slip into the cubicle and relax'.

I repaired to said cubicle, feeling more than a little tense. The walls were made of hankies and sweat. Inside was a chair, a radio and a table. The radio was turned on, which is more than I can say for myself. There was also a large pot of tea. This was telling, I thought. The English must surely be the only race in the world who regard tea-drinking and masturbation as mutually complementary leisure activities. There was also a plate of biscuits. Custard Creams was the brand name. The possibilities were absolutely endless.

On the table sat an 'adult' magazine, through which I began to leaf, contentedly unsticking pages and making detailed mental notes. I should point out to English readers that in Ireland, the backward and uncivilised country where I live, such artistic and educational magazines are not widely available, and so we are all reduced to reading the literary works of James Joyce, Samuel Beckett and William Butler Yeats instead. (Needless to say, we are all hoping and fervently praying to catch up with the English some day.) Anyway, this glossy publication featured in its centrefold spread the undoubted charms of a young woman called Rayleen who, according to the accompanying text, had 'hidden talents'. She certainly wasn't hiding too many of them that morning, I reflected. The article went on to list Rayleen's 'personal qualities' as 'shyness and intelligence'. This was indeed food for thought. Rayleen was the only shy person I'd ever seen who could fellate a hose-pipe while placing both ankles behind her head and getting paid for it. This last was the intelligence part, I guess. After a brief enough time, I closed the magazine and put it under the chair. It was nothing personal. Rayleen was one of the nicest girls I'd come across in ages, but somehow I just didn't feel like coming across her. The truth is, I just didn't think Rayleen and I would respect each other in the morning.

Reader, I unbuckled and sat there, waiting for something to happen. But you know how it is. There you are, hot to trot, in the mood for love, when some little thing just goes and spoils the ambience. In my case it was the radio, which suddenly started to belt out the old Max Bygraves number 'You Need Hands (To Hold Some One You Care For)'. That just put me right off, dunno why. I am somewhat constrained here by the laws of good taste, but let me just say that I found it more than a little hard – a wildly inappropriate adjective in the circumstances – to concentrate on the matter in hand. I tried, I tried. I summoned up every shatteringly exciting fantasy I could. A reasonably progressive and yet economically competent government for Great Britain, for instance. The studio where they make *Neighbours* being struck by a large thermonuclear missile. But nothing stirred down there in the penile department, despite the fact that my wrist soon felt like it had recently played all of Vivaldi's violin concertos in enthusiastic fortissimo. After twenty minutes of frantic activity, I paused, took a sip of tea and stared grimly southwards. A gallon of Guinness, a prawn vindaloo and an evening in front of the television watching old reruns of *Roseanne* have rarely had so total an effect.

Determined, I tried again. Here I am in a foreign Protestant land, I thought, the seething den of our ancient tyrannical enemies. That's what's bothering me. But I won't be beaten down! I thought of Michael Collins. I thought of the 1916 Rising. I thought of the Republic of Ireland beating England one–nil in the European Football Championships. That seemed to do the trick. Pretty soon, if I'd laid down on my back, I could quite easily have been mistaken for a single-masted schooner. Yes, yes, yes, I thought. With my free hand I reached out and turned off the radio. But just as things were really hotting up, disaster struck again. With a disconcerting sense of increasing deflation, I realised that I could now hear Lillian and Dora's conversation through the flimsy partition.

'Mabel's goin' in next week to get 'er feet done.'
 'Ohh, noooo, is she ray-ly? The poor dear.'
 'That woman's a martyr to 'er feet.'
 'Oohh my Gawd, yes. Has bin for years.'
 'You should see those bladdy varukas she has. Her feet look like sumfink out of an 'orror film.'
 'Do they? Do they rayully?'
 'Yes. They do. She said she'd sue, you know. But her husband's seek.'
 'Is he? What's wrong wiv 'im?'
 'No, no. He's a Sikh. From India. They don't believe in it.'
 'In wot, dear? In varukas?'
 'No. In suing people. It's against their religion, see.'
 BUZZZ BUZZZ BUZZZZZZZZ!!!!!!
 'There's the bell. Go and get the door, will you, dearie?'
 'Oh, I'm busy love, can't you?'
 BUZZZZZ!!! BUZZZZZ!!!
 'Alright. Coming.'
 BUZZZZ!!! BUZZZZ!!! BUZZZZ!!!

'COM-ING. I said I'm COMING. YESS. YESSS.'

Well, that was that, I'm afraid. I took a deep breath, fastened up the trews, vacated the cubicle and handed back my empty jar. Dora stared at it with the doleful air of a backstreet mechanic who has seen one too many broken-down cars. Out in the street, I used my last handful of coins to call my parents from the nearest public telephone and ask them to send me the fare home. Desperate measures just didn't suit me. And I didn't feel great about my failure, I suppose. But then, as Confucius once said, if love is a ten-course banquet, sad is the man who settles for a self-service snack.

One day last year, as I was halfway round the course of the Dublin Marathon, a strange thing happened to me. At about the thirteen-mile mark I always feel a bit tense. I just get a little lonely, being so far out there in front, leaving lanky Ethiopians and athletic Chinamen all coughing and spewking half a mile back in the ha'penny place. So that day, I stopped running and drifted over to the side of the street for a fag and a cheeseburger and a gander at the newspapers.

And I seen be one of the papers that day that The Average Man – whoever that elusive creature may be – thinks about sex once every twelve seconds!! Every twelve seconds!! I ask you now!! That means The Average Man thinks about sex almost as often as the Taoiseach thinks about getting into an aeroplane. Imagine! Me daarlin creature, The Average Man, has pondered doing the horizontal samba several times already in the course of reading this page. Can this be? Is it true that we fellows are all obsessed by sex? Or is it just a load of balls?

Up until very recently, I had not had much experience of 'sex'. I had read about it, of course, and I had seen diagrams, but personal experience of our old friend, the beast of two backs, had not come my way with any regularity. This is because, as you are aware, I was married twice before meeting the present Mrs O'C. Neither was a particularly happy union. I lost my first wife, Deirdre, a linguist from Sligo, only three weeks after the wedding. Losing her was difficult. It really was. I tried for ages, but she and the bloodhounds always found me again. In the end, one Saturday afternoon, I brought her into Bewleys for a sticky bun, slithered under the table in mid-chomp, tied her ankles together with sizel and cantered out of the joint doing 190 mph and singing 'Oh What A Beautiful Mornin'. No good though. Boy, could that broad hop. Zebedee with highlights.

My second spouse, Elaine, was a different kettle of piranhas. There are some very nice women in the world, and Elaine was definitely two of them. We did have sex at first, but hey, in the end we just lost that lovin' feeling. It was the small things that got me. Like, I know you're not supposed to mind someone falling asleep while you're making love to them, but really, you'd think a person could stay awake for all of three minutes. Too much to ask? God now, you'd only be biting your toenails before hopping into the connubial scratcher and she'd practically be in a coma. Our marriage ended when I had to bury poor Elaine in January 1991. By the time they dug her up in mid-February she had gone off me. She promptly fecked off to Amerikay with a garrulous, cross-eyed, counter-lepping troglodyte who used to recycle teabags and sing 'American Pie' at parties. And to think I gave that woman the best fortnight of my life.

I am currently cohabiting, as you all know, with my lovely wife, Jennifer, whom I met three years ago in a Leeson Street 'discotheque'. We started doing a line right away, but her cocaine habit is clearing up nicely now, and the police eventually agreed to community service. She moved in two years ago, and overnight a funny thing happened to the bathroom. Suddenly there were expensive moisturisers and skin lotions all over the shop. And there were tights everywhere. Our bathroom now looks like I'm married to a bank robber with acne. It can get depressing. It's so funny, as Cliff Richard once put it with almost Keatsian poignancy, but we don't talk any more.

The other night I was feeling a bit blue about this, when my colleague from the *Sunday Tribune*, Mr Aodghán 'Touchy' Feeley rang and invited me out for a quiet jar. We met in the saloon of the well-known hotel in town where Aodghán keeps a room permanently rented, if you get my drift. It was good to see the old dog, I must say. He was very consoling. But then something difficult happened. Aodghán came sprinting down from the bar looking uptight. 'Sacred Heart of the livin Jay,' he gasped, 'I'm after saying an awful thing to that barmaid.'

'What?' I said. 'That Fianna Fáil represents a credible alternative government for our divided nation?'

'Worse,' he said, 'I went up to her nibs, Joe, and I said, '*Petal mo chroi*, two thighs of Guinness please.' Holy God, was I mortified! I meant two pints of Guinness, but I said two thighs of Guinness. A Freudian slip, you know. It's when you want to say one thing, but what you're really thinking just slips out. I haven't been so embarrassed since that incident with the married sister's hoover hose and Horatio the hamster.'

'I've had those Freudian slips myself,' I said. 'In fact, I

had one the other morning. I was sitting there lurrying into the breakfast with Jennifer. And she said, 'Would you pass the cornflakes please?' And I looked up at her. And I said, 'You've ruined my life, you wagon.'

'I know,' sighed Feeley. 'It's awful when that happens. Anyway, cheers. Here's wishing you health, wealth and a penis.'

You see, 'sex' is all around us, whether we know it or not. So allow me to give active readers some advice on the ins and outs, as it were. OK, OK, so you finally got lucky. Last night you scored. You don't know how you did it, but you did. Yippee! Look, there, beside you there in the scratcher. There they are. (I don't mean 'they' plural, unless you got very lucky indeed: I just don't want to keep writing 'he' or 'she'.) The divine creature that seemed so lovely last night, that made you laugh, that thrilled you to the very core of your sexual being. Look at them now, reeking of stale lager, snoring like a motorbike, hair like a madwoman's fanny, tongue lolling out of their mouth. Last night they looked like an angel out of paradise. This morning they look like Garth out of *Wayne's World*. As you peer and yawn and try to feel tender, they suddenly fart, stick their thumb in their gob and roll over, taking the duvet with them. With a terrible surge of panic and disgust you realise something: oh my God, they're still wearing their socks. What on earth happens now?

Yes, modern sexual etiquette is a funny and complex old game, yet it is really very important to master its rules, codes and mores. So here are a few basic tips:

Flirtation: It is very important to learn how to flirt effectively. Flirtation is all a question of tact and suggestion rather than direct propositioning. You do not, in other words, just blunder in saying 'Listen, gorgeous, ya wanna get buck naked and fuck?' Subtlety is the best approach. Pay compliments. Make eye contact. Buy drink. Make conversation. Quote some poetry. Buy more drink. Then say, 'Listen, gorgeous, ya wanna get buck naked and fuck?'

Avoid gender stereotyping: Women sometimes feel that all guys want to do is get them into bed. This, of course, is a terrible mistake. Given the right amount of booze, most guys would settle for the back of a car, or, failing this, an alley.

Kissing: Many a potentially shattering banquet of carnal fulfilment has been abandoned halfway through the hors d'oeuvres, and all because of an inability to indulge properly in tonsil hockey. (Consider the following verse by Mr Cummings: 'She frowned and called him Mr./ Because in sport he kr./ And so in spite that very night/ This Mr. kr. sr.') But it is important, too, not to get carried away. It is considered impolite to kiss your partner as though you are trying to taste what they had for breakfast yesterday. Experts agree that the socially correct way to kiss these days is to put your tongue into the other person's mouth, but not to swop spit.

Foreplay: This is the technical term for taking your shoes off.

Oral sex: In the old days, of course, oral sex was considered a bit taboo. Now, however, attitudes are changing in Ireland and oral sex is going on right under our very noses.

Exploring your fantasies: It is considered quite OK these days to share your fantasies and desires. Ask your partner if it's OK for you to think about someone else when you're making love. Be open. Don't worry. If said partner replies, 'Yes, dear, it'll make a change from you thinking about your fucking self anyway,' worry.

Contraception: The Catholic Church is, of course, opposed to artificial contraception and the present Pope has compared condom use to murder. Certainly, anybody who has ever tried to put on a condom half-pissed in the pitch blackness of a malodorous Rathmines bedsit will agree. Sheer bloody murder is the only word for it. Nevertheless condoms do protect you from numerous social diseases and unwanted pregnancy, and these days they come in a wide variety of interesting flavours. Indeed, flavoured condoms, when not being used for prophylactic purposes, make a very good and reusable alternative to chewing gum. Do not be tempted to use clingfilm for contraceptive purposes. In the heat of the moment you can get confused. Wrapping the male member in clingfilm will not actually do it any harm, but wrapping your picnic lunch in a condom can sure wreak havoc on an egg-salad sandwich.

Other precautions: It is obviously very important indeed for mature adults in sexual situations to be responsible and take adequate precautions. So many younger people these days suffer distressing consequences by their failure to follow a few simple rules. We've all been there. We know what it's like. The heat of the moment, the raw surge of passion. It's so so easy to forget precautions. Don't make this mistake. Remember: if you're staying over at her place and have to leave your bike outside, please, *do lock it properly*.

Sexual positions: Experiment. Be bold. It is quite acceptable in these modern and liberated times to suggest your favourite sexual position to your partner. I may tell you candidly, being something of a red-hot lover myself, that I have tried every single sexual position there is. Yup, both the one with the woman on top and the one with the man on top. So there. Wild and crazy guy, huh?

Doing it 'Doggy Style': This means rubbing your groin enthusiastically against a visitor's leg while panting and letting your tongue hang out.

Masochism: Give this up immediately. You might start enjoying it too much.

Bondage: If you tie somebody to a bed, it is quite important that you do not then go down to the pub and forget about them.

Orgies: The conversation does tend to be limited. But then you can't have everything. And it is rude to talk with your mouth full.

Spanking: Can be good fun between consenting adults, but do be careful to avoid confusion. The phrase 'bring back the birch' is actually current Fine Gael crime policy, not an invitation. (Nor is it a slogan for a campaign to save deciduous trees.)

Achieving orgasm: The name you call out as, and when, and if you reach orgasm should be the name of your partner, not the name of any previous partner, your pet or your football team. On no account should it be your own name.

The post-coital stage: Most modern sex therapists agree that the few minutes immediately after making love are very important indeed, and that it is vital to hold your partner at this time, to tell them you love them, cherish them and care for them deeply. For many Irish men this is a little difficult, as by this stage they're on the bus home with a bag of curry chips and a spiceburger.

Honest communication: Do not use sexual euphemisms. When I was an impressionable lad in senior school, the priests told me all about 'the birds and the bees'. As a result I took an albatross to my debs.

How to handle the morning after: This is really a very complex matter. You have done the most intimate things it is possible to do with another human being – at least, I'm assuming it's a human being – and you don't even know their second name. Or their first name. Or anything else about them. At all costs, do not admit this. While they're in the shower, search their bedroom for something that has their name written on it. If you can't find anything, you may have to resort to pet names. 'Funny Bunny', 'Cheeky Chops' or 'Snuggle Face' are all considered acceptable. 'Poxbottle', 'Hair Oil' or 'Damp Arse' should probably be avoided, at least initially.

How soon to ring: This is really a very tricky one and has been the undoing of many a promising relationship, including, I may say, several of my own. There are no easy answers to this. Just remember one vital thing: when Irish women say, 'Will you ring me?' they mean, 'Will you ring me tomorrow or the next day?' No problem.

Perfectly clear. The difficulty is that when Irish men say, 'Yes, I promise that I will ring you really soon,' they mean that they will ring you at some point before they die.

The root cause of this difficulty is that many Irish men are stark staring mad. They tend to feel that women who have slept with them will want to marry them. The logic goes: if I ring her, then we'll probably go out again, have sex again, go out again, and before you know it, be putting down the deposit on a bungalow in the suburbs and getting a cat and complaining about the young people of today and buying the Sunday newspapers on a Saturday night. Thus, if a woman really does want to see a man again after having sex with him, it is very important that when he asks, 'Can I ring you again?' she should laugh maniacally before spluttering the words, 'Are you serious, you sad fat loser?'

If she does this, I guarantee, he'll have moved in by the end of the week.

II   Old Flames Can't Hold a Candle to You, Unfortunately

THE HISTORIANS TELL US THAT FOLLOWING HIS OVER-throw Napoleon III fled France and died in awful agony in the south of England, where, oddly, a lot of people live in awful agony. And this week I got a letter from an old girlfriend of mine – well, she's not old actually, she's twenty-seven – who has the poor fortune to inhabit that flat and arid portion of Limey Land. Gloria was her name, and indeed it still is.

I met her one night in a country music nightclub in Dublin. It was a rough joint. The kind of joint where they searched you for weapons on the way in, and if you didn't have any, they beat the crap out of you. As soon as our eyes met she burst into applause. Little did I know that this would certainly not be the last clap I'd get from Gloria. Yes, we broke up in difficult circumstances some years ago, but hey, let's forgive and forget. The rash only comes back really badly when I've been overdoing things, the pustules hardly ever leak since I've been taking the penicillin and in any case it was nice to get her letter. My mind went back to the old days. Ah, how did the noble bard once put it? 'Gloria, Gloria, you made my life a fairy tale: fuckin' Grimm.' But no, I jest. Life was pink and soft back then. Once, shortly after we met, I remember we took a ferry from Dun Laoghaire to Holyhead together for a long weekend. It was a lot of fun, but Sealink were a tad annoyed when we got back with it.

But, ah, what days. Her family were a little strange. Her dad was a quiet man. His face was so incredibly wrinkled that sometimes I used to shudder to imagine what his testicles must have looked like. Her mother insisted I smoke in the kitchen. Which was a pain, as I didn't actually smoke. To complicate matters, there was a lot of sexual friction between us. But I have to admit that we had our bad times, too.

She said I was cruel. I was brutal. I was acerbic. And I'm certainly not. I'm Croatian. (Chortle.)

Our love was doomed though. The night Gloria moved into my flat we got burgled. She insisted we buy an Alsatian first thing next morning. We drove to the pet shop and looked in the window. Suddenly, this enormous yellow budgie came flapping out the door and into my honey's hands. It was touching to see how she caressed it and fondled it and threatened to 'fookin mill it into the shagginwell floorboards' if it didn't stop struggling. I thought it was, oh, I dunno, sort of symbolic of our love. After a moment we entered the premises. The assistant glanced up and said, 'Jesus, love, where'dja get that ugly-looking pig?'

And Gloria said, 'That's not a pig, that's a budgie, yeh eejit.'

And the guy said, 'No, I was talking to the budgie.'

I did laugh, I must admit. Gloria didn't get it. I tried to explain.

'No, Fluffylips,' I sighed, 'don't you understand? The joke is, "Where'dja get that ugly-looking pig?"'

There was only a short silence before the budgie chirped, 'I dunno, pal, it was waitin' for me when I flew out the fookin door.'

Anyway, after she had chomped its head off, we had a look at one of the Alsatian pups. It cost two hundred quid! The guy said it'd protect our valuables. We didn't fecking have any! We'd just been burgled, for God's sake!! If we'd bought the bloody dog we'd've had to get something to protect it.

This had not occurred to Love Bunny, unburdened as she was by any surfeit of grey matter. I would come home at the end of those cold winter days and say, 'Chilly outside, darling.' And the poor wagon would get out a bowl.

In the end, things between us grew tense and violent. 'Is your face hurting you, Cup Cakes?' she enquired one night near the end.

'No, Cutieboots,' I replied, 'why?'

She grinned. 'Because it's bleedin' killin' me, Burgerfeatures.'

Oh, God, the arguments. I knew it was over when she

said I'd smashed all her records. Which wasn't true. Although I had admittedly shaved point five of a second off some of them. Ah, poor Gloria. Gloria in Excelsis Deo. Where did you go to, my lovely? I know, I know. To East Grinstead. Boo bleedin hoo bleedin hoo.

III Matri-Money

FOLLOWING A RECENT COLUMN ABOUT MARRIAGE, I have been inundated with requests from (two) readers for further clarification of the ins-and-outs, and, indeed, the ups-and-downs, not to mention the whys-and-wherefores, of wedding etiquette. And I can understand why. It is impossible to overstate the importance of wedding eti-quette. Well, it's not actually impossible. I mean, I could claim that the bombing of Pearl Harbor was caused by wedding etiquette, or that the recently publicised soaring crime figures are caused by wedding etiquette, and, of course, I would be wrong. No, etiquette is not the most important thing in the world. The Eagles breaking up again, for good this time, with sworn and witnessed statements promising no further reunion tours, ever, on pain of crucifixion, is the most important thing in the world. But wedding etiquette is pretty important too, particularly at weddings. So here are the answers to some frequently asked questions:

Question one: What are the best man's duties? Most people feel that the best man's duties are to be nice to the groom and not to forget the ring at the crucial moment. This, as seasoned observers know, is not actually the case. The best man is there to humiliate the groom before, during and after the ceremony. Chief among his functions, of course, is the arranging of the stag night, an ancient ritual of tribal evolution during which the groom-to-be is derided, beaten, half drowned, hung, drawn, quartered and then resuscitated long enough to have his private parts stapled to a billiard table by a group of young colleagues from work humorously wearing stolen toilet seats around their necks. Next, it is considered polite for the best man's speech to be lightly peppered with witty anecdotes about the bride and groom, involving how they met, how they fell deeply and tenderly in love, how they decided to embark together on the great spiritual adventure of marital togetherness, and, finally, of course, what constitute their favourite sexual positions. (It is always an advantage for the best man to have a malodorous brother who works in some aspect of real estate.)

Question two: What are the bridesmaid's duties? The bridesmaid's main duty is to lose enough weight to fit into the ghastly pink velveteen-cum-leopard-skin lycra strapless backless puffball-cum-meringue garment that has been thoughtfully rented out for the day by the bride's family (see: Question three).

Question three: Who pays for what? Well-established tradition has it that the bride's family have the privilege of paying for the dresses, the suits, the cars, the flowers, the singers, the church, the altar boys, the cake, the food, the hotel, the drink, the band, the priest and the damage. The groom's family's contribution is 30p, if they need to make a telephone call from the hotel lobby to order a taxi home because they are too stocious.

Question four: What should the band play? This is a very important question. All good wedding bands will be proficient at playing both kinds of music, that is, country AND western. Everything they play will be rendered into a country and western style. Everything. From 'Amhran na Bhfiann' to 'I'm Too Sexy for My Shirt', the instrumentation will feature drums, bass, pedal steel guitar, fiddle, washboard and one of those monstrously large organs with cha-cha-cha rhythm built in. The play-list must be rigorously followed. The first set of the evening must always, yes, always, be 'Sweet Caroline' by Neil Diamond, segueing into 'Twist and Shout', followed by 'Bold Robert Emmet, the Darling of Erin', followed by 'One Day at a Time, Sweet Jesus', ending in 'Lady in Red' by Chris de Burgh and then 'Aon Fhocail Eile' by the Boston Symphony Orchestra. Any other sequence of songs is considered very bad form indeed. The one permissible variation is a charming little local custom, whereby later on in the evening the bride's father may be permitted to sing a merry traditional Irish post-ceasefire song of peace, brotherhood and reconciliation, such as 'Up Against the Fookin Wall, Yiz Durty Black and Tan English Bollixs'.

Question five: Who should be the first people to leave the wedding reception? The first people to leave the wedding reception should be the bride and groom. Their departure should be accompanied by ribald cries of, 'We know ware ye're goin,' and so on, by their friends, and whispered tearful murmurings of, 'I suppose a ride'd be owwa the question, wha?' by the best man to the bridesmaid. It is at this point, also, that the bride's mother should break down in tears, start drinking really heavily and muttering to the priest, 'Yeh know, Father, I never liked dat shower of miserable gombeen counter-jumpers' – meaning the groom's relations – 'between yune mean the wall (hic), I never liked them, Father. Never. Oh, I know dhat crowd well. I know dem. Know dem well dis many's de long year. I'm tellin ya. And I never . . .'

Question six: What should the married couple find in their room? The bridal suite should by now have been reduced by the best man and his associates to a smoking rubble reminiscent of downtown Sarajevo. The bed should be full of poisonous snakes, noxious frogs, exploding cigarettes, concealed knives, electric chain saws, thermonuclear missiles and other items of harmless marital fun.

Question seven: Who should be the last people to leave the wedding reception? The last people to leave the reception should be the police officers who have come to issue a verbal warning to the pageboy and arrest the bride's married sister for GBH on the lead singer of the band.

I hope this will have been of some help to all those intending to jump the broom in the foreseeable future. The last thing that needs to be said, of course, in these times of great secularism and unholiness, is that marriage is a wonderful institution. And if you believe that for one minute, the best man's brother has some prime real estate for sale. Seriously. It's a beautiful site, now, serio. I've a soft spot for it meself. A bog outside Termonfeckin.

Now that I am legally married myself, I feel I can discuss in print the difficult subject of contraception and birth control without giving scandal to anybody. There are those who would argue that Jennifer and I will not actually need contraception, in that now we are married we will not be having sex any more, but, you know, there is a smart aleck born every minute and a dignified silence is really the best response. The main question is, of course, what kind of contraception to use and how to talk about the whole subject without embarrassment? I told my wife that I was happy not to discuss the messier details at all, that I would be more than content to leave all that side of things to her. She didn't go for that, for some reason. Huh! I thought. The modern woman. There she is, never off Marion Finnucane's *Liveline* banging on about her right to control her own fertility and then suddenly when you say, OK, so dear, off you go and control it, she gets upset and before you know it, it's round to the shops with you quick-march to buy a big box of chockies before she throws you out of the house or something!! God now, I couldn't figure it out at all. But Jennifer was very insistent. She said that if we didn't discuss all available forms of contraception immediately, we'd find ourselves suddenly using the most traditional kind. 'What?' I twittered, 'abstinence?' She shook her lovely head firmly. 'No,' she sniffed. 'Castration.'

'We are the prisoners of infinite choice,' once wrote the great Irish poet Derek Mahon. Well, he might have had birth control in mind when he penned that perceptive truth. Good heavens, where does a person start? Contraception, like air travel and membership of the Fianna Fáil party, comes in all sorts of shapes and sizes depending on the pocket and the medical circumstances!!

Of course, the condom itself now comes in a staggering array of forms. You can buy coloured ones, textured ones, small ones, large ones, luminous ones, edible ones, flavoured ones. I'm serious now. Flavoured condoms. Myself and the War Department spent a lovely evening there during the week sampling them. Not making love or anything, just sitting out in the garden, enjoying the sunset as we passed the pack to each other and chewed. We began with a couple of peppermints and progressed inexorably through the assortment. Ultimately I favoured the strawberry, whereas Cup Cakes pronounced herself very taken with the chocolate chip and the kumquat.

Then there is the female condom, or Femidom, as I believe it is called. Now, the word 'Femidom', to me, sounds like the kind of illicit publication for which I am told you have to shell out a lot of money in Soho basements, but no, it is actually a female condom. Jennifer asked a married friend of ours what using this was like. Not so bad, came the reply, if you don't mind making love with a shopping bag hanging out of you. Hmmmm. This was all getting a tad difficult.

The pill was out, because Jennifer is iffy about that. 'I just wouldn't dream of putting anything so unpleasant into my body,' she said. 'Huh,' I thought. 'You didn't say that when you used to go out with that rugby player from Lusk.' What other options? Well, there was the IUD, to which I was opposed, because I'm not having my wife using a form of contraception that sounds like one of those new Dublin universities where all you can study is woodwork or journalism. There was 'the cap', which we barred because the doctor insisted on referring to it as 'the pubic frisbee'. Then, of course, there were the Billings or rhythm methods to be considered. Jennifer was attracted to these because she is a good Catholic, and as everyone knows, while Holy Mother Church objects to a person using physics or chemistry to prevent conception, for some bizarre reason she has no problem at all with biology. Still, though, these sanctified methods weren't much use, because you need an amazing array of equipment to ensure their success, for example, calendars, thermometers, rosary beads, alarm clocks, the complete works of Padre Pio, holy water, a copy of Dana singing 'Totus Tuus', etc.

The vasectomy option was briefly explored, but rejected by myself as being just a little on the final side. The doctor laughed and explained that actually I was wrong about this. The operation can be reversed, and anyway, it is possible for a goodly amount of one's spermatozoa to be preserved in a freezer in the event of them being required one day. But we weren't sure about this. Where we live, there are a lot of power cuts, and really, nothing would quite spoil your holidays like returning from abroad to find your last chance of fathering a child floating around on the freezer floor with several pounds of thawed peas, half a cow and a gallon of molten Häagen-Daaz. The bottom line is that we still have not found the form of contraception which suits us. We have thus been married for some time now and have still not got around to celebrating our love. It's getting desperate. If readers more experienced than myself have any constructive suggestions, you know where I can be reached.

IV Baby Love

TWO FRIENDS OF MINE HAVE JUST HAD THEIR SECOND baby, a cause for great rejoicing and bursting into tears and massed carnation purchasing for just about everybody they know, yet an occasion for black humour from them.

'I'm thrilled,' the mother said to me, when I went to

see her in the Ozzy, 'it's just that when you have a baby your sex life keels over and dies.' I guffawed dutifully at this point, thinking it was a hoary old myth, but she insisted that it was true. 'Seriously,' she said. 'After we had the first one we never had sex again. I don't know how we ever managed to make the second one. It must have been an immaculate conception.'

Her husband confirmed this with a rueful grin. 'One night there recently we were going to bed,' he said. 'There we were, just about to lep into the scratcher and celebrate our love with a good Jekyll and Hyde, you know? And I'm just taking me clothes off and getting into the posing pouch when the screaming and crying starts up. And yer wan goes to me, you better shut up with your noise or you'll wake that bleedin' baby.'

It is all a difficult business, it seems. The woman explained to me how the learned doctors had had to give her a powerful drug to induce labour. This was entirely appropriate, she said, in the sense that her husband had had to give her a powerful drug to induce conception. We talked for a while about the marvellous properties of this drug, Petosin by name. Imagine, I thought, a drug that induces labour. It should be given to TDs, I felt.

We sat by the bed fondly admiring the fruit of their loins, a tiny cute purple thing with weeny little fingers and a great frizz of matted hair that made it look like a member of the early Planxty. There was some discussion at this point about which parent the child looked like, but I couldn't see any resemblance whatsoever to either of them myself. But then again, I've never seen either of these two people wrapped in swaddling clothes and plangently wailing and sucking at their thumbs the way a dipso would suck at a bottle of gin, so I wouldn't really

121

know. I picked up the little bundle of love and dandled it on my knee, to the best of my abilities. It gaped at me in abject horror.

'Talk to her,' the mite's mother suggested.

'What'll I say?' I asked.

'I don't know,' she said, 'anything that's on your mind.'

I regarded the lovely little face. 'Well,' I began, 'it's an awful pity about global warming, isn't it?' The gorgeous features crumpled up, rearranged themselves and began to weep bucket-loads.

'Put her over your shoulder, you great gobshite,' sighed the mother.

I did. It puked all down my back.

But I didn't mind. I was kind of flattered, in fact. I thought it was a sign that she liked me. There is a certain species of South American parrot which, like certain species of baby, and certain species of Irishman, can only express affection by puking all over the admired one. And what's a little baby-vom between friends, after all? But anyway, there is a great and widespread myth around that women are designed by nature for the more or less exclusive purpose of having babies and that if they don't have them by their mid-thirties they develop that strange internal machine, the Body Clock, which drives them scats and makes them get up and eat chocolate in the middle of the night and encourages them to purchase demanding and flea-infested pets of the feline persuasion. I have rarely found this to be the case. Many of the women I know are too busy being better at their jobs than their male colleagues to have babies. Indeed, men these days seem to be far more clucky than women. Certainly, I do not mind confiding that I came out of the hospital that day with my own body clock ticking so loudly it could be heard several counties away. After about half an hour it began to sound disturbingly like a particularly excessive drum solo by the late Keith Moon.

I walked the streets of our capital for several hours in a very funny mood. I am thirty-one years old, I thought. If I was to become a parent tomorrow, by the time Junior was sixteen I would be forty-seven! Imagine, having to deal with all that business about spots and boys and girls and masturbation and mathematics homework and what's going to happen to the planet and why were there Nazis at the age of forty-bleeding-seven. I don't know if I'd be able for it. By the time I'm forty-seven I intend to be entering my dotage and causing serious trouble for everyone around me, not parked outside some appalling disco waiting to receive the tearful and disappointed progeny into the car before trying to convince them on the journey home that the pain of rejected love will disappear if only you give it time. And the questions you have to ask teenagers! Are you really going out dressed like that? (No.) Where were you? (Nowhere.) Who were you with? (Nobody.) Are you going to use the phone again? (Maybe.) Do your friends not have homes of their own? (Funny, aren't you?) What time do you call this to be strolling in here and your poor mother only off the blower to the guards and the hospitals? (I didn't ask to be born.) Do you think this place is some kind of effing hotel or boarding house? (Huh?) What would you like for your supper? (You hate me, Mother, and you have ruined my life.) And, of course, there is that great existential conundrum so often discussed by the philosophers and sages down through the history of thought: Who do you think you are, anyway? I was first asked who I thought I was anyway at the age of about seven, and I have to tell you,

123

I've given it a hell of a lot of contemplation in the intervening years and I'm still not exactly sure. I don't know. I think I'll go out and buy a bloody cat. Tick, tick, tick, tick, tick . . .

V Your Cheating Heart

YOU KNOW, SOMETIMES PEOPLE WHO WRITE FOR NEWS-papers get these things called press releases in the post. A press release is a single page of densely typed and frequently misspelled information plugging an event, a book, a record or whatever. It is one page, by the way, aspiring publicists take note. Sending a journalist a press release that is longer than one page is a total waste of time; you will get no publicity at all if you do this. In fact, if you have ever in your life done something really bad and sinful and immoral and you really do not want anybody to ever find out about it, you should write a two-page press release in which you confess everything and hold nothing back and then send it in to your local newspaper. Believe me, if it's two pages, nobody will ever hear a single thing about it.

But anyway. Sometimes the press releases you get are more interesting than others. I got one recently about a book called *The Jewish Guide to Adultery* by Rabbi Shmuel Boteach. A copy of the book was attached.

The press release was going for the hard sell. '*The Jewish Guide to Adultery* will stimulate any marriage, however contented,' it proclaimed, 'and could save those in danger of collapse.' Being more or less in perpetual danger of collapse myself, I felt the book was really aimed at me.

I am a great believer in self-help books. I remember

124

once reading one called *I'm OK, You're OK*. I'm writing my own self-help book now. It's called *I'm OK, You're an Almighty Screaming Pain in the Arse.* (It works for me.) But anyway, back to Rabbi Shmuel. This wise and holy man has spent many years studying adultery – nice work if you can get it, huh? How come I spent many years studying Peig fucking Sayers and he spent many years studying adultery?! – and his conclusion is that extramarital equestrianism only occurs when the partners in said union have lost what the Righteous Brothers once famously called that lovin' feelin. It's not that you're not fond of each other any more. You are. In fact, your fondness for each other is part of the problem. It's simply that over the years you have become just good friends. There is no glamour or excitement or sexiness to your union. (You may perhaps be in the Transport and General Workers.) Your partner used to give you funny butterflies in your tummy, now all she or he gives you is a vague headache and a Vicks rubdown when you've got a chill. You don't have sex any more, and if you do, it is unsatisfying. This is a persuasive enough theory, if not exactly an original one. 'I don't know anything about sex,' admitted Zza Zza Gabor many years ago, 'because for most of my life I've been married.'

Well, I was interested in all this, because adultery has been in the news a lot lately. To judge by the popular press, adultery is as popular as ever. Movie stars, pop singers and royals, they're all at it. Didn't we even have the artist formerly known as Prince (Charles) leppin in and out of the extramarital scratcher with the lovely Camilla for years? Some Anglican bishop over beyond in Blighty got himself into hot water there recently when he appeared to argue that adultery was not exactly sinful, per se. Many people were very shocked by this, but I was not. The way the Church of England is going these days, doing your granny in with a lump hammer and then dancing about on her grave singing 'Paranoid' by Black Sabbath is not exactly sinful per se either.

But what is it about adultery that we find so fascinating? When I was in America two years ago at the World Cup I remember reading a survey about adultery in the *New York Times*. Self-confessed adulterers had been asked about the circumstances in which they had done the bould thing. The majority of respondents had met an adulterous partner 'in work'. Many more had cheated on their spouses by sleeping with a former lover. The most interesting statistic was that twelve per cent had said that they had committed adultery 'by accident'. I remember sitting there wondering how in the name of God a person could commit adultery by accident? Now that is something I would like to see. Good heavens, you could actually sell tickets to something like that.

My own view on adultery is that monogamy is about as natural for human beings as line dancing is for goldfish. But the fact that it is not natural does not mean, of course, that it is not good. I can think of many natural things that are not good at all. Spiders, for instance, and spinach, and natural yoghurt. And I can think of several unnatural things that are truly marvellous, such as heart surgery and motorcars and a number of other things that you couldn't possibly mention in a family publication. Monogamy belongs in this latter category of human experience. It is unnatural despite the fact that it is good. In fact, it is good precisely because it is unnatural. For surely this is the important thing about marriage. On paper it makes no sense whatsoever. How in the name of

God could it ever work? It is totally irrational and it derives its humanity precisely from that. We profess ourselves disappointed when marriages break down in disorder, but we have got it the wrong way around. People who have long and happy marriages should be regarded as extraordinary adventurers who have scaled the Everest-like heights of emotional experience, rather than being the norm. They should all be sending out triumphant press releases about themselves, if you ask me. (On one page, if you please.)

VI This is a Man's Man's Man's Man's World

YOU'LL ALL BE FAMILIAR WITH THE CONCEPT OF THE New Man, I'm sure. Like communism, it's a great idea in theory but it just doesn't work in practice. The New Man is supposed to be sensitive to his feelings – well, men have never been bad at being sensitive to feelings, if those feelings are their own, of course – just try removing a beer from one and see what happens. Feelings are what will happen. But New Men are also supposed to be sensitive to the feelings of women, children, pets, etc. They are supposed to be able to express emotion, to be nurturing and supportive, to be able to cry in public. This is difficult. It takes a lot of practice and time. As one woman friend told me recently of her Irish New Man husband: he can cry like a baby alright, but he still can't put up a bookshelf. Maybe he should join one of those new groups for men, I said, where men can play bongo drums and make pottery and run around the forest stark naked in the middle of the night. She scoffed.

'What's the matter?' I asked her. 'Don't you believe in clubs for men?'

She grinned. 'Only when other forms of persuasion fail.'

So, if it's hard to be a woman, it's hard to be a man, too. Specially an Irish man. Take the recent survey in a well-known Irish newspaper about Irish men. The organisation asked 35,000 women all over Ireland the following question: do you agree that the average Irish man is an indolent shit-bag who never thinks about anything but his gut and his mickey and would have sexual intercourse with a diseased aardvark if it would iron him a shirt afterwards?

Ninety-two per cent of women agreed with this. The other thirteen per cent noticed that Irish men were also bloody useless at mathematics. By spending a little time scientifically analysing these results, we can conclude that Irish women do not appear to have a high opinion of men. And who can really blame them? Yes, Irish women seem to have problems trying to figure out how they think. Well, I'm going to spill a few trade secrets here and let you women out there know how to deal with Irish men.

The question of communication is vitally important if you are going to have a relationship with an Irish man. I cannot stress this enough. Communication is a real problem. And so, one important thing: no matter how close you become, remember, never *ever* ask an Irish man to communicate. Never ask an Irish male to tell you about his deep and sensitive thoughts. There is a very good and crucial reason for this.

He doesn't have any.

Well, he does. But they are mainly deep and sensitive

thoughts about himself. For example, I met an old college friend for a drink recently. I've known this guy for ten years now and I like being in his company because he is always in such a good mood. He is tall, this fellow, and confident and good-looking. He is articulate and bright and relatively rich. And yet, that night, he seemed depressed and despondent. At first I assumed that some major disaster had befallen him – he'd pranged his Porsche, perhaps, or wasn't able to manage his third holiday of the year. But no, he said, the problem was his girlfriend. I sighed and prepared myself for what I somehow knew he was going to say.

'She's cleverer than me,' he sighed. 'She earns more money than me, she has more friends than me, she's more interesting than me, she's healthier than me, she's a better human being than me . . .' He paused and sipped miserably at his pint. 'Damn it,' he hissed, 'she's hornier than me, if you want to know the truth.' He peered up at me. 'Don't you ever just wish you were a woman?'

This was odd, because it is a question a lot of my male friends seem to have been asking each other lately. They've all read the papers, seen the figures. Men are having trouble keeping their heads above water – as lovers, fathers and as workers. The number of men in work has dropped by three million over the last twenty years, while the number of working women has actually increased by two million. Men want to be women now. It's getting as predictable as Monday following Sunday. Wherever two or three men are gathered these days, you can bet your bottom dollar it will only be a short time before they end up discussing how much they'd like to have a baby. I don't mean father one. I mean actually give birth to one. 'Lucky bitches,' these poor men sigh, as the wonderful miracles of conception, gestation and labour are rehearsed yet again. In the old days, large groups of socialising men talked a lot about women's breasts. They still do. It's just that now they actually want to have them. This is getting scary. I mean, what kind of world is it where a twenty-stone former second-row rugby player can look you in the eye and openly tell you that he has fantasised about suckling his young?

This, I suppose, is a poignant example of the crisis of male identity about which newspapers and magazines have been telling us for some time. The statistics are there to be scrutinised by terrified male eyes: women are more employable than men, more intelligent and more creative. They live longer, they are far less likely to die in accidents and they tend to do better in school and at college. For God's sake, even that last great scapegoat of the male chauvinist and the crappy comedian – the bad female driver – has been made redundant. Women's car insurance is now cheaper than men's and that, believe me, is enough to give your average possessor of a pair of gonads a serious coronary, never mind an identity crisis.

This crisis of masculinity has spread into all aspects of contemporary culture. Recent novels by Malcolm Bradbury and Martin Amis have taken the essential awfulness of modern manhood as their central focus. Movies like *Thelma and Louise* and *The Piano* have openly portrayed men as ignorant boorish oafs, while promoting the notion of the creative and moral superiority of women. A whole new breed of women rock and rollers, from Courtney Love to Björk, have taken the most quintessentially male art form in history and simply expropriated it, leaving the boys to their air guitars and their drum machines. Be honest now. Who would any normal person rather get stuck in a lift with? Juliana Hatfield, or one of those effete little boy-bimbos who front English rock bands these days? From comedy to politics, from sports to journalism, it is women who are making the running.

Poor men. Poor, poor babies. How did any of this happen to us? Fifteen years ago we still ran everything. We had it all to ourselves. All we had to do was not screw up. Back then, soul star James Brown was able to boast, 'It's a man's, man's, man's, man's world.' If he tried that nowadays, intercontinental ballistic missiles rather than frilly knickers would land on the stage around him.

And we wouldn't mind, us poor, poor men, only we did try to be good. We tried to be New Men. This is what women wanted, we were told. Men who could talk about feelings and be nice to puppies. Men who could watch television commercials for panty liners 'with wings' without blushing, laughing or waving their arms up and down. We went into therapy, we got in touch with our karma and we even bought a book by Maya Angelou, which we displayed prominently on the coffee table, just in case we got lucky and managed to persuade somebody to come back to the digs for a cup of (Nicaraguan) coffee.

But it didn't shagging well work, did it? Oh, no. None of it worked.

Because we forgot something very important, which is: women are always, always several evolutionary steps ahead of us. Thus, just when we got to the point where we were fully paid-up members (if I may use such a penetrative word) of the New Man club, women went and decided that they didn't want that any more. Just as we started being able to cry and express our vulnerable side and talk openly about thrush, women decided that the New Man was just the same old creature in modern threads. The New Man was merely another way for men to be weak and vacillating and generally useless, and now women wanted men – if they wanted them at all, which was frequently not a given – to be strong and sure and built like The Chippendales.

I do not think I will ever forget the full horror that flooded my veins when, one night recently, a close woman friend said to me, 'This New Man thing – it's all bollocks. They think if they know who Andrea Dworkin is, you'll go down on your knees and give them a blow job out of sheer bloody gratitude.' It was awful. I argued with my friend. I said women these days want men who can be soft, strong and very, very long, like Andrex toilet paper. She scoffed and said I was living in the past. 'That's not what I want. I want a bloke with a twelve-inch tongue who can breathe through his ears, and that's more or less that.' (I do have her number, by the way, if any iguanas amongst you want to write in.)

On my way home that night I was confused, I have to admit. I decided I would talk to the Better Half about this. Previously we had enjoyed a large number of fascinating conversations on the subject of male power and patriarchal oppression, usually while I was doing the dishes or cooking her dinner. But anyway, when I got home that night Herself was sprawled on the sofa watching television. The show she had on starred a man with a face like an old shoe, a man who looked like he would beat up his own grandmother for a packet of Tayto and a six-pack of Newcastle Brown. His name was Jimmy Nail and he most decidedly did not look like he had recently got in touch with his feminine side. But there she was, the feminist, independent, successful love of my life, practically fainting with raw desire. 'Jayzus,' she sighed, licking her lips, her pupils visibly dilating with excitement, 'I'd eat chips out of his Y-fronts.' She looked up at me then. 'Go and make me a cup of tea,' she said. I told her sweetly she had forgotten to use that one special word. 'Now,' she said.

I left her to it and went off to do a little light ironing. The New Man, I realised, was definitely redundant.

I spoke to another male friend about all this recently. 'Don't get me started about being a man,' he sighed. 'It's a shaggin' nightmare these days. We don't know what we're supposed to do any more. If you get out the Black and Decker and put up a shelf, you're being a sad, macho bore. And if you ever, ever say you don't want to have sex every single night of your life, you're a wimp.' So it's true? There is a crisis for men? 'Well, yeah,' he nodded. 'But a crisis for men is gonna be a crisis for women, too, in the end. OK, we're confused about what we are, but so are they. In fact, we're confused about what we are, *because* they're confused, too. They haven't a clue what they want from us any more. They keep saying they want to appropriate male role models. I wish a few of them would try being the strong, silent type.'

Another friend I talked to was a little more definite. 'What they want is actually very simple,' he said. 'They want to spread our balls on toast and I can't even blame them. The male game is up now. They've won. And they want to just humiliate us for a little while, just for, oh, a couple of decades, to make up for what we did to them over the centuries. And then, when we're successfully emasculated, they'll forgive us and send us to work down the salt mines. It's very simple, really.'

Things have got so bad for men now that over in the United States many of them are actually taking courses on how to be men. This is odd, because you cannot actually take a course on how to read, write or add anywhere in the modern US educational system, but you can do a course on how to be a man. The guru of this new form of masculo-therapy is Mr Robert 'Iron John' Bly, a fine fellow who, if facial hirsuteness is anything to go by (and it isn't always), has absolutely no problem with his maleness, thank you very much indeed. But anyway. The Iron John theory is that us men are deeply screwed up, threatened and defeated by feminism, cut off spiritually from our fathers and other masculine role models. Mr Bly and his followers have evolved a number of spectacularly expensive courses to remedy all this and teach biological men how to be real men. Thus, every weekend, the forests and glades of the United States pulsate and echo with the sound of stressed, topless, sandal-wearing, suburbanite manhood clambering through the bracken, banging bongo drums and generally trying to avoid getting pricked by the nettles or nettled by the pricks.

I spoke recently to a friend who had attended an Iron John course. 'Half an hour of it was enough to have you pining for a bit of Catholic reserve,' he told me. 'I mean, fuck it, we all had to strip off and hug each other and forgive each other and forgive our fathers and whinge and then do more hugging. And, I mean, the guy hugging me had tits on him like Sharon Stone's. And we had to pay for it. It was supposed to make us feel empowered, but it made me feel like the biggest gobshite on the whole planet.' What did he mean? I asked. Wasn't it even vaguely therapeutic? Hadn't it helped him deal with his crisis of masculinity? Yes, he said, it had. In the sense that it had made him resolve not to waste his money and time on his male anxiety any more. So male anxiety was a media construct after all? 'No,' he shook his head. 'I'm not saying there's nothing to it, but I hate my own uncertainty. And listening to all these goms wanking on about it makes me hate it even more. Yeah, yeah, yeah, so being a man is hard sometimes, big deal. The way I see it now, who ever said we had a right for it to be easy? I mean, my old man learned to be a man by being one, you know? He didn't have time to explore his bloody feelings about masculinity because he was too busy working hard to make sure we didn't starve.'

But that's the whole point, I said. Back then, men knew what was expected of them. That was then. This is now. Back then men derived their socioeconomic and political power from a corrupt social system based on enslavement and domination and subjugation where women were seen as cooks, mothers or endlessly willing bed-mates. His eyes clouded over with dreamy nostalgia. 'Yeah, imagine,' he sighed, 'and Manchester City were at the top of Division One.'

He grinned and began to laugh as he finished his pint. But I knew he was just being flippant to hide his inner grief. Because I don't remember Manchester City ever being at the top of Division One. It may not be a man's world any more, but, let me tell you, some things really never change.

Chapter 6

The Irish Male at Home and Abroad

I   Ireland in Exile

'When one realises that his life is worthless
he either commits suicide or travels.'

Reasons of the Heart, Edward Dahlberg

ONE DAY WHEN I WAS IN MY FINAL YEAR AT UNIVERSITY
College Dublin a man arrived out from town on the bus
and began to wander about the campus assailing bemused
undergraduates. It turned out that he was a photographer
who had been commissioned by the Irish Industrial
Development Authority to take pictures for a newspaper
advertisement that would persuade wealthy foreign capi-
talists to come and open factories all over the Irish
countryside. He wanted images of handsome and clever-
looking students who would be willing to dress up in
tweed jackets and Laura Ashley frocks and peer into the
lens of his Leica and grin like clams and appear to forget
about the fact that they would never be able to find jobs
in their own country despite the fact that the PAYE
workers of that country had shelled out considerable

bucket-loads of folding stuff in order to subsidise their chances of so doing. He wanted young people who would embody the bright new Ireland about which journalists were wittering on at the time. None of the people I knew got selected.

Some months afterwards, a friend arrived at my flat with a copy of this IDA poster, which he had cut out of a newspaper. The slogan beneath the image announced proudly: THE REPUBLIC OF IRELAND: WE'RE THE YOUNG EUROPEANS. As it turned out, my friend knew one of these young Europeans, a very talented engineer from a small town in rural Ireland, who had just upped and offed to Saudi Arabia, having failed after much effort to find work at home. My friend went through all the faces in the photograph, indicating to me that this person was in America, that one in Australia, several were in Spain or France or Germany and, of course, many more were in England. Most of the young people in the poster had fled the country precisely because of the almost laughably suicidal economic policies that same poster was attempting to advertise. Those who were still living in Ireland were unemployed, and, believe me, in the summer of 1985, they had an ice pop's chance in the Kalahari of finding a job. My friend and I talked for a time about this IDA poster. It seemed strange that all these good-looking young people who were supposed to embody Ireland had actually been forced out of the country simply in order to survive. We had both studied English literature, my friend and I. We had been trained to recognise an irony when we saw one.

We had also studied Irish history. We knew all about our country's unique history of emigration. Famine, de-population, the coffin ships, the ghettos of Kilburn and

Boston, the statistics, the lists, the death of the Irish language, the way emigration became a tradition in Ireland, not just a phenomenon, but actually a way of life. It had been a way of life for our parents' generation and now it was a way of life for us, too. The day we graduated, we practically got handed a plane ticket to London along with our degree. We knew about Irish emigration from reading all about it. As my pal and I sat talking about it that afternoon we didn't know – or perhaps we did know, deep down – that soon we would both know a little more about Irish emigration from personal experience. Soon we, too, would be leaving, like just about everyone else we knew.

It is ten years since I first saw that poster in my friend's newspaper, and I spent eight of those years living in London. Whenever I would come to Ireland during those years I would find myself thinking about that poster. Up until quite recently, a version of it was still running. Last time I saw it, it had the same old picture but a new slogan: THE REPUBLIC OF IRELAND: THE QUALITY BUSINESS BASE IN EUROPE. You would see this ad in the Irish newspapers, or in in-flight magazines. And you would often see it in Dublin Airport.

You might be coming home for a family celebration or a funeral. Or to see a friend. You might just be coming back to Ireland because you were so lonely and freaked-out where you were that you couldn't stick it any more, and you would have rented your own grandmother out by the hour to be back home in the pub by nine on a Friday night having fun and telling stories. Or you might be coming home for Christmas, like the hundreds of thousands of Irish emigrants who come back to this island every year at this time to celebrate, to share, to remind themselves why they ever left in the first place.

And there it always was, this IDA poster, illuminated at the end of the corridor that leads from the air-bridge gates to the terminal building; the ghostly faces of those beautiful Young Europeans. It always seemed so poignant to me, this pantheon of departed heroes, so hopeful and innocent, so frozen in their brief moment of optimism.

You would meet your friends the night you got home, the people who stayed behind in Ireland to tough it out. You'd talk to them about what was happening, you'd get all the news. Some of them would have got married to people you never would have met, because you didn't live in Ireland any more. Some would have broken up with boyfriends or girlfriends. Most would still be trying to find decent work. You didn't really know what these scandals and bits of gossip were, about which people were laughing so knowledgeably as they sipped their pints, but you laughed, too, because you didn't want to feel left out. You pretended you knew what your friends were talking about, because you still wanted to belong. And sometimes there were rows as the night wore on, because you didn't keep in touch as much as you should have, and your friends resented you a little for going, and if the truth be told you resented them a little for staying, although you could never really put your finger on why. But the conversation flowed, as much as it could, with only a couple of awkward moments. When you used the word 'home', for instance, or 'at home', your friends sometimes didn't know where exactly you meant. Sometimes you didn't know yourself.

Before you were aware of time passing, it would be the middle of another Christmas Eve, or the eternal Friday night. Hysterical – almost desperate – joy all around you. The pub full of smoke. The smell of beer. The jukebox on loud, playing The Pogues, U2, The Cranberries, Van Morrison. The Chieftains. Mary Black. Traditional singers. What would the songs be about? People like you. People who left. The Wild Colonial Boy. The Green Fields of Amerikay. The Wild Geese. Thousands Are Sailing. The joint would be jumping. You'd have all your best friends around you, all the people you know and love and it's Christmas Eve and everything is fine now. You're home. You know the score. More drink. Another drunken chorus of Paddy's Green Shamrock Shore. My Love is in Amerikay. Everyone is glad to see you. It's familiar. You're home. And then an extremely odd sensation begins.

Suddenly, about half an hour before closing time, you find yourself looking around the pub and becoming frantically uptight. It's weird. You're feeling completely out of place, you don't know why. You don't get it. Somehow, despite the crack, something is wrong. You're home in Ireland, but you're not home really. Your heart is in London or New York or Paris. But the rest of you is in Ireland. How did this happen to you? It's not that you're unhappy exactly. It's Christmas, after all. You wanted to be here, didn't you? But it's just not right. Take a swig of your drink. The music seems louder, oppressive, raucous. You close your eyes and try to fight back the almost overwhelming urge to be somewhere – anywhere – else. And you realise in that moment that you really are an emigrant now. That being an emigrant isn't just an address, it's also a way of thinking about Ireland.

Some mornings later you'd be back at the airport to fly home – ah, that difficult word again. You'd be hungover so bad you'd look like downtown Sarajevo on legs. Your head would be pounding with tension and confusion as you'd say your goodbyes, embrace your loved ones. In the old days, emigrants went for ever when they went, or came back once in forty years. So different now. Air travel is cheap now, you could come back really soon, and you'd say you would, although you knew you probably wouldn't. And you'd see that bloody poster of The Young Europeans once more, as you trudged your way back out of the country, on the wall of the corridor that runs parallel to the duty-free shop. How they would stare down at you, those pure virginal faces, as you shuffled through the plastic racks of Irish whiskey, clingfilm-wrapped smoked salmon, Tayto crisps and Major cigarettes, wondering what to buy with your mountain of leftover change. You always have a lot of change whenever you've been in Ireland. It's because you drink too much when you're in Ireland, and drinking, if it means anything at all, means the accumulation of change. So you'd be weighed down like a racehorse. And sometimes, just sometimes, as you rattled your coins and felt light-headed with emotion, you'd find yourself wondering what on earth they must be thinking, those speculative faces. But you'd know what you'd be thinking yourself, because it was so very simple in the end. You'd be thinking: run. You'd be thinking: Christmas is over now. You'd be thinking: Go. Run. Don't stop. Get out. Just get on that plane and vanish. Before you change your mind.

We are now, as we have always been, a land of exiles and wanderers. 'The history of transport,' muses a Paul Durcan poem, 'is there any other history?' Well, it's a very Irish question. Ever since James Joyce claimed that the shortest way to Tara was via Holyhead – he clearly didn't do honours Leaving Cert geography – hundreds of thousands of us have followed the unwashed and bright-eyed Dedalus junior on that heartbreaking, exciting and frequently stomach-churning journey across the snot-green scrotum-tightening sea.

Emigration has changed, admittedly, over the years. The sons and daughters of the middle classes emigrate now, in search of higher wages and better career prospects, and, also, if the truth be told, to get away from their parents. Ireland must be the last country in the world where people have to leave the country in order to get their own flat. They fly back home at the weekends to parties in Killiney and Montenotte, these young and successful people of the Ryanair generation. Their parents think it's good for them to be out of Ireland for a while, they figure it broadens their minds. They're right. It probably does.

But we also continue to export our poor, our unedu-cated, our weak. We throw out our suffering, our home-less, those who are as utterly dispossessed in their own country as any refusenik. We expel those who are incon-venient to our fabulous dream of ourselves. That dream used to be of a post-revolutionary Celtic Erin, where we would all without exception be rural, Catholic, hetero-sexual, conservative, in a family as nuclear as the Wal-tons. It would be an Ireland where we would all know our places, respect our elders and betters, wear bawneen jumpers and Aran knickers, smoke pipes and write turgid poetry in Irish about fishermen. Yeats said independent Ireland was no country for old men. How breathtakingly, unusually wrong he was. For the last seventy-five years that's exactly what it's been. A country where being old and male really did clock you up serious points.

More recently, the dream has been of a post-Maastricht, utterly dehistorified tax haven for rich tourists and pop stars, with sixteen channels of satellite TV, full employment at low pay in prefabricated factories and smooth new roads paid for by the Germans. Things are changing now; we can all see it. Ireland is introducing civilised laws, recognising that it needs to be humane in its social arrangements. Some of the emigrants I know will come back. But for others, it's too late. They feel that dreams change, but in Ireland waking up is always the same. Always was. Always will be. For ever and ever, Amen. Which is why they like waking up somewhere else.

Emigration is as Irish as the dear little shamrock or Cathleen Ni Houlihan's harp, yet it is only since the sixties and the generation of Edna O'Brien that Irish writers have written about the subject at first hand. It has been taken as read that emigration and exile are important themes in Irish writing, like the Big House or the Catholic Church. But if they are, they are intermittent and inconsistent preoccupations. Where are the first-person texts of Irish emigrant life in the latter part of the last century and the earlier part of this one? With one or two notable exceptions – Robert Tressel's *Ragged-Trousered Philanthropists*, say, and the bleak, spare poems and novels of Patrick Magill – they're not there. At the heart of the Irish emigrant experience is caution, a refusal to speak, a fear of the word.

Our emigrant culture has traditionally been described in songs rather than novels, plays or poems. But a friend said to me recently that he was sure all those sententious and mawkish ballads about grey-haired macushlas and shagging shillelaghs were written by people who had never been out of Portlaoise, never mind Ireland, in their lives. I suspect he would well be right. No one who ever really lived in Californ-aye-ay wrote 'Spancil Hill', I'm sorry. Silence, exile and cunning, Joyce maintained, were the true weapons of the writer. But the exiles have been silent too long. Perhaps we will give them voting rights. Perhaps not. In either case, the politicians whose manifest failures have perpetuated Irish emigration would do well to ponder the words of Coriolanus. 'Long my exile, sweet my revenge.'

What the English Sunday newspapers call the 'New Irish Literary Renaissance' has begun to fill the exile's silence with a torrent of words. Now there are green fields all over the planet, and at last they are beginning to appear in Irish fiction. The poet Louis MacNeice wrote about celebrating 'the drunkenness of things being various'. This younger generation of writers is claiming the right to celebrate an Ireland that is various also, in terms that are primarily aesthetic, but also, by implication, profoundly political. The silence of the Irish exile is over now. That is important.

'We are the blacks of Europe,' observes a character in Roddy Doyle's novel *The Commitments*. But that isn't really true any more. Being Irish is something worth talking about, if you're on someone else's turf and lucky enough to be making enough readies to socialise occasionally with the natives. These days an Irish passport seems to give you what people in the advertising industry call a reachier punch, I don't know why. I suspect it's more to do with Gabriel Byrne and *Riverdance* and Van Morrison than Synge, Beckett or William Trevor. People envy you these days in New York or London or mainland Europe if you're Irish. That's been my experience anyway. It's extraordinary. The whole world longs to be oppressed and authentic and post-colonial and tragically hip and petulantly Paddy, whereas many of us Irish just want to be anything else. Still, being Irish abroad – half-invader and half-native – is a fine thing for a writer to be. It means you probably won't get shot in the event of an aeroplane hijack, and it certainly helps you understand just how very Irish you are. Indeed, it sometimes seems to me that you almost have to get out of Ireland to be Irish at all, in some important sense, that those who stay sometimes turn out to be the real exiles, whereas those who go are the natives. But for a writer that's material. So no complaints.

We have gone about the world like wind, Yeats said. Wish you were here. Wish I was there. Well, sometimes anyway.

II   The Lizards of Oz

'Australia: The Koala Triangle: a mysterious zone
in the Southern Hemisphere where persons
of talent disappear without trace.'

A Nice Night's Entertainment, Barry Humphries

Wednesday, 18 October 1995, 4.30 a.m.: Somewhere over Australia. The in-flight video is showing a very interesting television programme about the natural world. It features wonderful scenes of maggots making endless love in slow motion to Mozart. (Well, not actually to Mozart, but . . . you know what I mean.) I switch off the video. I have had enough insect porn for now, thank you very much. If I was a maggot myself, no doubt I would find this very entertaining, but no, I am not. I try to think straight. This is hard. I left Dublin the day before yesterday, got delayed, flew to London, got delayed, flew to Singapore, got delayed, now I am flying to Australia. Yes, Australia!! The other side of the world. I mean, I admit it's true that writers will do almost anything to avoid writing. But a book promotion tour? Of bloody Australia?! Isn't that taking things a little too far? I turn the video back on. Two nasty-looking spiders are engaging in serious heavy petting. Thirty seconds later, just as I'm getting interested, one eats the other. I guess they just lost that lovin' feeling.

5.30 a.m.: Melbourne airport. I arrive and am met by the very friendly and professional young woman in charge of publicity at my publishing company. She explains to me that Melbourne is 'the cultural capital of Australia'. This is very fascinating indeed, but I'm finding it just a tad hard to concentrate. After twenty-three hours on the plane I have jet lag the way Abba had flares. My head is pounding. My feet have swelled up to the size of watermelons. My tongue feels like a slab of sandpaper. My skin is not so much dry as desiccated. I look like a stressed prune. I feel like Limerick on legs. The car radio says it is five-thirty in the morning, but my body clock knows different. My body clock knows that it is either half past four next Saturday afternoon or some time in the late 1820s. As we cruise gently into the city, *Good Morning Melbourne* comes on the radio. It is presented by two young Australian chaps who make Beavis and Butthead seem like Umberto Eco.

'G'day, Mite,' one says. 'Hawaii yah this morning?'

'I'm blardy good, Mite. And you?'

'I'm good, too, Mite. I'm the best, or so the woif tells

me anywaze. HA HA HA HA. And tell me. Did yah perform your abbo-lutions this morning, Mite?'

'Moi what, Mite? My . . .?'

'Your abbo-lutions, Mite. Your ABBO-LUTIONS! It's a poloyt word for taking a poo, Mite.'

It is very nice, I must say, to be here in the cultural capital of Australia.

The hotel is the kind of hotel in which writers only ever stay when they are on book promotion tours and somebody else is paying. This is the kind of hotel where the staff ask how you are feeling today, how your flight was, what kind of newspaper would you like delivered to your room every morning. That kind of thing. Most of the hotels I have ever stayed in are not like this. In my usual type of hotel, the walls are so thin you can hear your next-door neighbours' inner doubts. In my usual type of hotel, if I get an 'Ah, shut yer trap, poxbottle, I told yeh we're out of bleedin' drink' from a waiter, I feel I'm doing quite well. I settle into my room, which is bigger than my entire flat at home. I try on the fluffy white dressing gown and attempt to iron my overcoat in the automatic trouser press. I run a bath, get into it, fall asleep in it and wake up an hour later thinking that I have died in it.

Thursday, 19 October: Wake up feeling absolutely dreadful and stagger out for a stroll. 'In Sydney,' wrote the great Australian playwright David Williamson, 'people spend their whole lives trying to find a house with a nice view. But in Melbourne, they know there is no point, because there are no nice views. So the pace of life is easier.' Looking around the city I can see what he was on about. Melbournites are friendly and hospitable people,

147

but the place they inhabit is not so much a city as one big airport terminal. It has the transient and prefabricated air of a place that could be taken down tomorrow and shifted fifty miles north. People who live here are obsessed by the weather. If you comment that it's not a very nice day today, they will tell you the exact temperature, the relative position of nearby slow-moving cold fronts and the precise wind-chill factor correct to fourteen decimal points. The other thing they seem to like talking about in Melbourne is their personal problems. Perhaps this is because living in Melbourne means you have a lot of personal problems, I don't know. But certainly, Melbournites outdo even New Yorkers when it comes to spilling the lurid details of their personal lives. For example, the chap behind the bar in the café tells me he is upset because his wife keeps threatening to leave him. And she hasn't yet.

'The only difference between my missus and a Rottweiler, Mite,' he explains, 'is that when a Rotty starts to savage you, it locks its bloody jaws shut.'

This afternoon, as part of the Melbourne International Literature Festival, there is a public forum on 'Irish Writing and God', at which I have been invited to speak, along with the Irish novelists Brian Moore and Frank Ronan. On the plane to Australia I spent time reading a long article about 'the new multiculturalism' in the country and how 'great efforts are now being made to combat racial stereotyping'. I am utterly fascinated to see how Australia's new anti-stereotypical approach applies itself to the Irish. Three Irish writers, oooh, what'll we get 'em to talk about? Leprechauns? Harps? Foster and Allen? Oh, I know, God. Very imaginative. I look forward to the next reading by an Australian writer in Dublin so that I can ask him about the enormous influence of the boomerang on his work.

The audience today seems to be full of nuns. I have not seen so many nuns since I last watched *The Sound of Music*. I stand up and begin my speech by gamely telling my favourite religious joke. How do you know Jesus was an Irishman? Because he hung around with the lads all the time, he thought he was God and he lived with his mother till he was thirty. This goes down very well indeed, as you can imagine. I manage to get out of the building without being stoned to death or crucified.

As I am led to the police car with the blanket over my head, I am very glad that I didn't tell my second favourite religious joke. How do you know John the Baptist was made of elastic? Because he tied his ass to a tree and walked forty miles into the desert.

Friday, 20 October: Wake up feeling appalling. This evening I am doing a reading in the Melbourne town hall. One of the other speakers is 'New Zealand's greatest living poet'. As I listen attentively to her performance I am in two minds about her poetry. I cannot decide whether I dislike it, or, on the other hand, whether I hate it. This person writes the kind of poetry we all wrote when we were fifteen and then had the good sense to stop. Each line seems to be made up of the same list of words simply rearranged more or less at random. (These words are: I, feeling, moon, me, emotion, pain, self, emptiness, grief, spots, listless, my, heartbeat, nipple, parents and bastard. Just try reading them out repeatedly in any order you like and you'll probably get a large grant from the New Zealand Arts Council.) One of her poems is about how love is like a kangaroo. I swear to you, I'm not making this up. Me, I have never noticed before how much like a kangaroo love is, but now, having listened to her, I can see how wrong I was. Love and a kangaroo are, of course, practically identical. One is a big, bouncy, unpleasant and unreliable brute that initially seems cute but can actually kill you. The other is a kangaroo. Thanks be to God (him again!), New Zealand also have the All Blacks.

This evening after the reading I discover that the most common Australian slang word for having sex is 'rooting', or 'having a root'. (Yes, yes, yes, you can calm down now. I discover this because somebody tells me over a glass of wine.) This makes one or two things about Australia fall suddenly into place. I had been wondering, for example, why the audiences on this trip have cackled and hooted with ribald laugher whenever I refer to my 'Irish roots'.

Here is an Australian joke, which I now understand. Why is an Australian man just like a koala bear? Because he eats roots and leaves.

Saturday, 21 October: Wake up feeling banjaxed. A local freelance photographer arrives to take my picture. He is an affable cove. As he snaps and clicks at my still jet-lagged self, he tells me an interesting story. When the Queen was last in Australia this photographer fellow was commissioned to cover the royal visit by an Australian newspaper. 'Her Madge', as he insists on calling HRH, turned out to be 'a friendly enough old buzzard'. He tells me all about how he actually met her. One afternoon during a royal walkabout he was snapping away at Her Madge, when suddenly she came strolling over to him and began to casually chat. I ask what she wanted to chat about. The weather mainly. And photography. Her Madge was very interested in photography.

'Do you know,' said Her Madge to my new friend, 'I've got a brother-in-law who's a photographer?'

'And what did you say to her then?' I ask him.

'I said that was a bladdy funny coincidence, Mite,' he grins, 'because I've got a brother-in-law who's a queen.'

Sunday, 22 October: Wake up still feeling bad. This afternoon I fly to Sydney for the second stage of my book tour. The man sitting beside me on the plane has the worst facial tic of anyone I have ever seen. It is quite astounding. Every time his face tics, the plane practically goes into a nose dive. Later, we share a taxi into the city. I don't know whether the excitement of being here in Sydney has affected the tic in some way, but the poor guy is now bouncing uncontrollably around the back of the taxi like a steel ball in a pinball machine, his head banging off the windows. Later still, at a bar near the hotel, I meet the first Sydney journalist who wants to interview me. The interview does not get off to the best of starts:

'So. You're Sinead O'Connor's brother, aren't you?'

'Yes,' I answer, 'as you so perceptively point out, by far the most important thing about my work is that I am Sinead O'Connor's brother.'

'But she's so beautiful,' the interviewer says, and she peers at me, with a mystified look in her eyes. I have the uneasy feeling that devastating irony may not be that big in Australia.

Monday, 23 October: Wake up feeling poorly. This morning Viceroy John Hayden has given an interview to the *Sydney Morning Herald*, explaining how he doesn't feel Australia should have an elected president. He seems to seriously want this country, which is 12,000 miles away from England, to continue being part of the British Commonwealth and having Her Madge as first citizen. He finds the Queen a very friendly and supportive person, he says, the most friendly and supportive person he knows. He can talk to the Queen more openly than he can talk to anybody else in the whole world, he says. Wow. I find myself wondering how Mrs Viceroy feels about this. Australians feel a strong emotional link with the British Royal Family, the viceroy explains. Hmmmm. I think about this and wonder if it's true. Most of the Australians I've met don't seem to feel a strong emotional link to anything much except perhaps beer and, of course, the weather. I wonder exactly how you would persuade your average Italian- or Croatian- or Malaysian-Australian of the mystical emotional link she or he is supposed to feel with Prince Charles and his mum. This is not a job I would like to have.

The point about modern Australia is that it has completely transcended its Anglo-Celtic origins and is now comprised of people from all over the planet. Melbourne, for example, contains the largest Greek population of any city in the world except Athens. These days Australia, like I told you, is obsessed with multiculturalism. As a result, Australians do tend to go on a bit about the level of multicultural social change they have achieved. I am suspicious of this. The last place I visited where people talked long and loud about the level of multicultural social change they had achieved was Alabama. A bit of local investigation revealed that what this amounted to in practice was giving black citizens a twenty-minute head start into the woods before letting loose the bloodhounds.

Yet, in the case of Australia this multiculturalism does

indeed seem to be a reality. It is not Utopia, by any means, and in the past absolutely horrific crimes were conducted against the Aboriginals. Yet these days it is certainly a less truculent and fitful society than America or Britain when it comes to issues of race. I ask an Australian friend how his country has managed to achieve all this. How is it, for example, that there have never been race riots in Australia? He considers for a moment. 'Apathy,' he says.

Tuesday, 24 October: Wake up feeling a little better. This morning's interview begins with the question 'Do young Irish writers see themselves as the voice of the new Ireland?' When I have finished laughing, I think about this. Maybe it would be nice to be the voice of the new Ireland. Perhaps we could take it in turns. Anne Enright could be the voice of the new Ireland one week, then Colm Tóibín, then Dermot Bolger, then Pat McCabe, and so on. And during the weeks when we were not being the voice of the new Ireland we could be some other body part. The foot of the new Ireland, or the armpit of the new Ireland, maybe. I myself would like to be the bum of the new Ireland, but that is another story.

Wednesday, 25 October: Wake up feeling almost normal. A week into the tour and the humiliation begins in earnest. Having spent seven days dealing with print journalists, a species I understand and mostly like, I am now doing local radio. Local radio interviewers are the same all over the world. They come in two varieties: (a) the type so emotionally disturbed and mentally subnormal that they went into local radio because they didn't have the personality to work at assembling car number-plates; (b) the type who was very clever in school and has a nice velvety voice and really feels they should be presenting an internationally syndicated show, and is only condescending to put in time in this crummy joint while waiting for someone who does present an internationally syndicated show to drop down dead or fall into a coma.

This morning, the interviewer, 'Happenin'' Henry Horovitz, confesses that he has never heard of me or my book, and that he doesn't actually like reading because it gives him a headache, and that they're only having me on the show because the guest they had originally booked, a part-time postman who can fart 'Waltzing Matilda' while accompanying himself on the Wurlitzer electric organ, has mysteriously cancelled at the last moment. But he's sure 'we'll be able to wing it'. The interview begins. We chat for a while about my book. It is called *The Secret World of the Irish Male*, I explain, and it is funny. 'Oh right,' he says, 'say something funny for the listeners then.' I try my best. Happenin' Henry peers at me intensely, looking every bit as amused as a person who is watching *Schindler's List*. Then he says he's going to take a few calls. Things go downhill from here.

Happenin' Henry: 'OK, yeah, Boris in Woolloomoolloo, you're through to Joe O'Connor, Mite. He's the voice of the new Ireland, Mite, HA HA HA.'

Caller: 'Hello?'

Happenin' Henry: 'Go ahead, Caller?'

Caller: 'Hello?'

Joe: (attempting the local lingo) 'Hawaii yah, Mite?'

Caller: 'Hello? Are you there?'

Happenin' Henry: 'Yes, Mite. You're through to our studio guest this morning, Ireland's Joe O'Connor, author of *The Male Secret of the Irish World*.'

Caller: 'Hello? Am I through?'

Happenin' Henry: 'Go ahead, Caller.'

Caller: 'Yes. Can you hear me?'

Happenin' Henry: 'Hello? Hello?'

Joe: (getting desperate) 'HAWAII-YAH?'

Caller: 'Hello, yes? Am I on the air now? HELLO?'

Etcetera, etcetera. After a few more minutes of this, Happenin' Henry begins to lose it a bit. He begins rocking back and forth and snorting with maniacal laughter. And I do mean snorting. Happenin' Henry is very possibly the individual for whom the adjective 'stertorous' was originally coined. As the full contents of Happenin' Henry's nostrils come rocketing across the studio table as though they have just been discharged from a double-barrelled cannon, I can't help but feel, phew, the sheer bloody glamour of the writer's life.

Thursday, 26 October: Wake up feeling just about OK. I do a reading with the wonderful American writer John Berendt, who has the following true story to tell: while stopped at traffic lights in his hired car in downtown Sydney he is approached by a large and attractive black woman who asks him for a lift. He opens the door and she sits demurely in the passenger seat. They begin to chat. She has a flirtatious and rather physical manner. She keeps running her finger down his thigh and calling him 'Baby' or 'Sugar'. Her name is Chablis, she tells him, (pronouncing it Sh'blee, with the emphasis on the second syllable). 'That's a nice name,' he tells her. 'Ooooh, yes, Baby,' she drawls, 'a cool sophisticated name for a cool sophisticated lady.' They drive on, her hand lightly stroking the back of his neck, her lips intermittently blowing gusts of perfumed air against his face. He feels a little uneasy. His playful passenger begins to explain that Chablis is actually not her real name, it is a name that she chose for herself. 'And what was your real name?' John asks her. 'I mean, before you changed it to Chablis.' She peers at him for a moment. She grins. 'Frank,' she says.

Saturday, 28 October: In Australia, just like in every other country in the world, local TV is even more badly organised than local radio. An hour after I have turned up at the studio, the producer for my interview, a very pleasant but harassed-looking young man in a black polo-neck jersey, comes in and explains that they are still building the set. I ask if he would like me to give them a hand.

Another hour later I am summoned to said set, which is designed like a suburban dining room. I make an impressive entrance by tripping on the carpet, somersaulting over the velour sofa and almost demolishing the attractive coffee table. Once we fix the set and get going, the interview proceeds quite nicely. I'm sure both viewers enjoyed it very much indeed.

Sunday, 29 October: Wake up feeling marvellous. Yippee! A great night's sleep. At last I am over my jet lag. I spring out of bed with the easy grace of a young gazelle. At last I can start enjoying myself. Yessss! Now what do I have to do today? An awful realisation dawns. Of course. I have to get the plane back to London today. Twenty-three more hours of nonstop fun and airline food and bugs bonking to bloody Mozart. I promise, I'll never try to find an excuse not to write again.

III   Amateur Traumatics

IT IS TWO MINUTES TO EIGHT ON A TUESDAY NIGHT. I am sitting in the Tricycle Theatre, Kilburn, London. I am terrified. My brother is sitting beside me. I am gripping his arm so tightly that his eyes are bulging like gobstoppers. My stomach feels like I swallowed a pogo stick. My brother is telling me to calm down. He is telling me to take deep breaths. He is telling me that everything will be alright. Thank God I have been on a diet for six months now, otherwise passers-by hearing the conversation would take one look at me and assume that my waters had just broken. The reason for all this anxiety? In two minutes' time the curtain will go up on my very first play, *Red Roses and Petrol*.

I use the word 'curtain', although one thing the Tricycle Theatre, Kilburn, and myself have in common is a bit of an ambivalence where curtains are concerned. So, in two minutes' time the stage lights will be illuminated and actors will come on and start saying things and in the course of the following two hours and twenty minutes the product of months and months of hard work by a quite large group of people, myself included, will be watched by an audience of real people, and then judged by the critics. They will poke it, prod it, tweak its chubby cheeks, hold it upside down by the ankles, spank it lightly on the backside and pronounce it either a handsome little creature with a bright future or a bit of a fucking turkey.

How did any of this happen to me? I never wanted to write a play. And yet, almost a year ago now, I agreed to do so. I should have followed my instinct and said no when I was asked. But I didn't. So here we are. I think back to the long nights of composition. For most of the play's period of gestation I was suffering from a bad writer's block. Let me tell you, there were times when the influence of Samuel Beckett on this play of mine was going to be considerable. It was going to be a very meaningful work indeed, instead of the utterly hilarious, yet oddly affecting, little family drama it ended up as. Here, for the sake of posterity, is the entire first draft:

Curtain up on an empty stage. Enter Actor A, naked, except for a luminous condom. He sits on the floor for half an hour in silence, eyes bulging. From time to time he scratches his crotch. Enter Actor B, dressed as a tramp. He drops his trousers and stands on his hands for half an hour in silence, except for the occasional bloodcurdling scream. Curtain down. Fifteen-minute interval for sipping of gin in the foyer, commenting on how fashionable everybody looks and publicly congratulating the anxious author before privately whispering that he really should have stuck to what he is best at, that is to say, the penning of puerile gags of a dubiously sexual nature in *Esquire* once a month. Back into the theatre. Curtain up. Enter Actor A and Actor B, dressed in black tartan kilts, white stilettos and Republic of Ireland soccer shirts. Actor A: 'I can't go on. I must go on.' Ten-minute silence. Actor B: 'I feel that I will die soon.' Actor A: 'Me, too.' Member of audience: 'You're shagginwell dyin' already, boys.' Fifteen-minute silence. Curtain down. Wild cheers.

But that was fantasy. This is the real thing. The lights come up. The actress Anne Kent, who plays the mother of the family in the play, strolls on and just looks amazingly calm. I cannot understand this. The reality of finally seeing her on a real stage is making me want to be hospitalised. Then her daughter, played by Kathy

Downes, comes on and says her first line. I'm sorry to use professional jargon here, but Kathy's first line is what we in the theatrical world sometimes call 'a joke'. She delivers it perfectly. Spot on. And nobody laughs. It's nothing to do with the way she said it. It's not that they didn't hear it or anything. They heard it and they just didn't laugh. Hmmmm. Kathy says her second line, another gag. Again, no laugh. I find myself silently assessing the relative merits of shooting oneself in the head as opposed to employing the noose, the gas oven or a Linford Christie-style high-speed canter down the nearest pier.

I am in the front row. The critics are all sitting behind me. There are a lot of them. They have notebooks! I glance over my shoulder. Rampant paranoia begins to descend. In the fragrant air of the Tricycle Theatre the scratching of biros begins to sound like the sharpening of machetes. Not that it matters what the critics say, of course. As Emerson put it, 'It is the job of those who cannot construct to take apart.' (That's Ralph Waldo Emerson, by the way, not Emerson Fitipaldi.) So I don't care whether we get good reviews or not. Oh, no. I am a serious artist, a miner hacking at the coal face of language, a blacksmith forging the uncreated conscience of his race, a second-hand car salesman extolling the merits of the national Fiat Uno, a professional cyclist getting in his spoke for . . . (Could we get the hell on with it here – Ed.)

Suddenly there is another joke. And the audience laugh. It's not a big howl or anything, more of a speculative titter. I breathe in deeply. Quite soon there's another gag. A guffaw from the audience. I breathe out. I look at my brother. He is practically in tears. I am touched by his fraternal loyalty. I thank him profoundly. 'It's not that,' he hisses, 'but please, if you don't let go my hand soon I'll have to scream with the bloody agony.'

I release my brother's hand, which he clamps into his armpit. The audience settle into it. (The play, that is, not my brother's armpit.) More laughs. At half-time I have a drink with my father. He is very encouraging. I know I should not really refer to this fifteen-minute break as 'half-time'. It's not as if the Territorial Army Brass Band are going to march on in formation and play 'Abide with Me' or anything. 'Interval' is the proper word. This theatrical business is going to be difficult to get used to.

Back in for round two. It goes well. The audience, possibly fortified by copious amounts of free drink, continue to laugh in almost all the right places. Then – another piece of sophisticated technical jargon here – we get to what Arthur Miller in his seminal work *The Meaning of Modern Theatre* (University of Massachusetts Press, 1957) once called 'the sad bit at the end'. Anne Kent is so moving that all around me hardened critics are gulping with either emotion or asthma. When the play is over I go to the pub with the actors. I have been off the drink since New Year's Eve and this does strange things to a person's metabolism. After two pints of lager I am pissed. After four I am kissing the actors. After five I am out in the street and kissing lampposts. Things get a bit hazy then.

Next morning the phone rings at dawn. I wake up and recognise the lamppost beside me. I must say, it is not nearly so attractive first thing in the morning, but I make up my mind to respect it anyway. My father is on the phone. He has read a review in one of the morning papers. The massive financial inducements, offers of sexual favours, etc., seem to have worked. The review is pretty good. Relief is not the word for what I feel. I don't think I have been quite so overjoyed about anything since the tragic death of Andy Gibb. I make a light breakfast for the lamppost and myself. And I sleep, for the first time in days. Never ever again in my whole life will I complain about the difficulty of writing an article for a newspaper or magazine. After what I've just been through, I'd be happy to write the whole magazine, every month, for nothing. It's the one truly great thing about being a journalist. You don't have to sit there and sweat while people are reading you. Although, now that I think of it, I do feel a little bit light-headed at the thought of you finishing this page. So read it again. Go on. It's better the second time around. Honest.

IV   Come Fly with Me, Aaargh!

AS READERS WILL HAVE GATHERED BY NOW, I SPEND A good deal of my time in the air because of the exciting and interesting nature of my job. I'm a flu germ.

No, seriously, today I think we should have a talk about the vexed subject of international air travel. Do you like it? I don't. I mean, the only time in my life when I ever pray is on an aeroplane. On terra firma I am the biggest atheist going. I am a pagan and hedonistic rationalist who can dismiss millennia-old belief systems with a scarcely discernible raising of one eyebrow and a light scoffing curl of the upper lip. Once the plane takes off, however, it is a very different story. I am fingering the bloody glaze off those rosary beads. I am praying with a white-knuckled fervour that even his holiness, Pope John Paul II, would find just a tad over the top.

I know all about the statistics. I know you have more chance of winning the lotto and a greater probability of being battered to death by Armenian terrorists than you do of dying horribly in an air crash. But that's not going to be much consolation, is it, when you find yourself plummeting towards the ground in a metal box that is moving at five hundred miles an hour, and you have not even had the opportunity to enjoy your duty-free?

It's just not safe, is it? You are sitting in something the size of your house and it is fifty thousand feet above the sea, moving at three times the speed of a racing car. How in the name of God did something like that ever make it off the drawing board, never mind the runway?! And if proof of what I am saying were needed, just think of all the famous people who have died in plane crashes. Stevie Ray Vaughan. Buddy Holly. Patsy Cline. Terrible, isn't it? All that dead talent, and we can't even get Celine Dion onto an airline.

It is always the same story. Before you take off, the captain comes on the radio sounding like Liam bloody Neeson or something out of a Martini commercial. He is Mister Smooth, Mister Sophisticated. He tells you he is glad that you have made the decision to travel with whomever it is, and that the weather today is perfect flying weather, and that you'll be there at your destination before you know it. He tells you the ground temperature at the airport of your destination, for God's sake, as though you give a fiddler's feck. What he does not tell you is: I was out on the razz with the mott and her auld wan last night, I have a hangover on me that would fell an ox, I feel only wojus, I've a ferocious dose of the runs, the co-pilot is a complete psychopathic maniac, I am sure he has got a gun, I need some heroin fast.

Yes, yes, the stewards and stewardesses do their best to reassure you as they go through the safety procedures. They point out the emergency doors, that is to say, the doors through which you will be sucked into oblivion if there is an emergency. They point out the emergency strip lighting on the floor. The emergency strip lighting winks at this point, with all the power of a sixty-watt light bulb in a heavy fog. Look, let me make it plain here. I want to see the kind of floor they had in the discotheque in *Saturday Night Fever*, not a solitary tube of feeble bloody neon! They point out the location of the life jackets. The life jackets float, you are told. Oh, great. Hallelujah. The only reason the life jackets float is that you bloody don't! There is a tube to inflate the life jacket 'by mouth'. Oh, that's handy, isn't it? As I flail around in the pitch-black ocean dodging the sharks, I'm really going to be calm and collected enough to blow up my life jacket 'by mouth' as though inflating a comedy balloon at a toddlers' Christmas party, aren't I? Perhaps I'll twist the bloody thing into an amusing sausage dog shape, shall I? There is – and how the hell they can say this without blushing I'll never know – a whistle for attracting attention. Attracting attention? You have just fallen screaming out of the sky and are actually on fire. I would have thought attracting attention would be the least of your bloody problems.

I used to have this trick whenever I was on an airline that hit a patch of turbulence – whenever, in other words, I felt my buttocks beginning to clench like an industrial vice – I would look at the flight attendants. If they looked happy, then I would be happy. Hey, I would tell myself, they do this every day, these people are professionals, they know when it's only turbulence and they know when it's real trouble. I thought I was the only person in the world who did this. But I was wrong! Everyone does it. I've asked around. Furthermore, I have a good friend who is a flight attendant and she told me recently that flight attendants are trained, for God's sake, to always look calm! The bloody plane could have a fire going in all four engines, it could be about to sink as quickly as a willy joke in a convent, the entire undercarriage could be rapidly turning into molten steel, and the staff would still be looking relaxed and offering you more drink and the pilot would still be burbling away on the intercom about the shagging wind velocity and the interesting view below. The interesting view below, in the meantime, is about to get a hell of a lot more interesting, in that it is about to get a hell of a lot nearer your window in a hell of a short time.

The simple truth is that there is just no way of knowing what's going to happen to you on an airline. It is absolutely unpredictable. Except for one thing. Every single person on an airline will be reading a book by Roddy Doyle and guffawing loudly and turning to each other with tears of merriment in their eyes and saying how terrific Roddy Doyle is, and how they can't imagine how any sane and normal person, anywhere, could read anything that wasn't by Roddy Doyle, ever, and how every other young Irish author going is only in the ha'penny place beside Roddy Doyle. Not that that has anything to do with my dislike of airlines. Honest.

V The Italian Job

> 'By 1948 the Italians had managed to pull
> themselves together, demonstrating once more
> their astonishing ability to cope with disaster
> which is so perfectly balanced by their absolute
> inability to deal with success.'

Matters of Fact and Fiction, Gore Vidal

LAST YEAR I WENT TO ITALY WHERE I WAS DOING A
reading and also speaking at a debate with the tall,
talented and impossibly thin Northern Irish novelists
Eoin McNamee and Glenn Patterson at the Turin Book
Fair. (My not-quite-so-tall but admittedly perfectly
formed fellow Southerner, Aidan Mathews, was there,
too.) The debate was about how awfully challenged and
culturally oppressed young Irish writers feel, coming, as
they do, from the country that produced James Joyce, and
how young Irish novelists in particular find life unbear-
ably tricky living in the shadow of the master. I don't
have this problem myself. I can tell you candidly that I
very rarely wake up at three o'clock in the morning
sweating about James Joyce. My own view is that *Finnegans Wake* bears precisely the same relationship to a
work of art that masturbation does to lovemaking; that
is to say, it's quite nice to experiment with from time to
time, and it won't do you any harm if you don't overdo
it, but it's not nearly as good as the real thing. When I
said this at the debate, however, nobody laughed, except
Glenn Patterson, who was sitting beside me and who is
obviously a very kind person. Hmmmm. Perhaps it lost
a little in the translation. Reader, I do not know if you
have ever sat in a room and been stared at by a hundred
Italian Joyceans, all of them in black polo-neck sweaters

and tight trousers, but, take it from me, pleasant it ain't.

Turin itself is an interesting town, particularly when you are in the company of foreign novelists. I speak no Italian myself, and so I had to rely on Glenn and Eoin, who had each learnt a few key phrases. One day I asked the boys to each tell me their most useful bit of the lingo. They thought for a moment or two. Then, Glenn said that large groups of Italians, like large groups of any nationality, tend to be a bit disorganised and vacillating, and so he had found the phrase '*andiamo*', which means 'let's go', to be pretty handy. Eoin, for his part, pointed out that people at the Turin Book Fair would inevitably ask you what you had written, and so he had found '*ha scrittoro una romanza*', which means 'I have written a novel', a good thing to know. I learnt both off by heart, and, indeed, I found them a useful and very multipurpose combination. Taken together, 'I have written a novel, let's go' seemed to be so much more than the sum of its parts. I recommend it to readers who are heading off on the hollyers soon. (It is particularly effective when accompanied by the waving in the air of a package of prophylactics and two large glasses of Campari and soda, each containing a paper umbrella and a slice of cantaloupe.)

Anyway, I don't know if you've ever been there, but Turin is a really nice town. It has perhaps a surfeit of factories and hideous power stations, and, of course, it is practically owned by the Fiat Corporation who have their headquarters there. Yet, it also has lovely squares, gracious fountains featuring armless marble broads with serious cellulite and a good hefty chunk of the Po, which is, you will recall from jogger class, the longest river in all of Italy. Strolling by the banks of that long and lovely river at night in Turin is an interesting cultural experience. The sheer variety of drugs for sale is quite staggering. Drug dealers approach you with menus the length of something very long indeed. During one brief stroll I was offered ecstasy, hashish, cannabis, cocaine, heroin and tranquillisers. Since I always feel tranquil anyway when I am in Italy, I declined. But it was nice to know that every taste was being catered for. Except the one for nicotine. Turin is the kind of city where a ten-year-old child can purchase with its pocket money enough hallucinogenic narcotics to keep a former Beatle happy for a six-month, but a fully grown adult has to pound the streets for hours looking for a place that is licensed – 'licensed', I ask you – to sell cigarettes. But nowhere is perfect, I suppose. (Look at Portlaoise, if you doubt me.)

On the Sunday morning I went along to the cathedral to have a gander at the famous shroud, only to discover that the holy men in whose trust it has been placed keep the thing in a big jewel-encrusted box which they only open once every hundred years or so. What a swizz! I had been hoping to have my photograph taken in the cathedral, preferably while actually wearing the shroud. I thought it would have made a very attractive souvenir. But no such luck. If I was an enterprising Turinian I would be setting up on the cathedral steps with one of those cardboard Brighton seafront panels with the face cut out, the entire thing made up in the image of the shroud so that tourists could put their heads through the holy hole and smile and look divine.

I do not mean to be blasphemous, and, in fact, I am not being so, because to whomsoever the shroud belonged in the past, it was certainly not Jesus. It is admittedly a truly remarkable object, but electro-carbon research has now proved beyond any shadow of doubt that it hails from the fourteenth century, and even allowing for a pretty generous margin of error I have to say that this does put old J.C. well and truly out of the picture. In any case, the real question about the shroud is: how did anybody ever think for even a moment that face could have belonged to our Blessed Saviour? I mean look at it. Carefully. And then look into your heart. Who does it remind you of? Who is it really? You know, don't you? Is this the face of the son of God or is it the face of Finbar Furey?

Yes, Italy is a wonderful place, a fine country for mind-blowing political corruption, Vespa scooters and swanky Renaissance paintings full of skinny-dipping babes. Italy is perhaps the most stereotyped European nation of all. There is, for example, the myth that all Italians are good-looking. In reality, the attractive ones all got out years ago. I can tell you candidly, you would need a bloody licence to keep your average Florentine in the house. There is also the notion that Italians are inherently stylish. Well, if gangs of drunken ululating carbuncular teenyboppers wandering the streets and publicly interfering with each other and screaming 'Ciao, bella' at your girlfriend is your idea of style, you would love Italy as much as I do. But I do have many happy memories of that fine country. Last Easter Sunday morning in Rome was a marvellous spiritual experience, I have to admit. It was lovely being in St Peter's Square, all of us together, singing hymns, saying rosaries and queuing up to kiss the Papal ring (the lip ointment really is working well now). In my view, there is only one thing really wrong with Italy and that is the currency. The current exchange rate for the lire is about 2,700 to the pound. This makes life very difficult indeed. A newspaper costs several hundred lire, a beer costs five grand. In Italy a person would need to be a millionaire to be an alcoholic, not that that seems to bloody well stop them. The mental calculation needed to purchase anything at all is quite phenomenal. Thus, many's the night, as I propped up some dodgy piazza speakeasy singing ribald choruses of 'Bandiera Rossa' and 'Nessun Dorma' with the locals, I found myself, not for the first time, disagreeing with Mr John Major on an important aspect of fiscal policy. I found myself saying: why oh why can we not have the ECU?

Now, as regular readers will know, I am not exactly blessed when it comes to the study of economics. When the other boys were doing double economics at ten past nine on a Monday morning I opted for art. Art class was really interesting. There was one boy who was actually talented at art, there were three or four indolent little skivers, and there were twenty-five saddos whose eyes were just a little too close together and who delighted in assembling turd-shaped objects made of plasticine and trying to ignite each other's burps with cigarette lighters. I will leave it to intuitive readers to discern the category into which I fitted myself. But anyway, economics? You could tell me that John Maynard Keynes was a blind blues guitarist from the Mississippi Delta who once jammed with Muddy Waters and Clarence 'Gatemouth' Brown on a scorching live version of 'Ah Can't Get No Grindin' Baby (What's the Matter with the Mill?)' and I would believe you. To me, Supply, Demand and Curve were a progressive rock-combo from the mid-seventies. All I know about the ERM is that they are a great old band, and that 'Losing My Religion' is a catchy little number to warm up a party attended exclusively by social workers. But one thing I do know. After a week in Italy I am all in favour of the ECU.

ECU, of course, stands for 'European Currency Unit', depending on whom you are talking to. But like Mr Major, I, too, have always had ambivalent feelings about the ECU, ever since a friend who works in the film business confided to me that the acronym ECU, in pornographic movie circles (and this is apparently true) stands for 'ejaculation close up'. Thus, even if we did introduce the ECU we would have to be cautious indeed. You would have to be pretty careful, for example, saying to a barperson, 'Can I have an ECU in the change please, I want to make a telephone call?', particularly if you did not know the barperson very well, and if you had not been out to the pictures with him or her (well, him, I suppose really) at least twice. I've come across a lot of angry barmen in my time, but I really would not want one of them to come across me.

But introducing the ECU would cut out an awful lot of bother, would it not? In the whole sorry business of foreign travel, there is nothing quite as bad as the worry about the currency. It doesn't matter how cosmopolitan you are, you are doomed to get it wrong. Picture the scene. It is the end of a pleasant evening in the local *trattoria*, *bodega* or *bierkeller*. You are feeling very post-Maastricht indeed, if you get my drift. You get out the wallet, extract a suitable banknote emblazoned with many zeros and a portrait of some moustachioed old Fascist. You shell out the tip, only to find when you have returned to the hotel that the amount you have so blithely handed over would pay the national debt of Zimbabwe and keep the landlady in stockings for about thirteen years. Either that, or you will have erred on the side of ferocious meanness, and the next time you visit the premises the barstaff will regard you the way they would regard a basin full of warm sick. In addition, not having spoken any English at all the night before, they will have suddenly and mysteriously acquired enough knowledge of the great tongue of Shakespeare to tell you under their breath that you are 'a tight-fisted old shit-head'. The ECU would sort all this out. It would give us the marvellous power to be tight-fisted old shit-heads in up to twelve different languages. And if that isn't European integration, I just don't know what is. *Ciao, bella*.

Speaking of languages, I read a while back that some committee of overpaid Eurocrats have made a truly important decision. No, it's not straightening bananas or anything as significant as that. It relates to the fluent and skilful use of the English language, and so it concerns all of us in this country, except perhaps Mr Charlie McCreevy TD, who speaks such a remarkable language of his own making. Anyway, it seems that English is to be finally adopted as the one, true, universal language of Europe. And not before time! Yes, some people would argue that what is so wonderful and mysterious about English is its breathtaking variety of spoken and written forms. Some people would foolishly contend that it's marvellous that Bob Marley and Dolores O'Riordan and Salman Rushdie and LLCoolJ and Maya Angelou, to name but a few English speakers chosen at random, all share the same language and yet make it so profoundly their own. Furthermore, some would say that the very reason why so many of the greatest writers in English have come from Ireland is that ever since English was forcibly introduced to this island as a vernacular, the people who live here have defiantly spoken it in their own way, with their own rhythms and cadences and meanings and nuances, that we Irish both possess the English language and are possessed by it, and that out of such a dialectic have come Joyce and Yeats and Heaney and all them lads. But, no, they would be wrong, these poor gobdaws who would say this. For the Europeans have decided not just that we must all speak English in the new future, but that we must all speak a new standardised European English. How right they bloody well are!

The Eurocrats have also decided that some changes will have to be made toute bleedin' suite in order to allow for the more full Europeanisation of the ancient tongue. The problem is spelling. Spanish and Italian are, broadly speaking, phonetic languages. You say the words more or less the way they look. But you will have noticed that this is not true when it comes to English. Consider, for example, the letters 'gh' in the word 'ghost' – tell us this and tell us no more – why do you need the 'h' at all? You do not. It is redundant. And, while we're about it, how do you explain the wildly varying 'gh' sounds in the words 'enough', 'plough', 'lough', 'through' and 'thorough', if you're so smart? You see? It can't be done. A little experiment now, if you still doubt me: let us spell out the word 'fish' taking the 'f' sound from 'enough', the 'i' sound from the way English people say 'been' (to rhyme with 'tin'), and the final lovely 'sh' from the beginning of the word 'chiffon'. What do we have? We have the word 'fish' spelt 'gheech'! Gheech and chips, please, my old scout, and a batterburger when you're ready?! Well, exactly. It's a pronunciational jungle out there, in need of serious clearing.

The enlightened Eurocrats have decided that the English language needs a more simplified form of spelling. To begin with, the soft 'c', as in the words 'certain' and 'cellophane', will be abolished and replaced with the much more sensible 's'. The pluralising 's' which comes at the ends of words – such as 'ends' and 'words' – will be superseded by the more phonetically correct 'z'. This newz will be reseived by English speakerz all over the world with tremendous happiness, I feel sure. Shortly after this, the letter 'c' will be phazed out altogether – just think of the money we'll save on smaller typewriter keyboardz – and we will all drive our kars, or, should I say, karz, on the right – I mean the rite – hand side of the rode. But then there is the problem of the superfluous 'e' to be addressed, which klingz on to our language like a useless appendix. If this new report is implemented in full there will be no more 'e's at the end of wordz such as 'here' or 'more'. No, it will be the new era, of the far more praktikal 'hir' or 'mor'. From then on it will be plain sailing and we will all be as happy as a dog with two mikiz. We will hopfully be abl to eradikat the kumpletly unnecessary and ugly double konsonants which skar such otherwiz fin wordz as 'parallel' and 'tomorrow'. Thez wil be spelt 'paralel' and 'tumoro'. The skem wil be veri popular indid. By the yer 2000, it iz hopd that totali fonetic speling wil bi awl the raj and the langwij, as a risult, wil bi far mor izy fur evribodi tu unerztand!!

Ov korz, sum pipul r surtan to bi unhapi abowt dis. Sum pipul fil zat zis almity showr ov overpad shagrz wud hav betr thingz tu bi duing with zemselvz. But then, sum pipul wil olwayz bi a payn in the ars wen it cumz to Uropin progrez!! No dowt, zey wont lik the nu Uropin nashunal anthim ithur. Tumoro bilongz tu mi.

VI The Emperor's New Clothes

OH MY GOD. HERE I AM. AT LONDON FASHION WEEK. I am in a tent waiting for a fashion show to start. Last time I was in a tent I was singing 'Ging Gang Goolie' and wearing a woggle. How the hell did this happen to me? The woman standing beside me must surely be a model. She is astoundingly beautiful. I have seen more interesting-looking women in my life. I have seen more sexy women. Hell, I've even seen more attractive women. But if it's pure old-fashioned beauty we're talking about, she's got it, big time. She is the High Priestess of Babelonia. I look at her. I stare at her. You could hang a hat on her cheek-bones. I practically start hyperventilating. She goes away.

Look, I don't have a lot of experience with the fashion industry. You're talking to a guy who thinks a supermodel is something really nice you make with an Airfix kit. And designer diffusion is something on which you pour hot water to produce a refreshing drink. Although I did meet Claudia Schiffer once. Well, I say meet. I was in LA to do a job. Sounds real glamorous, I know. When I tell you the job was to interview Billy Idol you may not be so impressed. Anyway, I'm staying in this nobby hotel in LA. I am not used to this. The kind of hotel I usually stay in, they knock on the door at eleven o'clock at night and shout, 'Time's up, Mac.' But anyway, I'm in this posh hotel and I figure I'll go for an early morning swim. So there I am, floundering around the pool, overweight, jet-lagged, spluttering, eyes streaming with chlorine, and I'm doing my best to swim along underwater, but suddenly I swallow about a gallon of the rank chemical liquid with which the pool is filled and I start to choke. Up I come, spitting and flailing, swallowing back nausea, nose running, hair in my eyes, swimming togs wedged tightly between my pendulous buttocks. And there she is. Claudia Schiffer. Sitting on the edge of the pool. Dangling those legs in the water. Claudia Schiffer. Wearing not so much a bikini as several pieces of deftly arranged dental floss. I gape at her. She looks like some kind of goddess crossed with some kind of angel. I feel my mouth opening and closing like a goldfish. I am a fully trained novelist. At this point I should be able to think of something really charming, smart and amusing to say. What I actually say is, 'Um, um, y-y-you're . . . um, I m-m-mean, aren't you, um, er.' Claudia Schiffer looks at me. What Claudia Schiffer says is, 'Do you think you could swim a little more gently, please. You're making me wet.'

I have told all my male friends the story of how I met Claudia Schiffer in LA and how she told me I was making her wet. OK, OK, I may have been a little creative with them about the actual facts of the story leading up this memorable punch line. But still. I met her and that's that.

Anyway, here I am, at the Pearce Fionda show. Don't ask me who the hell Pearce Fionda is. Perhaps it is two people, Pearce *and* Fionda. Perhaps 'Fionda' is a misprint of Fiona? I really don't know. There are people milling around with mobile telephones and walkie-talkies. Everybody seems to be wearing black. Many people are wearing sunglasses. At the end of the catwalk is a pen, the kind of thing in which a zookeeper might keep wild slavering rabid animals of some kind. In this pen there are at least sixty or seventy cameras with long protruding lenses. Behind them are sixty or seventy cameramen. (They *are* almost all men.) The lights go out. There is silence. Then suddenly the music starts. David Bowie's 'John, I'm Only Dancing'. The lights flash back on. A model appears at the end of the catwalk. She is wearing a cream trouser-suit. She begins to walk down the catwalk, although I don't know if walk really is the most accurate verb to describe what she is doing. Her hips are swaying like a bell. An audible murmur of appreciation surges through the crowd. The cameras are all clicking and flashing now. The sound of seventy cameras clicking is weird. It sounds like some kind of terrible insect. The flashlights flicker. 'It's very lonely,' sings the sound track, 'when you're a thousand light years from home.' Another model appears and sashays down the ramp in a brown knee-length dress. She has spiky hair. She looks sensational. The audience's heads turn to the right, following her to the end of the catwalk, then to the left, as she returns. It's like watching a tennis audience in slow motion. More girls appear, wearing lime-green jumpers, print patterns, Regency-style jackets, black and white patterned fabrics that look like Bridget Reilly paintings. On the sound track David Bowie is now singing 'When You're a Boy'. The creature that has just shimmied past me in the see-through chiffon shirt is no boy, I can tell you. Or if he is, he has a very severe oestrogen surfeit. I look at this model, wondering how it is possible for any human being to be so beautiful. How can it be the case, for example, that Jim Davidson and that astoundingly lovely creature now swishing past me are actually part of the same species? If that is a boy, believe me, I've just turned gay.

A few hours later, and I am trying to get in to the Red or Dead show when I see the High Priestess of Babelonia arriving in a taxi. She sweeps through the crowd, up to the door, gets in. I feel cold and lonely. The invitation to

176

the Red or Dead show is an A3-size piece of red paper. A3, in case you don't know, is the size you would get if you opened up a magazine and held it upright. So it's a big enough piece of red paper, is what I'm saying. And it's completely blank, except for a tiny circle, about the size of an old 10p coin, in the bottom left-hand corner, in which is contained the date, the venue and, most importantly, the information that the show will start at 3.45 p.m. prompt. This is very interesting to me, because it is now ten minutes past four and there's no sign of any action. You do tend to wonder how these designers can design clothes a full year in advance but can't start a fashion show on time. But anyway.

The venue is the Royal Horticultural Hall, a vast splendid room with an arching glass roof. It is very impressively laid out. There is a line of androgynous dummies lined up on one side, leaning, sitting, crouching, as though watching the show. This makes me laugh out loud. There are also little clusters of dummies wearing Chinese army-style costumes. And there are three enormous banners with Cyrillic Russian script. Backward Ns and Rs. The room looks like one of Ronald Reagan's worst nightmares.

It sounds like one, too. As I shuffle through the crowd of black-clad people to find my seat, the PA is playing a song called 'Detachable Penis'. (I promise that I am not making this up.) 'Even though it's sometimes a pain in the ass,' the singer clarifies, 'I like having a detachable penis. Though I really don't like being without my penis for too long.' There's a sentiment many of us can agree with.

At 4.15, a full half-hour late, a slightly disconcerting noise comes screaming from the PA speakers. It sounds a bit like an airline crashing. This accompanied by various assorted buzzings, rattles, drillings and sirens. A male model has appeared in the aisle. He is wearing a white vest-style shirt, grey trousers and a thin black leather tie. A girl follows wearing a similar outfit, followed by another girl in an amazing red and black dress. The Red or Dead models are pretty intriguing to look at. In fact, they are pretty *and* intriguing. They're all stunningly attractive, of course, and they have futuristic *Blade Runner*-style haircuts. But they have an earthy quality, too. They seem like real people you might actually see in the street where you live. If the street where you live happened to be Elm Street. Or Sesame Street.

There's a chap in a yellow and orange T-shirt and black trousers, another in a really nice tight grey suit, a girl with cropped hair in a red woollen dress. There's a black and red skirt, a few very sexy evening frocks. A svelte bloke in a long grey coat with epaulettes, another in a black string vest. There's an industrial theme – cogwheels and images of Chinese workers – but there also seem to be elements of glam in the purple tie-dye style trousers and the low-cut black leather dresses. There's a cool sophistication, too, in the classy navy and gold mini-dresses. There are fishnets, feathers, false manes of hair reaching down to the ground and stilettos. The whole thing is done with humour, style, street-smartness and drama. 'Bella Lugosi's dead,' roars the singer on the sound track. Maybe so. But if he wasn't, he'd certainly like this show a lot. He'd probably want to be in it. The High Priestess of Babelonia liked it anyway. I heard her say that to this really good-looking geezer linking her arm as they swept from the room together. 'It was very fun,' she is saying, 'wasn't it?' He is agreeing with her. 'Yes,' he says. 'It was very fun.' I stare at him. He looks like Brad Pitt. But I bet he has not got a good personality and sense of humour like me.

Later that night I attend Philip Treacy's show, which is being held back at the tent. Indeed, I am standing beside a television crew just inside this massive tent that has been erected inside the grounds of the Natural History Museum when something exciting happens. The cameraman's mobile phone rings. He answers it.

'Drop everything,' he barks to his crew. 'Kylie's here.'

'Kylie. Fuck. Where?'

'She's outside. Now. She's willing to talk to us. Quick. Come on, for fuck's sake.'

They begin to take apart the camera and pack up their equipment. A man in a red suit appears and begins to shout. 'What are you doing?!' shouts the man in the red suit.

'I thought you said we'd got Kylie,' shouts the cameraman.

'Not Kylie, you fool,' sighs the man in the suit. 'It's *Katie*. Katie Puckrick. From *The Word*.'

The cameraman sighs. He turns to his crew. He shrugs. He begins reassembling his camera.

I look around. A short man has arrived in a leprechaun hat. A woman comes in with a large black feather appearing to protrude from her head. It really doesn't suit her. She looks like a stressed chicken. Boy George and Jasper Conran and Simon Le Bon are here. Simon Le Bon walks right past me. He's *that* close. I could have reached out and single-handedly strangled the man who wrote 'Wild Boys', but I didn't. History will not give me this chance again. Bryan Ferry arrives. He is immediately swamped by photographers, reporters, cameramen. The television lights cut swathes through the darkness around Bryan Ferry. He is sitting in the front row. Minutes later a person who I think is Noel Gallagher of Oasis arrives wearing a white jacket and looking a bit like a waiter. He is mobbed by the media. Bryan Ferry has now been left on his own. It is a slightly poignant sight, for some reason, Bryan Ferry glaring gloomily down the row of seats at a person whom I think is Noel Gallagher of Oasis being swamped with attention.

The show begins. More wonderful weird exotic hats. There are hats like giant shells and crowns and platters and yashmaks and masks and veils. Incredible. Suddenly I see the High Priestess of Babelonia again. She is standing just across the aisle from me. I smile at her. She seems to be smiling at me. My God. She is actually smiling at me. *This is it.* I grin back like a lobotomised zombie. I find myself thinking back to the Claudia Schiffer incident. I'm not going to make the same mistake again. I breathe in deeply, suck in my stomach and take a step forward.

Unfortunately for me, the step forward also turns out to be a very steep step downwards. I topple, arms flailing at the air, and fall flat on my arse. My glasses go flying through the air and smash. As I try to stand up, I twist my ankle and fall over backwards, right through a flap in the tent. What I'm saying is that *I am actually outside the tent now*, in the darkness and the rain, my hands wrists deep in Kensington mud. I grope my way back in and start feeling around the floor for my glasses. When I find them I realise that I have lost one of the lenses.

The High Priestess of Babelonia looks down at me as though I am something malodorous she has just found stuck to the sole of her shoe. I grin optimistically. 'Oh, dear,' she says, and she turns away. Oh, dear. I guess my behaviour is not 'very fun'. I know it is not, in fact.

Next day I turn up early for the Clements Ribeiro show. The same camera crew are here from last night. I position myself beside them. They are talking in peculiar hissing sounds. 'Anyone good 'ere?' Pause. 'Nao. 'Aven't spotted anyone, 'ave you?' Pause. 'Tracey McCleod is over there.' Pause. 'Oo the fark is Tracey McCleod?' Pause. 'You know. That blondie bird off *The Late Show*.' Pause. 'What the fark is *The Late Show*.' Pause. 'Oh, forget it.'

The Clements Ribeiro clothes are all very nice, I must say. There are a lot of black-and-brown-and-check patterned things. The music is Latin-cum-Arab with a bit of Indian thrown in. She Who Must Be Adored is here with a bloke. Probably her brother, I tell myself. At one point she turns, puts her long, slender arm around his waist and kisses him so hard she looks like she's trying to suck off his face. Hmmmm. Obviously a very close family.

Later that night I head for East London to the Alexander McQueen show, which is taking place in a church. Everyone is talking about this event. It will be 'controversial' apparently. There are intimations of nudity. Perhaps this is why there are so many people here. If you could imagine an episode of *Absolutely Fabulous* directed by a Nazi, you would get some idea of the scene outside Christchurch, Spitalfields, as I join the brawling throng trying to gain entrance. There are perhaps five hundred people out here all dolefully waving their invitation cards in the air and looking miserable. There is one door, which was obviously designed for a very pious and thin Protestant to get through. I am not pious, thin or Protestant. After a while I decide to go for a walk around the block and come back. Spitalfields is a very interesting part of East London, I must say. On one corner stand three of the local girls, all dressed in miniskirts, thigh boots and low-cut blouses. They must be quite cold, I figure, given that a gale-force wind is blowing down the street. I wonder why they are wearing such charmingly revealing cozzies. They do seem very friendly, I must say. So friendly that they keep approaching the cars that pull up in front of them. They bend over and talk to the men driving these cars. What *can* they be doing? Giving directions, I suppose. They are *so* friendly, indeed, that occasionally they even get into these cars to give, I suppose, even more detailed directions. What a charming and jolly place the East End is.

Back to Christchurch, feeling very Pearly Queen. The scene has calmed down a bit now. I manage to squeeze into the church, which is full and decorated with a lot of candles. The *Elle* photographer has been ordered to take my photograph. This is very embarrassing. I have to plonk my anorak-which-is-missing-two-buttons-wearing self beside this very glamorous-looking woman while the *Elle* photographer snaps her flash at me repeatedly. After a while the glamorous-looking woman turns and asks me why I am having my photograph taken. I say I am writing a piece for *Elle* magazine. She looks at my anorak, which is missing two buttons. 'Really?' she says. If she grins any harder her eyebrows will disappear into her hairline. The show begins. The McQueen clothes are pretty wonderful. From simple enough grey hipster trews to big black woolly coats with flared sleeves, from grey flannel jump suits to dresses that change fabric mid-sleeve.

The show ends and everyone agrees that it was wonderful. The taxi driver is from Belfast and talks in a very attractive Reverend Ian Paisley accent. He asks me what I write about. 'Fashion,' I say. 'Aye, really,' he says, 'I like fashion myself.' I am astounded. This man is the only living entity I have seen in the last forty-eight hours who is actually less fashionable than myself. He is wearing a shell suit and filthy trainers and a tea-cosy hat. 'Oh, aye,' he says, 'I love fashion, I take a very keen interest in it.' I gape at him once again. I am utterly gobsmacked. 'Really?' I say. 'And tell me, what kind of fashion do you like best?' He pauses, grins, lights a cigarette. 'Salmon,' he says. 'Salmon fashion.'

The rain begins to fall more heavily now, as night comes down over the East End.

VII   Learning to Love the English, *Part One*

MANCHESTER? THE OLYMPIC GAMES IN *MANCHESTER*?! Excuse me just a second. AGH, HAHAHA HOHO, HEEHEE, EEARGHHEEE! Chortle. MANCHESTER? This was always a joke, right? Like, come on, it was a gag. Yet, all last year the British newspapers contended that Manchester was the favourite city to host the Olympic Games in 2000. When the news broke that it had got beaten into a poor third by the upstart Ozzies and the desiccated Stalinist fossils who run what is left of China, the British public seemed to be stunned.

Look, I actually like Manchester. And many people don't, God knows. There is a song by English rock band The Smiths that features the doleful chant 'Ohwooh, Manchester – so much to answer for.' But I *like* Manchester. I've been there a few times and it's fun, in a way. The way lying in bed for three days with a dreadful flu is fun, in a way. Mancunians are attractive, warm, terribly hospitable. Perceptive readers will now spot a 'BUT' peeping over the top of the page and beginning to jink menacingly down towards the start of the following paragraph.

BUT. You know the way Manchester looks in those drearily class-obsessed 1960s English kitchen-sink movies? The way it looks in *Coronation Street*? Well, *it's like that*. Don't be taken in by the promotional video, all verdant parks, twee pedestrian walkways swarming with mime artists. Manchester is Grimsville. If they are going to build a new running track, it should not be constructed in an oval. It should be constructed in a very long straight line, so that it leads all the way down to London. That way, Mancunians could at least gallop out of the place in comfort. If you plug in an electric toothbrush in Manchester the streetlights dim. I love the gaff, really. But there is only one reason why Manchester was not bombed more extensively during the war. Namely: that the Jerries looked down from their Fokkers and presumed it had been bombed already.

Manchester is also bloody dangerous. It is widely known to be the illegal gun capital of Britain. Listen, there is a nightclub in Manchester, which I'm not going to name because the libel lawyers would collapse and fall gibbering to the floor, clutching their hearts, if I did, but there was *armed gang warfare* going on in and around this Manchester nightclub last year. If you got drunk and sad enough to actually go to this establishment, your chances of enjoying yourself were broadly similar to your chances of getting back out the door without half a pound of buckshot lodged in your arse. That is to say, slim. You are far more likely to get yourself shot in parts of Manchester than you are in Belfast.

Manchester is also utterly drug ravaged. It is full of coked-up young people who think they are giant bananas. Mankies watch *The Magic Roundabout* a lot. They wear *flares*, for God's sake. Not just the relatively mild flares that young people wear in other cities. I'm talking great big flowery velvet bell-bottoms, the waists of which come up to their nipples, the hems of which droop right over the tips of their platform shoes and flap in the vicious Northern breeze like the wings of demented and psychopathic bats. Any city whose citizens all look like former members of Deep Purple should not be allowed to host the Olympic Games, I'm sorry. Like trousers, like mind, in my book.

Manchester is full of stern Industrial Revolution architecture, guano-spattered statues of obese Victorian philanthropists, plastic hamburger joints whose products give you botulism and salmonella to go. And Mancunians are forever whinging on and on about the North–South divide. Well, if I lived in England I would have one thing to say about this: let's build a bloody high wall right through the Midlands and *keep them out*.

You could not hold a Tupperware party in Manchester, never mind the Olympic Games. Look, I've been to Sydney, and they have their act together down there. In Sydney, they will have state-of-the-art fireworks displays, computer-driven laser light shows, giant inflatable kangaroos, revolving stages, huge choreographed extravaganzas involving hundreds of thousands of cute multiracial schoolchildren waving flags, holding hands and singing 'Waltzing Matilda' in harmony as President-elect Paul Keating unleashes five million white doves into the blue sky over the Opera House. In Manchester, they would have had a large plate of Spam sandwiches and a ventriloquist. It never would have worked.

Learning to Love the English, *Part Two*

YOU KNOW, PERHAPS ONLY ONCE IN A NEWSPAPER writer's life a column comes along which is so brilliant, so dazzling, so utterly sensational in every respect that the lucky reader has little choice but to fall down on the floor in a frankly worrying lather of appreciation and die of pure happiness. Until that happens, the readers of the *Sunday Tribune* may have to make do with columns like this, which is about going to an Eric Clapton lookalike concert in London. This lookalike thing is beginning to catch on in Ireland. In London it's huge. Any night of the week you can see a phoney Phil Lynott, bogus Bee Gees, an ersatz Elvis or simulated Rolling Stones. But an imitation Eric Clapton? I mean, good Lord, why would anyone bother? This I had to see.

Picture the scene, my dears. There are a lot of men in the room over the pub wearing Eric Clapton souvenir bomber jackets and Q magazine T-shirts over the trousers of their suits. There are some women too, accompanying some of these men, and generally these women look either patient or bored. But what you really notice are the men. Men in groups, men with their mates, men by themselves. Men everywhere. You can almost smell the testosterone. You feel that if any one of these women was to breathe in quickly, she would probably get pregnant with quads.

At eight-thirty a man who looks vaguely – and I do mean vaguely – like Eric Clapton strolls in, murmurs a laconic greeting, plugs in his guitar and begins to pound into an chunky acoustic slide blues. The man beside me becomes almost apoplectic with pleasure. As the gig proceeds – a few more solo Robert Johnson numbers before the band troop on and begin to crank up the pace – my neighbour enters the state of nirvana. He is bald, this man, and quite startlingly circumferentially challenged, and he will never see fifty again, except, perhaps, on a hall door, but he is soon screaming and whooping like an inebriated teenager at a Boyzone gig. Not only is he singing along with every single word of every single Clapton song, he is also singing along note-perfect with the note-perfect guitar solos. It is frighteningly weird. His right hand is strumming his trouser zip with his car keys, and his left hand is in the air, fingers working on invisible frets. 'Wee yeee awaawaaaway, aweee awaaaay,' he shrieks, his head thrusting back and forth, his eyes bulging, 'a bam bam beeeargh, unghawaaaay, eeeghaeeee, ungh, ungh, ungh.' He looks and sounds like the Reverend Jimmy Swaggart praying in tongues. His wife is gazing admiringly at him while this is going on. It is a picture of pure, devoted love.

But the suspension of disbelief required to engage fully with all this is really a bit much. This chap on the stage is not Eric Clapton, after all. This is a man called Norman who works for British Telecom. And when he sings about being a po' boy and being lowdown and ornery and getting locked up in the goddang county jail, you never really find yourself forgetting that tomorrow morning he could be disconnecting somebody's phone. Mind you, when the real Eric Clapton does these things, you never find yourself forgetting that, actually, he lives in a palace in Surrey. Middle-aged white millionaires get the blues too, for sure, but bad impersonations of them emoting are not everyone's idea of a night out. But anyway, Norman at least gives it the full welly, as he prowls about the stage, eyes screwed shut in that Claptonesque expression of someone with bad piles manoeuvring a bicycle with no saddle down a pothole-filled country lane. What a pity that old Eric's most famous song of tortured desire is now so closely identified with a television advertisement for up-market cars that when Norman pleads, 'Lay-la-hah, ya got me on ma knees, aw Lay-la-hah, I'm beggin' dawlin please,' you can't help feeling that he is requesting the eponymous heroine to fasten her computer-controlled seat belt before she causes a serious prang.

Reader, I confess that there have been times in my life when I have felt I was losing control and going mad. But when two women backing-singers teeter on in identical black dresses, whoo-whooing and bopping from side to side in uneasy unison, one banging a tambourine against her left buttock, the other battering a cowbell with a short stick, I really do think I am finally destined for the place where the doors have no handles. By the end, the audience are on their feet, cheering and stomping and screaming for more and yelling 'Eric, Eric'. But as the house lights go up, and you hear the evocative jangling of five hundred Audi keys, you can't help getting the uneasy feeling that somehow the English are in very big trouble indeed.

Learning to Love the English, *Part Three*

ONE AFTERNOON LAST YEAR I FOUND MYSELF IN THE departures lounge at London City Airport, waiting for a flight home to Dublin. The airport was busy that day. England and Ireland were playing each other in Landsdowne Road later in the evening. There were a number of English football fans sprawled around the lounge, some wearing Union Jack T-shirts and Doc Marten boots, others wearing well-cut fashionable suits and brandishing mobile phones. It was about three o'clock and many of the fans seemed to be already quite drunk. Two or three of them were barking 'No Surrender. No Surrender. No Surrender to the IRA' in cockney accents, trying to get the others to join in. I noticed a middle-aged woman with a boy of seven or eight stand up and move away with an expression of suppressed anger on her face.

Near the main group of fans was a young man on his own. He was heavily built and was wearing a brown leather jacket that was a little too small for him. He had an air of shyness about him. He chain-smoked and drank coffee while he waited for the stewardess to call the flight. He gazed at the main group of fans, and for a while I thought he was embarrassed by them. But then, as they broke into a chant of 'UVF, UVF, UVF,' I noticed that his chubby face broke into a beaming smile and he quietly joined in. He clapped his hands a few times, in uneasy rhythm with the chant, and he blushed when nobody else clapped and he put his hands back in his pockets. He looked like a guy who just wanted to belong.

On the plane I sat beside two English fans. They were well dressed, and I had the impression from overhearing their conversation that they worked together, in some sort of junior management capacity at a factory. As we took off, they began a stream of anti-Irish invective. They didn't chant or shout or anything, but they laughed at the fans down the back who did, and they just kept talking enthusiastically to each other in fairly quiet voices about how thick and violent the Irish were, and how they would be taught a lesson for sure in Dublin. Every time a stewardess passed by in the aisle they would snuffle with laughter and make grossly sexist observations about her.

'Look at that Paddy bitch,' they would say, and they would chuckle together like naughty schoolboys. I guess it was just that famously ironic English sense of humour on public display yet again.

I felt angry and hurt listening to all this, and after a while I leaned over and simply asked the two men to stop, and they looked shocked, and for some reason they did stop. They looked a little shamefaced. One of them said he'd only been joking, and he had Irish relations himself, and that no harm had been meant. He actually wanted to shake hands with me, but I found that I wasn't able to do that, and I turned away. I tried to read a newspaper then, to take my mind off things. The newspaper was the *Daily Mail*, and it was full of stories about how Britain is going to be 'swamped' by a tide of immigrants in the next few years. I thought 'swamped' was an interesting word to use about human beings. There was another story about a public campaign in the north of England to have a number of mosques closed down, and a related editorial about how 'English values' should be cherished.

A few nights later, watching the match on television, I saw English values being cherished for myself. I had been enjoying the game enormously. It brought back pleasant memories, because I was lucky enough to cover the 1994 World Cup for the *Sunday Tribune*. And then very quickly everything went wrong, as the terrible sickness at the heart of that greed-obsessed and xenophobic society was dramatised once again for all to see. I watched on, feeling horrified and angry. And a strange thing happened. Suddenly, as the camera zoomed in on the crowd, I saw the heavy young man in the leather jacket I had seen in the departure lounge a few days earlier. I recognised him instantly, although something of a transformation had taken place in him. The quiet young man was screaming and roaring, his eyes were bulging, his clenched fists were waving in the air, he was jumping up and down. I saw him there on the screen, utterly consumed by his passion. I didn't see him throw anything, I just saw his plump gentle face, contorted now in rage and hatred, as he bawled his heart out and screamed and ranted. But the odd thing was, when he finally stopped roaring, he looked so happy. He smiled. He threw his arms around the man beside him in the crowd. They hugged and slapped each other on the back. And as the missiles rained down on the terrified people below, he looked like he finally thought he belonged to something.

VIII   An Alien in Managua

'THE IRISH,' THE FAT POLICEMAN SAID, 'ARE JUST LIKE us Nicaraguans.'

I coughed vaguely, unsure whether this was a compliment.

'Yes,' he expanded, 'in the Irlanda you guys were fight for your freedom from the Queen Victoria, yes?'

'Sí,' I grinned, a little relieved. '*No pasarán, eh!*'

'*Sí, hombre,*' he chuckled, forming his hand into a pistol shape, '*mucho bang bang.*' Then he held an invisible grenade to his teeth, pulled the invisible pin and lobbed it into the street, making, with the back of his throat, a loud exploding sound that sprayed beads of saliva all over my passport and the desk.

'*Viva Irlanda Libre!*' he cheered. I suddenly realised how difficult it must be working for the Irish tourist board.

It was my sixty-first day in Nicaragua and it was hot. Stupefyingly, brain-meltingly HOT. So hot that my stomach felt queasy and I didn't want to move and I probably would have stayed in my boarding house, *El Hospedaje*, talking to one of the spotty Berkeley students who had come down in the fervent hope of getting shot at by the Contra guerrillas, except that my visa has run out the day before, a Sunday, and I was now illegal.

That's why I had hauled myself down to the station.

So, next thing I knew, a little Lada came screaming to a halt outside the door, siren on loud. Two young officers stepped out, AK47s on their backs. One of them looked like Charles Bronson. So did the other one. My friend beamed behind the counter.

Sixty seconds later we were heading out of Managua at speed and I was feeling distinctly unhappy. I was much too hot for a start and the windows wouldn't open. My sunburnt face was stinging. Worse, I was beginning to get edgy. I thought I was getting sunstroke or *quebradura* or some vicious little CIA super-virus. My head was pounding a salsa rhythm and my tongue was dry. Still, I said to the guys that there was really no need to take me to the hospital, thanks a bunch. If they'd just bring me back home to *El Hospedaje* that'd be *muy bueno*.

'What *hospedaje*?' the sulky one pouted. 'You go to the jailhouse.'

'HO HO HO,' I chortled politely.

'It's no joke,' barked the other. 'You alien.'

The car halted outside a big white house over which flew the red and black Sandinista flag. The sentry beckoned us through the gate, waving as we passed with a vaguely disconcerting finality. I was left in a room for three hours before being asked whether I wanted to make

192

any statement. I couldn't believe this. The only statement I wanted to make was thankfully untranslatable
into Spanish, otherwise I might still be there now.

I argued and pleaded, but Jorge was unimpressed. He
told me very politely that I was an illegal alien and that I
would just have to stay here until enquiries were made. I
pleaded with Eneyda. I lied.

'Look,' I said, 'I've got to go to a wedding tonight.'

She said, 'Are you the groom?' and Jorge chuckled.
They said I was looking pale and I should eat. I told them
I felt sick. But they insisted.

I had tasted some pretty horrendous *gallo pinto* during
my two months in Nicaragua, but I took one mouthful of
this coagulated black mush of beans and rice and almost
retched on the spot. My eyes filled with hot moisture as
I tried not to gawk. I blinked at a portrait of the national
hero, Augusto César Sandino, as he scowled admonish-
ingly down at me. I swallowed manfully and took another
mouthful. I chomped away, praying hard to keep it down.
I took a third spoonful, gulped hard, and then it happened.

My bowels parted like velvet curtains. My bum felt
like it was imploding. As I simpered across the table at
Eneyda, my intestines began to empty themselves uncontrollably into my shorts.

Jorge very kindly agreed to drag me off to the toilet
block, dribbles of *gallo pinto*, which had made a very
brief tour of my colon, now trickling slowly down the
backs of my legs. Inside my head was a howling sound.
Coming from my mouth was a pathetic excuse for a
whimper.

Next thing I remember is Eneyda and Jorge standing in
the bathroom, watching me, looking concerned, babbling.
I didn't care. I had never felt so unbelievably sick or so

unspeakably, utterly HOT. I dropped my shit-covered shorts and sat down on the pan, groaning, head in my hands. Eneyda and Jorge started to shout insults at each other. She called him an *'hijo de cien mille putas'* – son of a hundred thousand prostitutes. But the pain chewing through my guts was so bad that I was too miserable to be impressed. Anyway, I knew things were going to get worse. I could feel it. I gulped. Eneyda stopped abusing Jorge and looked at me. I gulped again. I put my hand in front of my mouth. I groaned. She winced and put her hands in front of her face. Jorge shrugged. I slid off the can. I vomited.

All over my shoes, inside my shirt pocket, over my knees, over my back, into my hair, I managed to puke just about everywhere except into the toilet. They kept giving me this special drink to stop the vomiting. Every time I took a swallow, I vomited again, down my nostrils, out my mouth, back into the glass, into the sink, all over Eneyda's olive-green uniform skirt, which, by the time I had finished with it, had gone distinctly camouflage. For twenty solid minutes I slithered around the floor, puking like something out of *The Exorcist*, while diarrhoea gushed majestically out my other end. My sunburnt face felt like it was on fire. The toilet paper felt like sandpaper. 'Poor Irish,' soothed Eneyda, as I dabbed pathetically at my stinging fundament.

When it was all over I lay slumped across the sink, a gibbering, weeping, shuddering wreck, any last shred of dignity being flushed away with the remains of my spleen. I couldn't wash because the water had been turned off. This was the rationing, Jorge explained, it was all the fault of Ronald Reagan and his imperialist cohorts. I clenched my buttocks with revolutionary fervour and

194

limped back to the big room. I lay down on the floor, blinking at the somersaulting ceiling, every single part of my body in agony, genuinely wishing that I was dead. I dreamed about hell, an eternal inferno of sunburn, rancid *gallo pinto*, vomit, army-issue toilet paper and Reaganomics.

It was 3.30 in the morning when my shattered body opened its bleary eyes. When it got up and took a few tentative steps it made a kind of squishing noise. This was because there was vomit in my shoes. A strange kind of desperate calm descended over me when I discovered this. I knew things just couldn't get any worse.

Jorge brought me a drink of lemonade that he had made himself. He said my clearance had come through. I could go if I wanted to. He seemed vaguely disappointed when I confirmed that, hey, I wanted to. He called me a spoilsport. Eneyda called me a taxi.

I staggered out into the dawn, unshaven, filthy, plastered in shit, sweat and puke, stinking so horrifically I thought I'd make myself throw up again. The taxi driver gaped at me. '*Madre de Dios*,' he sighed, before spreading the literary review section of the Sandinista newspaper *Barricada* across the upholstery.

It was bright when I got back to *El Hospedaje*, and Señora Villagomez was sweeping the path in front of the house. 'Sorry I didn't come home last night,' I mumbled. She turned around, shaded her eyes and scrutinised me. '*Santa Maria de las Victorias*,' she whispered, utterly aghast. The taxi driver slowly reversed past us, holding his nose ostentatiously between his index finger and his thumb.

'I had to go to a wedding,' I explained.

'Oh, well,' Señora Villagomez tutted, shaking her head

195

as she returned to her brushing. 'At least you look like you had a good time.'

IX   The French Letters

Friday, 29 March 1996: South of France. *'Parlez-vous français?'* asks the woman behind the counter in Nice airport.

'Mais oui,' I reply. *'Je avais le certificat du départ.'*

She wrinkles up her nose in confusion. *'Quoi?'* she asks. I am astonished by her ignorance. Surely to God, everyone knows that *'le certificat du départ'* is perfect French for 'the Leaving Cert'.

I do my best to explain but she doesn't seem to follow me. This is upsetting. I am here in France because of this thing called L'Imaginaire Irlandais, I say. It is a big festival of modern Irish culture. It has taken two years to organise. She gazes at me blankly. I take out my dictionary and look up the word 'novelist'. It is quite a nice word. *Romancier*. I point to myself. *'Romancier,'* I say. She apparently is unmoved. I am in trouble now.

A few minutes ago I discovered something important. There I was, congratulating myself on my sartorial elegance. This is not something I do very often. Yet there I was, in the arrivals terminal of Nice airport, having just arrived from Paris, and was doing just that. Kneeling on the floor of the terminal opening up my suitcase and looking for my sunglasses. Where did these rather attractive multicoloured knicks come from? The awful truth dawned. I had somebody else's bag. I had picked up someone else's bag during the changeover in Paris!!! (Mr Gerry Brown of Dublin, the things I know about you. Ten grand in a brown paper bag and the negatives are yours.)

Thus, alone, weary, friendless and broke, I book into the airport hotel. The only channel in English is the twenty-four hour Flintstones channel. I am so miserable and lonely that after two hours watching, I begin to think that Wilma's actually got quite a cute smile. I am dying for a shave, but my razor, like everything else, is in a bag in Paris. I ring reception and ask if they stock shaving materials.

'Hello,' I say to the receptionist, 'can yeux send me up a hghazohgh, please?' ('Hghazohgh' is, of course, the correct pronunciation of the French word 'razor'.)

After I shave I go out for a walk. The only thing I have to say about Nice is that it isn't really. Nice.

Saturday, 30 March: Nice. After a fitful night, my case arrives from Paris and this makes me as happy *comme un chien avec les deux mickis*. Shortly after this, The Better Half arrives on a flight from London. This makes me happier still. While I've been waiting for her I noticed a town on the map of southern France called La Grande Motte. I am in a childishly gleeful humour this morning, possibly because after two days I have been able to change my clothes, and so I find the name of this town very amusing indeed. La Grande Motte. It sounds like the French translation of a Roddy Doyle novel. I decide to amuse the girlfriend by referring to her as 'La Grande Motte' from now on. She does not seem to find this even nearly as amusing as I do. This may be because she is English and everyone knows they have no sense of humour. Her real name is Anne-Marie Casey, she points out, and that's what she would like to be called. I study Ms Casey's expression. It is the expression of a Londoner who has been on an airline for too long, thank you very much indeed. I am suddenly and acutely aware that while we have been going out together quite happily for a time now, this could all go down the pan in the space of a millisecond if I ever *ever* call her 'La Grande Motte' to her face again. Good God, aren't women unreasonable sometimes?

We leave Nice for Saint-Tropez, where we are staying in a cheap hotel that claims to be a converted fisherman's cottage. (What the fisherman converted from is not made clear, but I suppose it was Roman Catholicism.) Brigitte Bardot made this town famous when she appeared in the film *Et Dieu Créa La Femme*, which is French for 'Brigitte Bardot capering around with no clothes on'. I like this town, I must say. And if I ever have a son, I'm certainly going to call him after a saint. Tropez O'Connor. Got a certain *je ne sais quoi*, huh?

Sunday, 31 March: San-Rémy-de-Provence. I notice that my French is getting better all the time. For instance, I am in a café having my mid-morning snack when I say to the waiter, '*Garçon, qui portay les choccies à la table? We. Vouz. Portay une grande piece de cet cakefaction à moi, sil voo play, et look vitement about it.*' It is funny how a language comes back to you with a bit of practice. Of course the other solution to the communications problem is the one being employed by the middle-aged English couple at the next table. Not speaking *un worde de français comme moi* they are reduced to the next best strategy: speaking English very slowly and loudly.

'YES,' they say, 'WEEE WOOOOD LYYYKE a CUPPP of COFFFEEEE, PLEEEEEASE.'

'Yes,' the waiter replies. 'I am not deaf actually.'

Monday, 1 April: Montpellier. The first day of my own participation in L'Imaginaire Irlandais. This is a pleasant small city, famous for having 300 days of sunshine per year. Unfortunately, today isn't one of them. Myself, John McGahern, Evelyn Conlon and Jennifer Johnston are reading tonight. This goes pretty well. I get a bit of a lump in my throat actually, watching these fine writers read, and then hearing their words read out in French. It's the proudest I've felt about Ireland for quite some time. Afterwards, the only drink available is Irish whiskey or French dessert wine, but I actually like waking up in the mornings without having spent half the night before vomming like a one-arm bandit, so I decide to have water. During the reception, some bald French geezer in a suit wanders over and starts going on about what a rare sight it is, an Irish writer drinking water, what happened to ze spirit of Brendan Behan, Patrick Kavanagh, Flann O'Brien, etcetera. The spirit hasn't really been the same since they drank themselves to death, I reply. Top Of Ze Morning, he says. May Ze Rhoad Rhize To Meet Yeux. Pogue mahone, I reply.

In the far corner a three-piece band are playing the kind of Irish traditional music that you only ever hear outside of Ireland. A woman in a black dress suddenly starts doing Irish dancing. I had thought hurling was a traditional Irish sport until this moment. I am standing in a breeze-block office building on the outskirts of a provincial French town watching someone *aon-do-tri* to Wolfe Tones covers. How did this happen to me?

Later that night our hosts, led by the splendid Mr Thierry Guichard, take us all out to a restaurant called L'Assiette de Boeuf. The rest of Europe is terrified to eat anything that has ever passed through a country where a cow has even appeared on the television, but here in good old no-nonsense Montpellier they give us a plate of beef carpaccio which practically has a swishing tail. It is delicious. The food is just sensational. This is great. *L'Imaginaire Irlandais, c'est magnifique.* We are all in a very literary state by the end of the evening.

Tuesday, 2 April: The Espace République, Montpellier. Tonight's reading features last night's line-up with the new added talents of Eoin McNamee and Hugo Hamilton. The reading is very well organised and attended. After the reading there is the launch of the L'Imaginaire Irlandais catalogue. Doireann Ni Bhraoin, the Irish commissionaire of L'Imaginaire Irlandais is here, and she makes a good short speech. Following her good short speech, a right-wing French politician makes a long bad speech. Ireland so cultural, blah blah, the New Europe, blah blah, unity in diversity, blah blah, unaccustomed as I am, blah blah, votez pour moi, blah blah.

My book *True Believers* is about to be published in French and I meet the two translators, Gérard and Pirique. They are wonderful chaps. We spend a pleasant half-hour discussing the difficulty of rendering certain Irish slang expressions into French. 'The old sod' was particularly challenging, apparently. *'Le vieux sodde!'* I suggest to the boys. French for me is *un morceau de gâteau*.

Another dinner laid on by our extremely hospitable hosts here in Montpellier. The local gastronomic speciality is a mashed potato dish called *alioli*, which has the consistency of molten rubber. *Alioli* would have come in very handy back in the bad old days when we couldn't buy condoms in Ireland. It would have made a much more natural and much more Irish substitute for clingfilm.

Wednesday, 3 April: Surprise, surprise, out to dinner again. French waiters are legendary for their stunning rudeness. The waiter tonight actually laughs when I ask if I could have a tomato salad. Like a tomato would be a very unusual thing to find in a restaurant. I notice that the French couple at the next table are almost as rude to the waiter as the waiter has just been to me. As a result they seem to get served very quickly and in a friendly and efficient manner. I guess the best way to get a French waiter's attention seems to be to act in an even more rude and aggressive manner than he does. Thus, logically, the *absolutely* best way to get the attention of a French waiter is to enter the restaurant, march straight up to him and staple his balls to a table before attempting to ask for the menu. I may try this approach later in the trip.

Thursday, 4 April: Arrive in Paris and check into the hotel we have booked. The room has a really lovely view of a brick wall and a barbed-wire fence. It also has one of those old-fashioned revolving fans that makes a noise like a helicopter. The room should be called 'The *Apocalypse Now* Suite'. I took one look at the bathroom. I had never known what 'a gorge' really is, but, take it from me, five seconds in that bathroom and I know mine is rapidly rising. Check out and move into the Hôtel Des Beaux Arts. This is the hotel where Oscar Wilde died. Given the prices they charge, I am not one bit surprised. He probably just took one look at his bill and keeled over in a gibbering heap. I am all for European integration but, really, fifteen quid for a continental breakfast would bring out the Eurosceptic in anyone.

*

I am reading George Orwell's *Down and Out in Paris and London* at the moment. When it was published in French it was called *La Vache Enragée*, which, funnily enough, is French for 'The Mad Cow'. Anyway, Orwell says that a person who doesn't want to get food poisoning should never stay in an expensive Parisian hotel. This is because chefs in expensive hotels consider food to be an art form. Thus, they stroke it, pluck it, knead it, arrange it on the plate, make sure all the prawns are facing due north, with the very same fingers they've been using previously to pick their noses, smear Brylcreem in their hair, etcetera, etcetera, and in France, believe me, etcetera really suggests myriad possibilities. In a cheap restaurant, Orwell tells us, they just chuck the food onto the grill, incinerate it, pick off the pubes and then scrape it onto a plate for you. I pass this on for what it's worth.

This morning I find myself chatting with a French journalist who is telling me all about his views on Ireland, which is very interesting for me and is exactly what I came to France for. He loves Ireland more than any Irish person I have ever met. Everything about Ireland is great. 'Even ze omeless people in Dooblin seem so much more appy zan ze omeless people in Paris,' he says. I am actually speechless by now, but he doesn't seem to care. He feels that in addition to having the happiest poor people in the world, 'the Irish invented the comic tradition in literature'. Oh, yeah, right. Et les monkeys might fly out of my cul. I have a sudden vision of an ancient Celt sitting in a cave trying to invent the comic tradition in literature. There he is, scratching his boils and going, 'So these three druids go into a pub for a pint of mead, right, and one says to the barman, take my wife ... no, these three members of Na Fianna go ... no, how

many Finn McCools does it take to change a light bulb
... no ... hey, a really funny thing happened me on the
way to Newgrange ... No. Hang on ...'

A large lunch with my wonderful agent, Ms Maggie
Doyle. The menu features all sorts of mad concoctions.
There is pork broiled in aspic, rabbit charred and minced
into balls, veal seared and shredded. It is hard to decide
what to go for. In the end, I decide to have lobster slowly
bored to death by the *maître d'*.

The waiter is a nice fellow who is unusually polite for
a person in the French catering trade. 'And would you
like a little more wine?' he asks.

'*Est-ce-que le Pope un Catholique!*' I reply, wittily.

On the way home, the woman taxi driver is delighted
to hear that I am Irish.

'Ze Quwanbayrheaze?' she says.

'?!' I say.

'Ze Quwanbayrheaze?'

After about ten minutes of this I manage to figure out
that she is asking me if I like The Cranberries.

'No,' I say. But it is too late. She has started to sing.

'Yeuz gut me rhapped arhound yer finger, ah hah hah,
deux yeux av to, do yeaux av to, do yeux av to, let eet
leenger.'

'HOHOHO,' I say. 'You can drop me here actually.'

Tonight I am doing a really prestigious reading at the
world-famous Georges Pompidou Centre. I have been
looking forward to this for months. When I arrive I find
that the venue for the reading is a room on the sixth floor
of the Pompidou Centre that has been converted into
something called 'Le Dublin Pub', complete with Bord
Failte-type posters, etcetera. It doesn't look like any

Dublin pub I've ever been in, and I don't just mean that the toilets are clean and flushed. As I look around I am a bit flushed myself. I am not sure about the idea of doing a reading in a pub. I mean, yes, I understand that lots of effort and trouble has been taken, but still, it's a pub. It is so important to support these events that help to overturn anachronistic stereotypes and truly reflect the changing new modern Ireland, I feel, as I nimbly dodge the team of formation-dancing midgets in leprechaun suits. (OK, I made that bit up.) But it's still a pub. I am looking forward to the next visit of a prominent French writer to Dublin so that I can turn up to the event wearing my stripy jersey, black beret and humorous string of onions.

After the reading, the friendly and extremely helpful people from the Pompidou Centre ask me if I enjoyed myself. I have, in a way. They are the absolutely nicest audience over whose drunken babbling conversation I've ever had the great pleasure to read, I aver. La Grande Motte, who is a very polite person, kicks me with unnecessary force in the right calf.

A traditional Irish band led by a man called Mickey Dunne begins to play now. I watch for a while, standing beside a woman from one of the local newspapers.

'Mickey is a common name in Ireland?' she asks.

'Yes,' I say.

'Yes,' she says, 'my husband say there are many Mickeys in Ireland. Particularly in traditional music.'

I feel there is really no answer to this.

Friday, 5 April: La Grande Motte and I get the Métro out to Créteil, a distant suburb of southeast Paris, where the great Québecois actor Robert Lepage is doing his piece *Elsinor*, a multimedia reinterpretation of *Hamlet*. On the way, a fully fledged French lunatic gets onto the train and starts screeching at the top of his voice, *'Chirac, c'est un merde, Chirac, c'est un putain de merde,'* which is French for 'I have certain mixed feelings about President Chirac.'

The reaction of the Parisian commuters is astonishing. They all look into their newspapers as intensely as medieval astrologers scrutinising the skies, every last one of them, while my nabs continues roaring and bawling on the subject of Jacques Chirac's apparently considerable deficiencies. These people make London commuters seem communicative. *'MERDE!'* he screams. *'CHIRAC EST UN MERDE!!!'* Then, when the train pulls into a station, one of the passengers lunges for the emergency cord and pulls it violently. The doors open. Six transport police materialise out of the walls and begin to discuss the more complex of Monsieur Chirac's policies with the insane man using a large number of helpful visual aids, namely, batons, handcuffs and slavering Alsatians. As the train pulls out of the station and you witness the ensuing debate, you sense that the loonie may change his mind about Monsieur Chirac's policies as soon as he relocates his kneecaps and gets them sewn back on. The man who pulled the emergency cord is reading his newspaper again. He is smiling to himself, I notice. Touching how the spirit of *liberté, égalité, et fraternité* is still as relevant as ever.

Elsinor starts half an hour late. All of the parts are played by two male actors, who, in between acting, manipulate the set, operate on-stage video cameras and do fencing. (I don't mean barbed wire – I mean, with swords.) The show is absolutely sensational, but quite long. Afterwards I am dying to go to the loo, where I have occasion to ponder the truth of Billy Wilder's famous observation that France is a country where the money falls to pieces in your hands but you can't tear the toilet paper.

After this, back into central Paris where LGM and I go to a café, on the Quai de Contes. The café is full of young compatriots of LGM, spotty Englishmen who are in a very Parisian state indeed, to judge by the conversation. They keep talking loudly to the waiters and waitresses about subjects of major contemporary importance to Anglo-French relations, such as Trafalgar and Waterloo. I find myself fervently wishing that the waitress would bring up the Battle of Hastings, but sadly she does not.

One young Englishman is humorously wearing a pair of plastic comedy breasts. ''Ere,' he says, to a passing waitress, 'Quai de Contes, right? Does that mean Quay of the Cunts?' There is uproarious laughter and affectionate applause from his friends at this point, but he is not listening. He is now leaning head forward, mouth open, throwing up copiously all over his comedy breasts and moaning, 'Oooh Ahh Cunt-Oh-Nah.' It is good to see the English sense of subtle ironic humour is alive and well in the new Europe, I remark to LGM. 'HA HA HA,' she says.

Saturday, 6 April: Les Bains-Douches. This is French for 'The Public Baths'. It is also French for 'the trendiest nightclub in Paris frequented by clotheshorses and eejits where the only way to get in if you don't want to be totally humiliated by the skinny bouncers is to book for dinner in advance and pay out a king's ransom for a dodgy hamburger'.

Perceptive readers may be able to guess which strategy

I adopted. I had no doubts about Herself's trendiness, you understand, but my own was distinctly dubious and I felt it would be bad for the relationship for her to be let in and me to be kicked out.

After the dinner we go to the bar, which is downstairs in the club. The drinks cost 100 francs each. That's thirteen quid. Each. Like, for one. I have actually gotten blind mad drunk on thirteen quid before, but tonight I don't think that's going to happen.

By about 1.00 a.m. the place begins to fill up. I attempt to put what I believe young people refer to as 'my funk into your face', but LGM points out before long that God did not put me on the earth to be a dancer. I'm inclined to agree. Indeed, I don't think I have danced since I was about sixteen, when dancing consisted of standing in a frantic rhomboid of young fellows in the hall of Presentation Boys School, Glasthule, and pretending to play an invisible guitar while simultaneously trying to dodge the snowstorm of flying dandruff. My teenage years also saw the outbreak of the punk rock pogo, a dance that was much favoured in Prez, because it was very close to actual physical violence. But we are a long way from Prez now. Trendy uptight Parisians dance like they have corncobs up their bottoms to 'dance' music, which may admittedly be catchy, in the very same way that certain virulent forms of the flu are catchy. I try to dance to this too, but my left hip does not seem to know what my right one is doing. I retire to the bar to get some drinks. The barman peers at me as though I am disturbing his evening. He is sipping a drink that looks like something out of the Amazon rainforest.

'*Bonsoir*,' I say, '*je suis un romancier irlandais*.'

He nods and takes another sip of his luminous drink.

'Vouz allez ici often?' I ask, rather coolly.

He looks me in the eye for what seems like a long time, although, in fact, it is not. *'Pees awf,'* he says, then.

I turn and gaze upon the sea of gyrating, designer-clad bodies. *L'Imaginaire Irlandais! Je ne regrette rien.*

X   Border Lines

IT WAS ABOUT FIVE IN THE MORNING AND I WAS SOME-where around the border when it happened. I had been in Donegal doing a reading, and I had had to leave very early the next morning to get back to Dublin. I crossed the border into the North to look for a garage that was open, and then I headed south. I was driving quite fast along the motorway. If I tell you the truth, I was breaking the speed limit. But I wasn't too worried, because at five in the morning there's no traffic at all. It was quiet and still, and in the distance I could see the sun beginning to come up over the fields on my left, and on the right the vast slumbering hulk of Ben Bulben. Van Morrison was on the radio. I was smoking a cigarette. I was enjoying myself. I didn't know what was going to happen.

I turned a bend in the road. The scene was like something out of a beautiful dream. There were cherry blossom trees at the edge of the fields all along the motorway, and the breeze was shaking the boughs and showering the road with white petals. It was an extraordi-nary sight, the white petals raining down on the motor-way like so much confetti. And then it happened.

When I recall the whole thing now, I think I first saw the bird when I was about a hundred yards away from it. There were other birds around, whirling around above the motorway, but I think I did actually see this one just

208

sitting still in the middle of the road. I kept going. I got closer and closer to this bird and then suddenly I was a few feet away from it.

It rose up from the ground and spread its wings wide. But then I think either a gust of wind caught it, or it got trapped in the air stream around the moving car, and for one awful moment it hung in the air as though suspended by some invisible filament before it hit the windscreen with a dull and sickening thud that I don't think I will ever forget.

The whole windscreen went red. It was as though someone had poured blood all over the glass. I jammed my foot down on the brake and the car swerved across the motorway and into the oncoming lane. I felt the adrenalin surging through my limbs and body like a drug. I got out of the car. I could feel my breath coming hard and I could feel my hands and legs shaking. The poor bird was lying on the bonnet of the car, croaking in agony. There was a trail of blood and black feathers all over the metal. The bird flapped its wing and thrashed its head and slipped off the front of the car and fell onto the ground. It was in terrible distress. I found myself talking to it. I actually found myself apologising to the bird for hitting it. It suddenly dawned on me that I would have to kill it.

I am a townie. In my whole life, I have never killed anything larger than a spider. It's not that I'm a big animal lover: it's just never happened. How do you kill a bird? What was the most humane way of doing it? I looked at the bird, trembling on the road, and I decided I just couldn't do it. I decided to leave it there. I went to get back into the car, but just as I did so it let out another terrified croak. I knew then that I would have to end its agony.

I stared at it. Should I try to break its neck or something? Should I just put my hands on its bloodied throat and twist the life out of it? I squatted beside it and went to touch it, but I just couldn't bring myself to do that. I felt ashamed of my own cowardice. I got back up and walked up the road for a while, trying to find a heavy flat stone that I could drop onto the bird. Maybe that would kill it. Finally I found one. I staggered back down towards the car with the rock in my hands. But by the time I got back to the car I was glad to find that the bird was dead. I lifted its broken body and threw it by the side of the road.

I wondered what to do about the blood on the windscreen and the front of the car. I looked in the boot, but I could find nothing to clean the car with. In the glove compartment I found a half-empty bottle of mineral water, which I poured down the glass. Then, with my bare hands, I started to try and wipe the blood away.

I got back into the car and drove on. It sounds pathetic, I know, but I was deeply upset by the whole experience. I don't know whether it was because I was tired and shocked, but I felt very close to tears, and I don't cry very easily. My nerves were jangling. I felt as though I had jumped through a plate-glass window. Shortly afterwards, things began to get even more surreal. I realised with a start that I was approaching the border checkpoint. I stopped the car. I didn't want to approach the checkpoint at some unearthly hour of the morning with my windscreen covered in blood.

I stopped the car again and got out. It was cold. The morning was very quiet and still. There was nobody around. I wondered what to do. I still had nothing to clean off the blood with. On the back seat of the car there was a copy of the book I had been reading from in

Donegal. I started tearing pages out and wiping the blood away, and then throwing the bloodstained pages on the ground beside the car. When I had done the best job I could, I got back in and drove on. In time I came to the checkpoint, which looked eerie. In fact, there were no soldiers or police on duty, or, if there were, they were hidden from view.

I crossed the border and drove home to Dublin. On the way, all sorts of crazy thoughts went through my mind. What I am most ashamed of is that I started to think what had happened would make a really good short story. I felt that the whole incident meant something. I ran it again in my mind. Falling petals, bloodstained pages of a novel, the sound of the dying bird, the silent checkpoint on an unfamiliar road. I felt it was all symbolic of something, but I couldn't think what. It's the most debilitating psychic disease which writers suffer from, the desire to turn unusual experience into the stuff of fiction. It's terrible. It's morally very dubious. But I think I did learn something important that morning. I learnt that some things are symbolic of nothing at all. They stand out starkly in their sheer haunting meaninglessness. I realised that the whole event had meant nothing. It was just a sad stupid thing that happened, that's all. It scared me, but in the end it meant nothing.

Chapter 7

Yule Always Hurt the One You Love

I Should Xmas Be Axed?

THE FIRST THING I REALLY REMEMBER ABOUT CHRIST-
mas is being in the Yuletide play in St Joseph of Cluny
School, Glenageary. I was six, and deeply in love with
my teacher, Miss Glennon. The plot took place on
Christmas Eve. Santa was ready to roam with the sleigh,
but the Weatherman had gone on strike, so there was no
snow. Obviously anticipating my keen interest in left-
wing politics, Miss Glennon cast me as the Bolshevik
Weatherman. A girl called Niamh played my wife, the
Weatherwoman. She had to hold my hand a lot. This was
fine, except she had a permanently snotty nose, and she
kept wiping it with the same hand she employed to
clutch my own so passionately. My hand, that is. Not my
nose.

I wore a cotton-wool beard and a crêpe paper suit
covered with silver stars. The reindeers wore underpants.
Behind their heads they carried bits of cardboard with
antlers drawn onto them. They thought they were really

something. They were, too. One morning, after rehearsal, there was a fistfight between the reindeer and the Holy Family. One of the quadrupeds had suggested to the Virgin Mary that she was so fat she should have been playing Bethlehem. All hell broke loose. In the ensuing mêlée, one of the Wise Men got sent home for spitting at a shepherd and breaking a leg off the Baby Jesus. The Baby Jesus was played by Roddy, one of my sister's dolls. But after his premature disfigurement, Roddy's thespian career was unfortunately curtailed. This is a shame, as Roddy had enough acting ability to have had an exciting career in Australian soap opera. Or even in *Fair City*.

I remember later Christmases with a strange mixture of pleasure and fear. There's something oddly disturbing about the day for a lot of children. I remember ghost stories, the sweet smell of pine needles from the tree, mountains of shredded coloured paper lying piled up on the floor. I remember going to the Gaiety pantomime, my first time in a theatre, listening to the magical sound of the orchestra tuning up, being utterly petrified by the villainous Vernon Hayden. I remember Maureen Potter as Aladdin saying the reason Ireland's emblem was a harp was that the country was run by pulling strings. A joke she could still use.

We used to go to my grandparents' house on Christmas Eve. My grandad let us hold our notes for Santa Claus in the fireplace and the rush of air would pull them out of our fingers. He said this was the hand of St Nicholas. It was terrifying, but captivating, too. And I remember my sister Eimear swearing that she saw Santa Claus climbing up our stairs with a sack on his back. I was sure she wasn't lying. I still am. Children always see things that adults can't. And all of us sitting in Glasthule Church solemnly intoning the words of the Bay City Rollers' song 'Bye Bye Baby' to the tune of 'Silent Night'.

Another year I got an infuriating toy football game: a small plastic box containing two pinball flippers and a ball bearing. I remember long nights, re-enacting the World Cup with my father on this infernal machine. I was usually Brazil. I think he was Poland. It says something that, back then, neither of us would have wanted to be Ireland.

That was Christmas then. Once you attain maturity, however, Christmas changes. It becomes an excuse for socialising. When you are a teenager, socialising is a euphemism for drinking, fornicating, regurgitating, exchanging bodily fluids and indulging in malicious and destructive gossip, preferably simultaneously. Socialising is a broad, generous term to the young. It includes not only gluttony, sloth and lust but all the other deadly sins as well. When you are older, however, socialising becomes a terrible chore. A night in the pub becomes dull. Whereas one used to admire the bar staff and silently imagine all the chat-up lines one would attempt if one were not so nervous – 'You've lovely dark hair all down your back. None on your head, of course, HAHAHA, but your back is like a bleedin' shag pile!' – one now finds oneself pining for a chicken madras and *NYPD Blue*. A spell in the nightclub becomes similarly wearing. What is this polluting sound that the young call, with devastating irony, music? What is this epileptic lurching that is called, I believe, dancing? What on earth is, or are, 'M people'? Does the 'M' stand for manky? Maladjusted? When one enters the third decade, a new set of socialising opportunities comes along, each one being even less fun than the last. Let us consider, for instance, that foul and toothsome tsetse fly from the malodorous armpit of Beelzebub's granny, The Dinner Party.

There is a lot of this sort of thing at this time of the year. Your friends, whom you have not seen since last Crimbo, when you grossly insulted them over dessert and puked into their aspidistra on the way home, have decided that it is your turn to have them over for 'supper', whatever that is. Begrudgingly, you assent. You then realise that your flat is not really suitable for entertaining. Is it too late, you wonder, to get a bit of flock wallpaper up? Could you possibly borrow a grand piano, or better still, a concert harp? Is that picture you have on the wall of a Spanish boy crying really going to give the best impression?

And what about the menu? Normally, you might have a cheese sambo for dinner, or, if it is a really special occasion, a toasted cheese sambo. You cannot offer such plebeian fare to your guests. You get out the recipe book some malevolent bastard – probably the one you're inviting – gave you for Christmas last year. You ponder the options. Hmmmm. Quail's eggs hand-rolled in badger dandruff? Zebra spleen splattered with desiccated polenta? Eye of stoat, toe of newt, fresh salmon lung in pee of disaffected Eurocrat? No, let's face it, you'll do lasagne again.

And who to invite? Well, I've read up on this in the gossip columns and it seems that no Christmas dinner party is complete now without a few celebrities. And the best way to attract celebrities to your party is to mention a disease of some kind on the invitation. Society people, particularly in Ireland, are very fond of disease because it gives them the chance to dress up and sashay about looking like Noël Coward characters without feeling guilty for being so rich. Some diseases, of course, are more popular than others on the charity circuit and have really been over-used. But a number of other diseases – scabies, shingles and gonorrhoea, for instance – are still available for inclusion as part of the attraction of your special evening. Some of the more minor ailments, though they cause not inconsiderable distress, have really been scandalously under-utilised. Take my own Christmas dinner party disease. 'Joe O'Connor invites you to an evening in aid of anal warts.' It has a certain ring, does it not?

Party games are obviously very important, too: charades, musical chairs, pass the parcel (or pass the buck, as it is known at the Oireachtas Christmas party). There's also, of course, Parlour Mastermind, a variation of the well-known TV quiz show where you pick a subject: say, for example, the British Royal Family, 1500 to 1939. Bertie Ahern, who I've always invited to my Christmas gathering, has a really good special subject: the Dunnes Stores' Anorak, £15.50 to £16.99.

Every year it's the same. The Christmas party season seems to start in October now. You have not got over Halloween yet, and already the time is here for getting scuttered and dancing around some subterranean fleshpot to a selection of abysmal seventies Christmas songs that you thought you had forgotten for ever. I am thinking, for example, of 'Wombling Merry Christmas' by, yes, The Wombles. There is only one good use for a womble, in my book, which is that it should be hollowed out and turned into a slipper. And I am thinking of 'So Here It Iz Merry Christmas, Everybodeez Having Fun' by Slade, a work that never fails to bring me out in a rash, although

I suppose you do have to respect the only dyslexic band in the history of rock and roll.

There is the wonderful myth that Christmas parties are good places to meet people. Well, I've been to a lot of Christmas parties in my time, and I don't think I've ever met anybody at one. You turn up full of hope. You talk all night to the people you came with, about the people who were supposed to come with you, but didn't. You go home alone and stare at the television test-card for an hour before falling asleep with a cigarette in your hand and setting fire to the sofa. There's nothing you can do about this. It's like age, gravity and the phone company; ain't no point in trying to fight it. Ordinary parties are bad enough. But the Christmas office party is a vile scraping from between the gnarled toes of Satan. You turn up in the pub at 6.00 p.m., full of resolve not to go too over the top. You have to work tomorrow, after all. By 7.30 you are already tipsy. By 8.05 you are laughing maniacally for no apparent reason. By 8.15 you are reciting Monty Python sketches. (Nudge nudge, wink wink, say no more.) By 9.10 you are having a vicious argument with your best friend about Bosnia, the North or Aston Villa. By 9.15 the manager is telling you that he doesn't care whether you're a regular or not, any more language like that out of you and you're bleedin' barred.

You go to the jacks to splash water on your face. You peer at yourself in the mirror. You look like an overgrown intestinal parasite. One of your colleagues is locked into a stall busily getting off with another one. It's not that you're jealous exactly. It's just that every time they take a break from snogging the living daylights out of each other, you can hear them blithely conversing about how strange you are. You notice, suddenly, that there is a cigarette vending machine on the toilet wall. You think this is a marvellous innovation. You have spent fifteen quid before you realise that you have accidentally blundered into the ladies and you are actually feeding all your change in the tampon machine. In the restaurant, you end up sitting beside the one person in the office you truly detest, but you are so drunk that you suddenly find them strangely attractive. You suggest just skipping dinner and going back to your place. You then spend several hours nursing your sore face and pondering the delights of fizzy potato salad and greasy ham. You go to a nightclub. You jig around like a recently released lunatic. Fighting your way up to the bar, you bump into somebody you used to go out with. They are now happily married, with a beautiful child. They have given up the cigarettes and gone into therapy and lost two stone. Hearing all this just makes your night. They ask you if your life is still as disastrous as it used to be, and you laugh out loud and say you always liked their sense of humour. But you notice that, funnily enough, they are not laughing.

When the nightclub closes you go back to the office to have a few more scoops. Before you know it, normally sober people whose professionalism you admire are removing their trousers and photocopying their bottoms. You turn on the radio. John Lennon is singing 'So This Is Christmas And What Have You Done?' You hurl the radio through the office window. You reflect that you should have actually opened the window before you did this. You stagger outside and indulge in that ancient Dublin Christmas tradition known as waiting two hours for a taxi. When one finally comes, you get in. You ask the driver if he's busy. 'Ah jaze,' he sighs, 'it's fierce fookin quiet this year, boss. But sure, it's for the kids really, isn't it?' You take a deep breath. You open your mouth. You scream.

And then it comes. And it goes in a day. And then there is the aftermath of the festive season to be undergone. 'How did you get over the Christmas?' is the bizarre question which Dubliners ask each other at this odd time of the year. The quirky enquiry assumes that Christmas is an obstacle of definable height, and that the struggle to get over it is akin to vaulting a barbed-wire fence, trampolining over a moat or lepping a brick wall with those bits of broken bottles on the top of it. It also assumes, by implication, that Christmas is something you could tunnel under, slip surreptitiously around or blow into smithereens using dynamite. Very sadly, none of this is true, however. Like torture, puberty or unrequited love, Christmas is something which must simply be endured. How did you get over the Christmas, indeed. I got over the Christmas the way the Christians got over the feckin lions.

There is only one answer to this question, by the way. The response to 'How did you get over the Christmas?' is now, was always, and always will be, 'Ah, it was quiet enough.' No matter what the actual volume of your Christmas was – if you spent the festive season in a padded cell, or if you spent it with your head wedged between two stereo speakers listening to the finer moments of the *Jimi Hendrix Experience* turned all the way up, Spinal Tap-wise, to eleven, until your ears bled – it was still 'quiet enough'. And no matter what happened to you over Christmas, no matter if the ceiling fell in and nearly set the poor Ma's heart astray, if you had both legs amputated following a bizarre gardening accident, if you accidentally blundered into Lillie's Bordello after the office party and managed to get off with Claudia Schiffer during the slow set, your Christmas was 'quiet enough', and no variation on this dialogue is permitted. Try it out yourself, gentle reader. Ask any Dublin taxi driver – assuming every last one of them hasn't fecked off to the Caribbean with the spondulix they made over Christmas! – ask any one of that proud body of peripatetic philosophers, 'Excuse me, driver, but may I be so bold as to enquire, how did you get over the Christmas?' and just see what he says. Anything other than a piteous snuffle, a resounding fart, and a murmured 'Ah, quiet enough' gets a night on the tiles, all expenses paid by New Island Books.

January makes you happy. You are well and truly 'over the Christmas' by now. At this stage your presents will have been enthusiastically opened, hyperbolically appreciated and then briskly fecked into the dustbin. Unless, of course, a pair of lurid socks, a bottle of aftershave that smells like a sick terrier's sputum and a remaindered copy of that very attractive coffee-table book, *The Complete Combine Harvesters of Bulgaria*, are genuinely what you always wanted for Christmas. It's all over now, Baby Blue! Ain't that grand?! By now you will have placated your last unpleasant relation, scoffed your last cold turkey sarnie, endured your last dismal rerun of the Morecambe and Wise 1973 Christmas show. Christmas is no more! The time is here for the making of New Year resolutions.

This, I must say, is the time of year when I am most full of resolve, and I don't just mean the fizzy stuff that tastes unpleasant and gets rid of a hangover. I love resolutions. My favourite resolution is, of course, to give up smoking. My second favourite is to lose some weight. My third favourite resolution is United Nations Security Council Resolution 705, full autonomy and independence for the Palestinian people.

But next year I think I will make a new resolution. I think I will go away to Cuba or China or some heathen place where Christmas is not celebrated and New Year resolutions are not made. It seems pathetic, does it not, being thirty-two years old and sitting under a dead pine tree wearing a paper crown and getting slowly scuttered? It is pitiful. And as for that Santa Claus fellow, I really and truly feel that he is often just not what he seems.

II   Sanity Clause

STARK STARING SCREAMING MAD. THAT IS WHAT I MUST be. Here I am, in Arnotts, on a busy weekend afternoon close to Christmas, dressing up as a fat old dipso with a white beard who consorts with reindeers and dresses like a Lower East Side pimp and lives in rural Lapland and drops down chimneys once a year. I mean, Jeez, what kind of a role model is that for kids? Still, I am trying to get into the part. I am trying to identify with the character. But it is not so much a question of Santa Claus as sanity clause. I must be bloody well bats.

I am utterly terrified. I am sweating profusely. The black boots are a size too big for me. The red floppy trousers are several sizes too small and they look, in any case, like something a member of Abba would have refused to don on the grounds of good taste. The false beard smells like a putrefying rodent that died of something profoundly unpleasant. I have not had anything quite so nasty near my mouth since I once dated a member of Young Fine Gael. To make matters worse, I have been told that I must remove my glasses. Santa Claus does not wear glasses, apparently. He is blessed with 20/20 vision, which is a very good thing, I guess, if you have to drive a sleigh, particularly at Christmas, when there are so many drunken bowsies on the roads. But without my glasses I am as myopic as a bat with a bag over its head. I am about to make a spectacle of myself, and I don't even get to wear my spectacles. The world is a blur. I am definitely getting onto the union.

The real Santa Claus is giving me some advice about the kids. You talk to them a bit, he says. You ask them what age they are, where they live, where they go to school, what they want to find in their stockings on Christmas morning, apart, of course, from their feet. You tell them they have to promise to be good. You don't promise to bring them exactly what they ask for, because even Santa feels the pinch in these difficult times, but you say you'll do your best. If they want to sit on your knee while they're getting their photo taken, you let them, but you don't suggest it, because parents have got a bit sensitive about that kind of thing in the last two years. I want to stop rearranging my beard and ponder the true sadness of a world where a remark like that could be uttered but I don't have the time because a long queue is already forming outside the grotto. There are several hundred shrieking children eating lollipops and ice creams, and hyperventilating and tripping out on sugar overdoses and yelling and singing and fighting and loudly demanding expensive presents and driving their parents nuts and indulging in that important stage of the early learning process known as grabbing your sister by the pigtails and yanking on them until she fells you gibbering to the floor with a brisk kidney punch. It is my job to pacify these monsters.

My heart is pounding as I grope my way towards my seat. My first punter appears, a lovely little fellow of three or four in dungarees and a Superman shirt. He totters towards me, grinning broadly, hands outstretched. 'Ho ho ho, little boy,' I say, 'and what do you want for Christmas?' He promptly bursts into tears of shrieking horror, steps backwards and performs a Fosbury flop into the arms of his mother. I am not doing very well.

The next customers arrive: two sisters aged four and five. I ask them where they live. 'What do you mean?' one says. I begin to panic. I hadn't realised it was a trick question. 'Emmm,' I say, 'you know, where in Ireland do you live?' The younger one gazes at me. 'In a house, of course,' she says. 'But where's the house?' She begins to giggle. 'In a road,' she says. 'And the road is where?' I say. 'At the end of a lane, silly.' That 'silly' has me worried. I suspect I may be losing a little of the fundamental respect on which the Santa–child relationship is predicated. 'And the lane is near a field and the field is in the sky,' the other one says and roars with laughter. 'Right,' I say. 'Well, girls, emmm, Merry Christmas.' More maniacal laughter. 'HAHAHAHA and the sky is in the sea and the sea is in the world HAHAHAHA and the world is in Ireland and Ireland is in a lake and . . .' Their father arrives to cart them away and inject them with sedatives. He shoots me a very accusing look. More punters arrive.

The sheer innocent credulity of the younger kids tugs at your heartstrings. The thing is, you've approached all this as a bit of a gas, but you realise that they really do think you are Santa Claus. You can see it in their faces.

They are so excited. Some of them are actually quivering with joy as they come up to you. Their eyes are wide as saucers. 'I love you, Santee! I love you!!' Some of them have trouble being able to speak, they are so awestruck. After twenty minutes of all this I am feeling seriously clucky. By the end of the first hour I have practically grown a womb.

They're not all cute, of course. One fellow comes in sporting a skinhead haircut and a Republic of Ireland shirt. He reminds me of someone, but I can't think whom. He spends most of our conversation with his finger inserted into his nostril up to the knuckle. When I ask if he will promise to be good, he stares at me. 'Do yeh have to be good all the time,' he asks, 'or do yeh have to just troy to be good?' It is a question I have asked myself often, usually while drinking heavily, but just at this moment it is a little early in the day for philosophical speculation. You don't have to be good all the time, I conclude, but you do have to try. 'But Santee, are you good all the time?' he asks me.

I don't want to give the kid a complex but I don't want to lie to him either. 'No,' I say, 'I'm bold sometimes, but then I'm sorry afterwards.'

He throws back his head and begins to chortle like either Beavis or Butthead, I'm not sure which. 'I'm bold sometimes too,' he cackles, 'but I'm never ever sorry. HUH HUH HUH I'm glad when I'm bold! HUH HUH HUH.'

It is slightly disconcerting to realise that actually he reminds me of Damien, the child from *The Omen*. Even without my glasses, I am convinced that I can see the numbers 666 tattooed on the side of his head.

Then there are the kids who kind of know the score.

They tend to be eight or nine. 'Are you the real Santee?' one says.

'What do you think?' I say.

'I don't really think you are,' he answers.

'Why not?'

He grins at me. 'Well, if you're the real Santee, then how come you're in Switzers as well?'

I think about this for a moment. It is a very good question. I decide to kick for touch. 'Magic,' I say.

He scowls. 'There's no such thing as magic. There's only one Santee Claus and you're not him, because there's only three weeks until Christmas, and if you were him, you'd be too busy gettin' all the toys ready to be in here talkin' to everybody.' I can see a bright future for this kid. I wonder whether he would like to be Attorney General one day.

A little boy wants 'a new book' for his baby sister. 'Because she's after eatin' the one she had already.' One little girl would like a toy truck, because she wants to drive trucks when she grows up, like her Da. But generally traditional sex roles seem to be as strong as ever. At least half of the boys want guns or toy cars. About two-thirds of the girls want Barbie dolls.

The children are full of questions. 'What do you have for your dinner?' one wants to know. 'Do you have a wife?' 'Do you like Zig and Zag?' 'Do you have any children?' 'Do you have any brothers and sisters?' 'Were you ever small?' 'What time do you get up in the mornings?' 'Are there angels really?' 'Can you sing?' 'Does the sun ever shine in the North Pole?' 'Why is there snow?' 'Do you like Manchester United?' 'What different languages do you speak?' 'What do you do when it isn't Christmas?' 'What age are you?' 'Are you ever going to die the way my granny did?' 'Where do you go on your holidays?' 'Do you know Jesus?' 'Are you the same thing as Jesus?' One particular question – 'But when you were a little boy, who brought presents to *you* every Christmas?' – is genuinely quite perplexing. All the kids have something to say to Santa Claus. Some tell jokes. 'Santee, did you hear about the Kerryman doin' the Riverdance? He drowned.' And then some of the things they say aren't so funny. I ask one little girl with haunted eyes what she wants for Christmas. She says nothing. I tell her she can whisper it to me if she likes. 'I want Daddy to come back home,' she says, quietly. 'And I want Mammy not to be crying any more.'

Then there are the older kids, who no more believe in Santa than the Pope believes in Motorhead. They come in to see you because they're accompanying younger siblings, or because they've been forced to by their parents. One kid of about ten strides over, looking sulky, chewing gum, hands thrust into his pockets. I ask what he wants for Christmas. His lip curls into an expression so mocking that he looks like a pre-pubescent Jeremy Paxman. 'Tell Santee what you want,' I coax. He folds his arms and scrutinises the ceiling. His mother lets out a roar, 'Tell him what you want, willya, I'm after payin two fifty for the photograph of yez.' He turns and regards her as though she is something malodorous he has just coughed up and then he turns back to me. 'You can whisper it to me if you like,' I say. He nods. He leans in close to my ear. 'Dja know wha?' he says. 'You're only a fat bollocks.' I am a little taken aback, I must confess. 'Ho ho ho,' I say, clapping him on the back. 'Your arse is bleedin' hewedge,' he says. I suggest that this is no way at all to address Santa Claus and that he may get an unpleasant surprise on Christmas morning. 'So will you,' he says, 'if you come down our chimney, coz you'll set your fat fookin arse on fire.' I consider my next move as I chortle seasonally through gritted teeth. But then the sight of Santee grabbing a ten-year-old by the throat, hoiking him clear off the ground and squeezing him until he starts to squawk may not be very healthy for the mental development of those impressionable toddlers around me.

By the end of my stint I have been visited by perhaps a hundred children. I have entertained fervent pleas for mega-drives and Barbie dolls, pistols and prams, teddy bears and board games, mountain bikes and surprises. My head is pounding and I am utterly exhausted as I take my leave of the wailing, caterwauling mass and retreat to the changing room. The real Santa Claus is there waiting for me, feet up on a barrel, watching the telly. 'Howdja get on?' he wants to know. I tell him I'd rather face Iron Mike Tyson than do that again, and he tuts at me. But fifteen minutes later, back in my civvies, I pass by the grotto and see the big guy in action. He is surrounded by kids, pawing his tunic, pulling his beard, screaming and yelling. The sound of wild unrestrained laughter resounds through the top floor of Arnotts. He's joking with them, he's patient and calm and happy. And I have to hand it to him. He's the real Santa Claus, after all. I guess there's some gigs only one guy can do.

III   Christmas Pavlova

NOW I'M NOT A SNOBBISH WOMAN, AND I BLOODY WELL resent you thinking I am. I'm in Amnesty International, and Jim's family are practically from Darndale, for God's sake. I write to a black man in Kansas who is going to be

227

put into the electric chair next St Patrick's Day. I have a poor girl from down the country who comes into the house once a week for a bit of cleaning. I know all about suffering. But there are certain things that just aren't right, and I would like to tell you about one of them.

The Christmas is a very stressful time really. I have never enjoyed the Christmas very much. It is something to do with over-excitement. Christmas, to me, is crowds of bowsies in Grafton Street and stupid films full of men acting like goms on the television.

Our Victoria got out of the College of Art a few years ago and really things went downhill a little. She has her French and everything now, but she couldn't seem to focus herself at all. She tried being what they call a conceptual artist for a while. She had an erection or an installation or whatever they call them at a little gallery in town. Jim and I turned up. There were lots of people in black polo-necks and quite frankly I'm sure Jim and myself were the only heterosexuals in the room.

We all stood around drinking Blue Nun and eating lumps of Calvita and pineapple on cocktail sticks. There was a speech by some woman who was on about abortion. Then all the lights went out.

Victoria comes in wearing this boiler suit and carrying a bucket of green paint. She takes off the boiler suit. Nothing at all on except the radio. I don't know where to look. Starts putting the paint all over herself, shouting out words that an itinerant wouldn't use and I wouldn't repeat. It was about Northern Ireland apparently, the situation and so on. I didn't get it. Jim said she was making a statement. I said you didn't have to put emulsion all over your breasts to make a statement, and since when was he an art critic anyway? Jim would think

228

Louis Le Broquy was a character in *The Godfather, Part Three*.

Victoria went off to the UK last summer to paint a big mural of Nelson Mandela on the wall of a block of flats somewhere and, well, something bad happened to her, and I don't want to go into it. She came back here for a few weeks, then insisted on going off to New York. Nothing would do her except that, so we let her have her way. Well, we didn't hear much then for a time, but really Victoria has always been a little bit of a loner, so eyebrows weren't raised, not for a while anyway.

Last week I got a letter from her. 'Mum, Dad,' letter said. 'I've been back in Ireland for two months. I'm living in Ringsend. I met a fellow in New York and we got married. I'd like you to meet him.' There was a little smiling face drawn in the dot over the 'i' in her name. When I saw that I knew that things were bad.

Now I have to say I was upset, but we invited them around to the house last night, for an early Christmas dinner. I got in a sort of precooked turkey breast thing from Quinnsworth and a couple of bottles of Chardonnay. I warned Jim not to start about anything.

So last night finally comes. Everything, I must say, is looking beautiful in the house. Jim has got the tree out of the attic. He says it looks like a toilet brush, but I tell him he doesn't have to deal with pine needles. At half-seven Victoria arrives. She has lost a little weight, but she looks well on it. She's wearing a lovely black dress. It shows off her figure.

And this gorgeous creature strides up the path behind her. 'Well, well, well,' I think. 'Not bad.'

Richard is about six foot one. His skin is very lightly tanned and his nails are beautiful, I notice, when he shakes hands. He is wearing a kind of a crumpled white shirt, and very tight jeans. You can practically read the dates on the coins in his pockets, if you know what I mean. He is all there anyway, that is for sure, you can practically read his Visa card number, if you know what I mean, and his shoes are beautifully polished.

'Richard, Dad, Dad, Richard, Richard, Mum, Mum, Richard,' Victoria says. We all shake hands. He has gorgeous eyes.

'I hope it isn't too awful for you, Richard,' I say, 'meeting your mother-in-law.' Well, you have to make an effort.

He takes my hand again, and his fingers are as soft as a girl's. He kisses my knuckles. 'If I'd've known she was so beautiful,' he says, 'I'd've made Vicky introduce us earlier.'

He turns around to Victoria. 'Bubble,' he says. 'why didn't you ever tell me your mother was like Audrey Hepburn.'

'Oh, now Richard,' I say, 'would you get up the yard with yourself?' But my face is very hot, and I feel myself blushing. I show them into the lounge. 'Help yourself to nibbles,' I tell them. He winks at me.

In the kitchen I pour myself a vodka and I put the sprouts on. I don't feel the best. I feel a bit tense. It is a very long time since I have been compared to anything at all, never mind Audrey Hepburn. Actually, I tell a lie, Jim does compare me to the Creature from the Black Lagoon sometimes, but that is just his manner, and I know that basically he is ignorant. I take another sip of vodka and I bring in the smoked salmon.

Richard is very bright. He is the kind of person who actually understands the Beef Tribunal. He is a member of the Dublin South East branch of the Progressive Democrats. He campaigned for Michael McDowell during the last election, he tells us. He seems to know all about transfers and quotas, that kind of thing. His voice is just beautiful. We all agree that it is great about Dr Bhamjee getting in. Jim is already quite drunk. He cracks a pretty second-hand joke about cowboys and Indians, and Richard has the decency to summon up a dutiful giggle.

'And where are you from yourself, Richard?' I say.

'Actually, Geraldine,' he says, 'I'm from space.'

Well, Jim practically vomits he laughs so much. Jim just thinks that is some kind of panic.

'No,' Richard smiles. 'I really am from space, Geraldine.'

I know I'm going to say something now, and I hope it comes out the way I mean it. 'Well now, we're all from space,' I say. 'Women more than men, actually. I often think women are very lunar.'

'Yes,' Jim says. 'You are anyway.'

Richard peers at me. 'I'm from a very small planet called Veeblax One,' Richard says. 'It's quite far away actually. It's a bit of a hike, but it's very beautiful.'

'Get away, Richard,' I laughed. 'You're a terrible chancer.'

'Will I show them, Lambchop?' Richard says to Victoria.

'Yes, Loveboat,' she says. 'Show them.'

So he opens up his shirt and this enormous tentacle, I suppose you would call it, plops out, a big long black thing like a hoover extension, jerking all over the table, sort of throbbing. It has suckers all over it, too. That's what got me. The suckers.

Jim, as you can imagine, is in hysterics now. There are tears rolling down his face.

Richard seems to be encouraged by that. He stands up and unscrews his head. I'm not joking you now. I just don't know where to look. His hair and his face seem to sort of lift right off. Underneath he is a big greyish-white bloated blob, like a jellyfish. He has no eyes at all to speak of. Of which to speak, I mean, sorry. He unzips his jeans and takes them down. He unscrews his false legs. Apart from his tentacle, which looks obscene, he is one big blob of jelly. He looks just like a dessert.

The one good thing is, it certainly wipes the smile off Jim's face.

'Jim, dear,' I say, 'I need help with the sprouts.'

Jim follows me into the kitchen. He has his hand down the front of his trousers and he is scratching his private parts, the way he always does when he is confused.

'Well, it's a turn up for the books,' Jim says.

'Jim,' I say, 'this is Glenageary. Be serious.'

'I know it's Glenageary,' he says. 'Could I ever forget?'

'And what are they going to live on?' I say.

'Veeblax One, I suppose,' he says.

I stand there with my arms folded, looking him up and down. I tell him he is terribly funny altogether, and I ask him if he has ever considered leaving the bank to go on the television. He just turns away.

'It's as long as they're happy surely,' he says.

'Happy,' I say. 'Don't make me laugh. Don't you happy me. No son-in-law of mine is going to have a tentacle, I'm sorry.'

Victoria comes in then. She starts on about how it is difficult to understand, but love is love and all the rest of it. I tell her not to be going on with nonsense. When

232

young people start going on about love is when you have to let them know what's what. You know nothing about love until you have lived with a man for at least ten years, in my book. When you have watched a man take off his shirt and smell his armpits every night for ten years, then you can talk to me about love.

'I'd rather you married someone from Darndale,' I say. 'That's how let down I feel about it.'

She starts to cry then, and I tell her I don't mean it, even though actually I do.

'What about, you know?' I say. 'You know, the physical side, what about that? I mean how would you make love to something like that?'

'Delicately, Mother,' she said, 'very delicately.'

I pour myself another large vodka. We are out of lemons.

'Can you not make an effort?' Victoria says. 'For me?'

Well, I go back in and I try my best, but I have to say the evening goes downhill for me. He is kind of puffing and swelling now, like something you'd see in that programme about the things that live under the sea. Victoria is unscrewing his arms. His mouth is a sort of flap of jelly and Victoria keeps chewing his food up for him before putting it in there. He has no arms or legs at all. No head even, just a little lump. A nodule, apparently, is the correct term, so Victoria tells me. He keeps slithering off the chair and onto the floor, bouncing like a bloody basketball. He moves about with his tentacle, sort of dragging himself along. Every time he rolls a bit he leaves a trail of black slime behind him, all up and down the carpet. It is definitely not very hygienic.

I have bought Jim a new wheelbarrow for a Christmas present and we have to put Richard into it, to stop him from flopping around. We do that, and then we chat a bit more about the weather and the price of eggs. Richard is a great admirer of Monica Barnes, he says. He thinks it is an awful pity that she didn't get in this time, and we all agree. Everything is grand, until the younger ones get back in from the disco. They get a terrible shock when they see him. Victoria suggests a breath of air.

'Oh, he does breathe, does he?' I say. 'Well, that's something.'

Victoria pushes him up and down the patio for a while, in Jim's wheelbarrow. And he is terribly upset, the poor fellow, because he thinks he has embarrassed everyone. Little blue tears are coming out the top of his nodule. Well, I feel awful then. We all have feelings under the skin, I say, even people who don't actually have skin so much as membrane. He stretches out his tentacle towards me and I give it a bit of a rub. 'Please don't tell the Progressive Democrats,' he keeps saying. 'Please don't tell Mary.'

When I go back inside the younger ones are crying, and Jim is trying to reason with them. I tell them they will understand everything when they are older, but they won't stop. I stand up then, and I'm afraid I shout at them.

'You will be happy,' I roar, 'or you know what you will bloody well get. CHEER UP, FOR GOD'S SAKE. IT'S BLOODY CHRISTMAS, ISN'T IT?!'

Victoria pushes Richard back into the living room. He seems to have gone a bit purple. 'Richard wants to sing a song,' she says, 'don't you, Sweety Drawers?' I close my eyes and say a prayer to Saint Jude.

Victoria goes up to get her old guitar from the bedroom, the one she had when she was in the folk group in

234

Sallynoggin Church with all those nice nuns who wear cardigans. 'Make it a good rebel song,' Jim says, and Richard laughs.

I am a fifty-year-old woman, I think. Both of my parents are dead now. I have four children. My husband works in the Allied Irish Bank at Number One Upper Baggot Street, Dublin 2. I live in Arnold Grove, Glenageary. It is the week before Christmas. There is an alien in my living room who is about to sing 'Wrap the Green Flag Around Me, Boys'. Where did my life go so terribly wrong?

Victoria puts her arms around Richard and lifts him up onto the dinner table. He is leaking all over the place. It is disgusting, I think, but she doesn't seem to mind. Richard starts to sing now, and Victoria strums her guitar, and he thumps his tentacle from side to side as he sings:

> O the Holly she bore a berry
> As green as the grass
> And Mary she bore Jesus
> Who died on the cross
> And Mary she bore Jesus
> Our Saviour for to be
> And the first tree that's in the greenwood
> It was the Holly.
> Holly, Holly, Holly, Holly
> O the first tree that's in the greenwood
> It was the Holly.

And he sings very beautifully, I suppose, but the Christmas is already bloody well ruined for me. I say this to Jim in the kitchen when the two of us are loading the dishwasher.

'What's to become of them?' I say.

He looks out the window, scratching his private parts again. 'Sure, if there's love there, anything is possible,' he says.

That starts me off. 'A lot you know about love,' I tell him. 'The way you talk to me in front of people. You seem to take pleasure in it.'

He turns around to me. His face is like a big white stupid moon. He comes over and he takes my chin in his hand. 'Oh, Geraldine, I'm sorry,' he says, 'you're the most beautiful creature I ever saw in my life.'

'Talk is cheap,' I tell him. 'Cheap, cheap, cheap.'

'You sound like a budgie now,' he says.

And I suppose I do actually laugh, even though he is so horrible to me. He wipes my tears away with his thumbs. He puts his strong arms around me and gives me a big hug and he measures my neck with kisses.

'I don't know why I ever married you,' I say. 'I could have married Brian Devereaux and gone to live in Dalkey.'

'Neither do I,' he laughs, 'but I suppose you're only human.'

'It's just as well someone is,' I say. 'In this family.'

And he takes me by the hand then. He begins to kiss me once again, and he holds me against his body, and I listen to the dishwasher chugging away in the corner. He keeps kissing me very softly on my mouth. He keeps telling me how fond of me he is, and that everything will work out to be alright, and that it's great that we're all here together, and that it will be the best Christmas we've had in years. He pushes my hair out of my eyes.

'You're so precious to me,' he says. 'You're so precious to me, Geraldine.'

That is the word, if you don't mind. Precious. I hold his body very close to me. I put my arms around his neck. We say nothing at all for a few minutes, but that is

236

alright. I hold his fingers in mine. I know that we will make love later on tonight.

And I think about getting the Christmas pavlova out of the freezer, and letting it soften up a little, before I put it into the oven.

Chapter 8

Banana Republic:
Recollections of a
Suburban Irish Childhood

IN THE SUMMER OF 1977 I WAS THIRTEEN YEARS OLD
and pretty miserable with my life. My parents' marriage
– unhappy for a long time – had finally disintegrated in
the most acrimonious circumstances. My father had
moved out of the house, applied to the courts for custody
of myself, my two sisters and my brother, and won his
case. On the day he had come back to collect us and take
us to our new home, I had asked him to let me stay living
with my mother. I felt sorry for her, I suppose, and I did
not want her to be left on her own. My father agreed that
I could do this. He was very good about it.

We lived in a five-bedroomed house in Glenageary, a
middle-class suburb of southside Dublin. There was a
large stain on the gable wall, which, if you glanced at it
in a certain light, looked like the map of Ireland. I always
thought that meant something important, but I could
never figure out what exactly. My parents, both of whom
came from working-class Dublin backgrounds, had
slogged and scraped hard to buy this house, at a time
when things must have seemed full of possibility for

them. They must have had great plans for what they would do in that house. But in the summer of 1977, with only myself and my mother living there now, the house seemed unutterably empty, haunted by lost expectations.

We fought a lot, my mother and I. She had wonderful qualities. She also had a passionate and mercurial nature, which the circumstances of her life had somehow forced down a wrong turn, so that it had taken the shape of anger. She possessed a capacity for doing great harm to people she loved, and that must have made her very unhappy. When I think about her now, I try to do so with compassion and love, because, like all unhappy people, she deserved that. But in those days, we hurt each other a lot, my mother and I. We didn't see eye to eye on *anything*. Sometimes she would throw me out of the house; other times I would simply walk out to get away from her. So what I'm saying is that I spent a good deal of the very hot summer of 1977 just wandering around the streets of Dublin by myself.

And an odd thing was happening in Dublin in the summer of 1977. All of a sudden, a strange thing called punk rock had arrived in town. People were suddenly talking about it everywhere you went. Up and down Grafton Street, in the arcades of the Dandelion Market on Saint Stephen's Green, in Freebird Records – a sleazily glamorous shop down on the quays of the River Liffey – the young people of my own age were all talking about punk rock.

At first in Dublin, punk rock was nothing much more than a feeling. I mean, nobody *knew* very much about it. It was said that it had been started over in London the year before, by a group called the Sex Pistols, who swore at people during interviews and were generally controversial. But nobody I knew had much more knowledge than that. Punk had been initially perceived as just another English invention, I suppose, another weird Limey oddity, in the same culturally wacko league as eel pie, pantomime dames and The Good Old Days.

But that summer, posters for homegrown punk rock groups – or, more accurately, groups that masqueraded as punk groups – suddenly started to appear around Dublin. I remember starting to notice them, in places like the Coffee Inn on Anne Street, where I used to go and sit for hours over a single Coca-Cola. Posters for The Atrix, The Blades, The Boyscoutz, Big Self, Microdisney, Berlin, The New Versions, Rocky de Valera and the Gravediggers, The Vultures, The Bogey Boys, The Virgin Prunes, The Radiators From Space. I may be wrong about some of these bands – I mean that I may have got their dates of birth wrong by a few months – but in my mind and memory, they all appeared in Dublin in the hot summer of 1977. I remember seeing the names of these new bands on these lurid posters, how exotic and mysterious the words seemed, how funny sometimes. There was a band called Free Booze, who had called themselves this because it was a good way to catch people's attention. And there was an odd little outfit of Northside born-again Christians who played Peter Frampton songs, and who, it was said, would never amount to anything. In the summer of 1977, they were just about to change their name from The Hype to U2.

All these bands had sprung up more or less overnight in Dublin, it seemed to me. And at around the same time, a disc jockey called Dave Fanning, who worked on a pirate radio station called ARD, had started to play punk rock on his show. Also, a strange new music magazine called *Hot Press* had just started up, carrying regular articles about punk rock, reviews of records, news of punk rock gigs. It was odd. But slowly, punk rock was starting to seep into Dublin. And in the summer after my brother and sisters went away to live with my dad, I spent many nights in my room listening to Dave Fanning, reading Bill Graham or Niall Stokes in the *Hot Press*, avoiding my mother and wondering what to make of my life, and of punk rock.

It is important to say that this was a time when Dublin did not really exist on the world rock and roll map. We had Thin Lizzy and Rory Gallagher and a Celtic heavy metal band called Horslips, but that was about it. Foreign acts simply did not play in Ireland. It would have been almost unheard of for a big American or British band to gig in Dublin. The city had no pop culture of any size or significance. But in the summer of 1977, when I was thirteen, into this vacuum stepped a monstrous and slavering spirit.

Punk had a notion of secrecy about it in Ireland, a vague redolence of semi-illegality. Someone once told me that when Freebird Records first got in copies of the Sex Pistols record *Never Mind the Bollocks*, for instance, the customs officers had obliterated the word 'Bollocks' with strips of red sellotape. And RTE, the national radio station, refused to play punk at all. 'Punk rock is junk rock,' announced Larry Gogan, then Ireland's foremost disc jockey. Punk felt kind of taboo. So to people of my age, it felt attractive.

I got a job that July, working as a teaboy on a building site in Dalkey, which was near where I lived with my mother. It was great to get out of the house, wonderful to have somewhere to go during the days. One of the labourers on the site was a tall scrawny fellow called Hubert. Hubert was about nineteen, I suppose, from the working-class suburb of Sallynoggin. His language was atrocious. He peppered his sentences with the word 'fuck', sometimes he would even insert it between the syllables of another word. One day, for instance, I heard him refer to his home town as SallyfuckinNoggin.

Hubert had worked as a bus conductor for a time, before being dismissed in mysterious circumstances and coming to lift blocks on the sites. There were two things that made his life complete. The first was pornography. He had a vast and comprehensive collection of *Playboy*s and *Penthouse*s, which had been sent over every month for some years by his brother in England. (Such publications were not then legally available in Ireland.) Hubert would cut pictures out of these magazines and sell them individually to the other men on the site, thus garnering enormous profits. It was fifty pence for a picture that featured a pair of breasts, I remember, and seventy-five pence for what Hubert called 'a gee' – a word I had never heard before, a coarse Dublin euphemism for a vagina. 'Seventyfuckinfive pence a gee-shot,' he would sigh, shaking his head and absolutely refusing to haggle.

The second thing that made Hubert's life complete was punk rock. He loved it. He absolutely adored it, and he would talk to me about it for hours at a time, while we were supposed to be working. He told me about an establishment in town called Moran's Hotel, in the basement of which there were punk rock concerts almost every night. Hubert seemed to know a lot about punk rock. It was all about being 'against society', he said, it was about 'smashing the system'. He himself was 'against society', he assured me fervently. There were legions of people in the basement of Moran's Hotel every night of the week who were also 'against society', and they had stuck safety pins through their ears, cheeks and noses to prove it.

The bands who played in Moran's Hotel were against society too, all of them. But the worst of the lot, Hubert confided, the mankiest shower of louse-ridden, no-good, low-down bowsies ever to plug in a Marshall, ram up the volume and hammer out a three-chord trick, was a band called the Boomtown Rats. They were 'fuckin' scum', Hubert would say, and he would smile in a fondly contented way when he said this, as though attaining the state of fuckin' scumhood was a development in which a person could take considerable pride. 'They don't even fuckin' wash themselves,' he would beam, although, how he was in a position to know such a thing was always kept secret.

I would have loved to go to Moran's Hotel, of course, but being under-age, I couldn't. Yet I was frantically curious about this crowd of licentious and festering reprobates, the Boomtown Rats. I wondered what they would be like. The only live act I had ever seen before was Gary Glitter, performing in a television studio at RTE. I wondered if these Boomtown Rats could possibly be as entertaining as Gary. One day Hubert told me that I would soon have a chance to find out. The Boomtown Rats had been booked to play a big outdoor show in Dalymount Park soccer ground. And there must have been a bit of a run on gee-shots that week, because Hubert had bought me a ticket as a present.

That August afternoon, having lied to my mother about my destination – I think I said I was going to a boy scouts' day out – I went to the concert with Hubert and his

243

girlfriend Mona. Mona was a healthy-looking girl, with the arms of a docker and a bewildering vocabulary of swear words. It was a very hot day and the stadium was packed full of people. Thin Lizzy and Fairport Convention were headlining the concert, but I did not care about that, mainly because Hubert had said these bands were not sufficiently 'against society'. So, like him and Mona, I only cared about the Boomtown Rats. When their arrival was announced over the PA, I thought Hubert was going to ascend body and soul into heaven, Virgin Mary-wise, so screechingly enthusiastic did he become.

I had never experienced anything quite like the phenomenal excitement as the band sloped onto the stage, picked up their instruments and began to play. I felt as though a lightning storm was flickering through my nerve endings. It's something you never really forget, the first time you hear the scream of an electric guitar, the thud of a bass or the clash of a real high-hat cymbal. The lead singer, Bob Geldof, looked like an emaciated and drooling Beelzebub, as he leapt and tottered around the boards, spitting out lyrics into his microphone. The keyboard player, Johnny 'Fingers' Moylett, wore pyjamas on stage, an act of the most unspeakable and unprecedented sartorial anarchy. The bassist, Pete Briquette, lurched up and down leering dementedly, as though suffering from a particularly unpleasant strain of bovine spongiform encephalopathy. And if guitarists Gerry Cott and Gary Roberts, and drummer Simon Crowe, looked relatively normal, you still would have had not inconsiderable reservations about the prospect of any one of them babysitting your sister.

They played their music frantic and fast, incredibly LOUD, with a curious mixture of passion, commitment and utter disdain for the audience. I loved them. I had never heard a noise like this in my life. I was nailed to the ground by it. When they thrashed into their first single, 'Looking After Number One', I swear to you, every single hair on my body stood up and promptly did the Mashed Potato.

> Don't give me love thy neighbour
> Don't give me charity
> Don't give me peace and love from your good lord above
> You're always gettin' in my way with your stupid ideas
> I don't want to be like you
> I don't want to be like you
> I don't want to be like you
> I'm gonna be like ME!

Now, this was what I called music. I went home that night with my head pounding and my heart reeling. My mother was waiting, of course, and she spent several hours yelling at me, which made my headache even worse. But I felt empowered by the music, I really did. It sounds so naive now, I know, but that's the way it was. I felt that I had witnessed a kind of revelation. I felt that life was actually very simple. All you had to do, if someone was getting on your case, was tell them to fuck away off, that you didn't want to be like *them*, that you wanted to be like YOU! I told my mother this and she didn't exactly see things my way, to put it mildly. But it was the summer of 1977, you see. It all seemed very simple.

Back in school, in September, I told my friends all about the Boomtown Rats. I had five friends: Andrew McKimm, Andrew Deignan, Nicky, Conor and John. I think we were friends because nobody else liked us. Also, John's parents were separated, like my own, and Conor's mother had died, as had Andrew Deignan's father. So we felt we had something in common, in some odd way. I think we felt we had experienced more interesting pain than other people, although, of course, being teenage boys, we didn't talk much about such things. It turned out that Conor, a shy and very good-looking fellow, had heard about the Boomtown Rats himself. He had read an article about them – he was the one of our group who used to read articles – and it transpired that several members of the band, Bob Geldof and Johnny Fingers included, had actually *been to our school*.

If I had been interested in the Rats before, my enthusiasm rocketed through the roof now. These leprous anti-Establishment scumbags had actually been to *my school*. Blackrock College, the alma mater of Irish President Eamon De Valera – this priest-run joint that had always been famous for taking in the carbuncular and prepubescent sons of the Dublin middle class and churning out obedient wage-slaves – had somehow produced the Boomtown Rats! How had this possibly happened? There was hope for us all, it seemed.

Now, Irish readers must forgive me for a moment while I explain something to our English friends. There is a television programme in Ireland called *The Late Late Show*. Its genial host, Gay Byrne, is a middle-aged man of polite manners and generally mild views. It is often jokingly said in Ireland that Gaybo is the most powerful man in the country, and, like many jokes in Ireland – as opposed to Irish jokes – it contains the seed of a profound truth. One evening that autumn, Bob Geldof and the Rats were booked to appear on *The Late Late Show*. Once again, I lied to my mother, so that I could get out of the house and go up to my friend's house to watch this.

The atmosphere in my friend's living room was electric as we uncapped the shandy bottles, passed around the solitary spit-soaked cigarette and waited for the Messiah to descend. Bob shambled onto the screen like an evil bedraggled wino and sneered his way through the interview, in a furtive southside drawl. He detested many things about Ireland, he said. He loathed the Catholic Church, he hated the priests who had taught him in Blackrock College, he disliked his father. He had only gotten into rock and roll in order to get drunk and get laid. Almost everything he said was greeted with horrified gasps and massed tongue-clickings from the audience, and wild cheers from myself and my friends. When the interview was over, the rest of the band came on and performed 'Mary of the Fourth Form', a feverish song about the seduction of a schoolteacher by a female student. As the number climaxed in a clamour of drums and wailing feedback, the studio audience was absolutely stunned.

'Well done, Bob,' smiled Gay Byrne, ever the professional. Geldof turned around, scowling, wiping the saliva from his lips with the back of his hand. 'Yeah, well, if you liked it so much,' he snapped, 'just go and buy the record.' Fuck! The guy was giving cheek to Gay Byrne now! Well, this was something new and dangerous. This was practically revolution.

In Ireland, in the late 1970s, this was absolutely astounding talk. This was the decade when one million people – a third of the entire population of the state – had attended a Mass said by the Pope in Dublin's Phoenix Park. This was many years before Mary Robinson, or the introduction of divorce, or the legalisation for gay rights in Ireland. You could not legally buy a condom in Ireland in the late 1970s, never mind go on the television and talk so blithely about getting drunk and getting laid and hating priests and disliking your father. And although I liked my own father a great deal, Geldof's pungent cocktail of motor-mouth arrogance, somewhat unwise trousers and utter disrespect for authority really did appeal to me. In time, I couldn't get enough of it.

Soon after *The Late Late Show*, my friend Conor got a copy of the Boomtown Rats' first record and he taped it for me. It wasn't really punk. It wasn't punk at all, in fact, it was just souped-up rhythm and blues played with a lot of aggression. But there were some fantastic songs on it. 'Never Bite the Hand That Feeds' and 'Neon Heart', for instance. The music was raw, brimming with verve and a crisp visceral energy. But there were other things I admired about it. The songs were full of characters. I liked that. It made the songs seem like they were about real people. And there was a surprising facility for language, a gutsy pared-down approach to storytelling:

> Sooner or later, the dawn came breaking
> The joint was jumping and the walls were shaking
> When Joey sneaked in the back door way
> Pretending he was with the band, he never used to pay
> He used to know all the people and know all the tricks
> Used to lie up against the wall like he was holding up
>   the bricks.

But on the Boomtown Rats' first record there was also a slow piano-based ballad called 'I Can Make It If You Can'. It was a tender song of vulnerability and longing. I kept the tape beside my bed, and I would put on 'I Can Make It If You Can' every morning as soon as I woke up. I felt that this was the voice of a survivor, a guy who knew about pain. I felt he was singing to me, and to people like me, and that there was an integrity to what he was singing about. I played the tape until it wore out and couldn't be played any more. And there were many mornings around that time, I don't mind saying it, when that song really helped me to get out of bed. I can make it if you can.

The thing is, I used to get very down in those days. It began as pretty typical adolescent stuff but it got steadily worse, until it got more serious, until it became real depression. I missed my brother and my two sisters. I missed my father more than I can say, and I wasn't getting on at all well with my mother. I was supposed to go and see my father every weekend, but my mother had gotten to the stage where she would simply not let me do this. She had begun to drink too much. She was also taking drugs, sleeping pills and tranquillisers of various kinds. She must have been enduring some dreadful pain, the poor woman, but at the time, I must say, I only cared about the suffering she was inflicting on me. Her temper, when she lost it, became ferocious and unpredictable. Sometimes she would even try to turn me against my father, and against my brother and sisters. She would insist that I was not to go and see my dad, and I would not, most of the time, because I wanted a quiet life. And often when we did meet – he won't mind me saying it – my father and I had to meet in secret. A father and son, having to meet in secret, in an Ireland that never tired of spouting platitudes about family values. It's a shame things had to be like that.

I was so full of fear in those days that I would often feel fear clenched up inside me, like a fist, literally, like a physical thing. My life sometimes felt meaningless. In time, it actually got so I could see very little future at all for myself. It is a terrible thing to feel so hopeless when you're so young, but I did for a while, and I have to tell you that honestly.

If my memory is inaccurate on this point, then I ask for forgiveness in advance. But thinking back now, I truly do not think that any teacher, priest or neighbour ever lifted a finger to help my family. There were three things, and three things only, which kept me going throughout those years. Chief among these was the nurturing love and support of my father, which was constantly and unselfishly given to me and to my siblings, again and again throughout those years and since. He never abandoned me, despite what he was going through himself. The second was the support of my brother, my sisters, my stepmother and my friends. And the third was Bob Geldof.

I would listen to his song 'I Can Make It If You Can', and I would believe it. I simply felt that I could make it if Bob Geldof could. I was naive enough to think that, but I'm grateful now for the naiveté of youth. I associated myself with Bob Geldof. He became a paradigm of survival, toughness and courage. He would never *ever* get ground down by anything, I felt, and thus, if I remembered that, neither would I. As time went on, I began to think more about Bob Geldof. It was the only thing I could do. I derived an active *personal* pleasure from everything the Boomtown Rats got up to. I bought everything they released – 'She's So Modern', 'Like Clockwork', then the album, *A Tonic for the Troops*. I really did think their success had something to do with me. I felt I was involved in it, inextricably linked to it, bound up with it in ways that nobody but I could understand. I felt they were singing to me. I thought of them as my friends, even though I had never met them. Isn't that funny?

In November 1978, anyway, the Boomtown Rats became the first-ever Irish group to get to the top of the British charts. On *Top of the Pops* that week, as he jabbered the words of 'Rat Trap' into his mike, Geldof shredded up a poster of Olivia Newton John and John Travolta, whose twee single 'Summer Nights' the Rats had just ousted from the number one slot. In school, my friends and myself were speechless with joy. Conor cut a photograph of Geldof out of the *Hot Press* and we stuck it up in the Hall of Fame, where the framed images of all the famous past pupils of the school had been hung. We stuck Bob up there, among the bishops and diplomats and politicians who had founded the state in which we lived. His gawky snot-nosed face fitted exactly over a photograph of President De Valera, and this fact had the kind of exotically cheap symbolism that appeals very greatly to fourteen-year-olds. It felt like a victory of sorts at the time, and if I am honest, it still does.

Soon after that, things in the life of my family began to worsen again. My mother took my father to court and somehow won back custody of my two sisters and my brother. It was a decision that would lead to great unhappiness for my family – some would say it was an amazingly stupid decision by the courts. But in holy Catholic Ireland, bizarre legal opinion too often takes precedent over the rights of terrified children, or it did then, at any rate. Things went from bad to worse in the house. There were constant rows, terrible arguments. My father was routinely and absolutely denied access to us, and nobody official ever did a thing to help him. And there was fear. We experienced terror, the four of us children. We never knew from one moment to the next how my mother would behave towards us. There were many times when she treated us well, with the affection and love that I know she had for us. But there were other times when she seemed to see us as enemies, and at those times, the atmosphere in the house was close to unbearable. I don't know how we got through it. I sure as hell couldn't do it now.

I listened to the Boomtown Rats all the time. I would listen to them for hours on end, and let them send me into a kind of comforting trance. 'I Don't Like Mondays', 'Diamond Smiles', I knew the words of their songs off by heart. I would recite them, over and over again in my head, over and over. There were many nights when I went to sleep with the words of 'I Don't Like Mondays' rattling around in my head, many mornings when I woke up still silently reciting them, like a prayer.

In December 1979, the Boomtown Rats came back to Ireland. They were supposed to play a big concert in a marquee in Leixlip, but they had been denied permission by the authorities at the last minute. The Boomtown Rats were seen as dangerous and anti-Establishment in Ireland, such was the murderous innocence of the times. The band took the authorities to court, and lost. That Christmas, my parents were back in court, too. I went along with my mother, but the judge told me to leave. When I came out of the court and into the huge circular hall of the Four Courts building in Dublin I was upset and crying. An odd thing happened, then. Fachtna O Ceallaigh, the Boomtown Rats' manager, was standing on the other side of the hall with his lawyers. I recognised him from the newspapers. His case was on at the same time as my parents' case. He was just standing there with his hands in his pockets, looking cool as fuck. He might have been wearing sunglasses, although I'm not sure. But I was very glad to see him standing there. I felt it was a good omen. It made me think of Bob.

Christmas was dreadful that year. Terrible. The atmosphere in the house was one of pure fear. Early in the new year the Rats released – unleashed would be a better word – the single 'Banana Republic', which deftly summed up their feelings about Ireland, by now feelings that coincided greatly with my own.

> Banana Republic, septic isle
> Suffer in the screaming sea
> Sounds like die, die, die
> Everywhere I go now
> And everywhere I see
> The black and blue uniforms
> Police and priests.

It was a devastating attack on a society whose achievements in posturing cant and hypocrisy had so far outstripped its achievements in morality, and it was delivered with force and power, at a time when it needed to be so delivered. Nobody but Geldof would have had the guts to do it. I don't know how anyone else felt about it at the time, and to be absolutely frank, I don't care. I admired Geldof for calling it the way he saw it, and I still do admire him for that.

But it was to be the last big single for the Boomtown Rats. Not long after 'Banana Republic', things started to wane. There were rumours of drug-taking in and around the band, I don't really know if they were true or not. One way or the other, I think the Rats simply began to lose their way as the tastes of the record-buying public started to change. But I still chart where I was in those days, and what I was doing, by remembering their singles. 'Elephant's Graveyard' was January 1981, the month after my parents' last court case. 'Go Man Go' was August 1981, just before my eighteenth birthday, the month my mother had to go into hospital for a fortnight.

We never told my father about my mother's absence. Instead, we stayed in the house by ourselves and we went pretty wild, my brother, my two sisters and I. We stayed up late, we did exactly what we liked, we painted the words BOOMTOWN RATS across the front doors of our garage. We were drunk with freedom. We practically trashed the house. We moved four mattresses into one room, and we slept there, with the door locked. That's the kind of dread we had. We left the Boomtown Rats on loud, almost all the time. That's what I remember now, the blankness in the eyes of my siblings, the intoxicating light-headedness of fear and freedom, the thud of the bass coming up through the floorboards, the nasal roar of Geldof's voice. When you are in trouble, it is odd where you find consolation.

When my mother came home from hospital, it was clear that things could never be the same again in the house. We had tasted something like liberation, and would not easily go back to being suppressed. One Sunday afternoon, three weeks after she came home, my two sisters ran away and returned to live with my father, where they were treated with the love, affection and respect they deserved. They never came back to Glenageary.

'Never in a Million Years' was released in November 1981, just after I started college. That month, things got too much for me at home and I moved out too. My father helped me to get a flat near college. I made some good friends in university but I wasn't happy. I had the habit

254

of telling people barefaced lies in those days, for pretty much no reason at all. I think it was something to do with our former existence at home. It had been an environment where lies had become the norm for survival, and where the truth was often to be feared. So I hurt some of the new friends I had made by carrying this bizarre approach to the notion of truth out into the real world. I also felt ripped apart with guilt and self-loathing for leaving my brother. I sometimes went to meet him in the afternoons – he attended a school just down the road from the campus – but, as had been the case with my father, we had to keep our meetings secret. One day when I went to see him he had brought along the copy of *A Tonic for the Troops* which I had left in my mother's house on the day I had finally run away. That tore me to pieces, I don't know why.

'House on Fire' was released in February 1982, when I was going out with a girl called Grace Porter. 'Charmed Lives' was June the same year, just after we broke up. 'Nothing Happened Today' was August 1982, just after I finished my first-year exams. Almost everything that happened to me in those days, I am able to mark with a song by the Boomtown Rats. They may not be the greatest records ever made, but they're memorable to me, because they were involved with my life, and with the things I was doing, and with the people I knew and cared about.

The single 'Drag Me Down' came out in May 1984. I remember this, because I bought it one cold afternoon in Dun Laoghaire Shopping Centre, before getting the bus up to Glenageary to visit my mother. She was surprised to see me, she seemed pleased at first. We talked for a while, although I don't recall much about what was said.

I remember she asked me if I had a girlfriend now, and I said no, I didn't, for some reason, although in truth I did. I smoked a cigarette in front of her, and she was shocked that I was smoking. We had an argument, then, and we parted on bad terms. It was the last time I ever saw her. My mother died nine months later in a car crash. It was a Sunday morning. She was driving to Mass.

I went to Nicaragua that summer. I was utterly bewildered and confused about my mother's death. I couldn't really figure out what to feel about it, besides a grief of such depth that I couldn't understand it. I think I was probably a bit crazy, and longing to find some kind of frame into which I could fit the events of the last few years more clearly. So I ran away to Nicaragua to be by myself. I took a tape of the Boomtown Rats' last album, *In the Long Grass*, and also a tape of their last ever single, 'A Hold of Me'. In some ways I wanted to forget about home, and in other ways I wanted to remember every last thing.

But it's odd, the stuff that happens. One of the first people I met in Managua was Lyn Geldof, one of Ireland's leading journalists, and also, *inter alia*, Bob's sister. She's a terrific woman, very smart and bright and funny, and I was lucky enough to get to know her a little bit while I was there. Now, Bob had said some pretty critical things about his family life, but he hadn't ever spoken about Lyn much. I thought she was really lovely, and that Bob was very lucky to have a sister like that.

That was the summer of Live Aid. Many people with left-wing views were uncomfortable with the idea of the project, and I was one of them, I have to admit. I felt that charity wasn't the best way to deal with the problems of the developing world. Maybe I was right, maybe I was wrong, I don't know any more. Like Woody Allen said, don't ask me why there were Nazis, I can't even get the can-opener to work. What I do know is that Geldof was clearly motivated by nothing but humanity, and that if those critics on the Left who took cheap shots at him had displayed something like the same humanity, both in their criticisms and in their politics, the world would be a better place.

I came back to Ireland and returned to college. Slowly, gradually, things began to calm down a bit in my life. But I often thought about the old days, and sometimes when I did, the Boomtown Rats would come into my mind. Their career seemed to have petered out by that stage. Geldof was probably the most famous person in the world, but the band hadn't made a record in a long time, and they seemed to have no plans to do so.

And then, in May 1986, amid rumours that the band was about to call it a day for good, they came back to Dublin to play at a charity event, featuring Van Morrison, U2, The Pogues, all the great and the good of the Irish rock world. The Rats played a stormer. They blew everyone away and received a tumultuous reception from the audience. After the main set, Geldof strolled up to the microphone for an encore. He seemed taken aback by the warmth of the crowd's affection. At first – unusually – he didn't seem to know what to say. He appeared a little lost as his eyes ranged over the crowd. 'Well, it's been a great ten years,' he muttered, then. 'So, rest in peace.'

The thundering drum roll began. The opening riff pounded out. The familiar chords: D, A, G, E. The last song the Boomtown Rats ever played in public was their first song, Geldof's hymn to snot-nosed anarchy and adolescent attitude, 'Looking After Number One'.

257

Don't give me love thy neighbour
Don't give me charity
Don't give me peace and love from your good lord above
I'M GONNA BE LIKE ME!!

It was at once a powerful homecoming, a stylishly ironic act of self-deprecation and a poignant farewell. And in some odd and quite profound sense, it seemed like a farewell to me, too, a final goodbye to a time in my life that was over now. As I watched the show on television that day, I knew that I would leave Ireland again soon, that I would not come back for a long time, that I would try to forget about most of my past.

I came to England four months after that. I went to Oxford to do a doctorate, didn't like it much, dropped out. I came to London then, decided to stay there because I liked its anonymity, its vast size. All the things that other people hated about London, I loved. It was a great place in which to get lost, and that's what I did for a while, just kept to myself and got lost.

Gradually I lost touch with my old school-friends. I had ups and downs in my personal life, times of great joy, too. I moved flat three or four times, and somewhere along the way I left behind all my old Boomtown Rats records. But I remember their force and power still, the healing power of their righteous indignation. And I suppose that sometimes the words don't seem quite as electrifying now as they did in Dalymount Park on a summer day when I was thirteen years old and breathless with discovery. But that doesn't bother me much. Because great pop music sometimes heals us in ways that we don't understand, or in ways that seem unbelievably trite or trivial when we look back. Great pop music is about the people who listen to it, and the circumstances in which they do so, and not really in the end about the people who make it. Maybe that's what's so great about it. I don't know.

A few years ago I wrote a novel called *Cowboys and Indians*, about the love of rock music, among other things. In the winter of 1991, after a reading I did in Dublin, a girl I used to know in the old days came up to me and said that my friend Conor, who had given me my first Boomtown Rats tape, was dead. Things hadn't worked out for him in Dublin, she said. He had left Ireland, like so many of the young people I knew. He had drifted around for a while, ended up in Paris, and been happy enough there. But then something bad had happened to him – she didn't know what exactly – and he had died.

I was so shocked. I could not believe what had happened. I had a lot to drink and I lay awake for hours, just thinking about the past, unrolling images from my childhood as though looking at a film. I cried that night. When finally I fell asleep I dreamed about poor Conor. Sometimes – very occasionally – I dream about him still, and when I do, it's always the same happy dream. I see his laughing shy face on the day we stuck the photograph of Bob Geldof up in the Hall of Fame in Blackrock College. I hear him whispering, 'Let's do it, Joe, come *on*, don't be afraid.' It's not the worst way to remember him. And I'm sure the Boomtown Rats are up on the wall in Blackrock College officially now. But we beat the authorities to it, me and my friend Conor. We beat them by a whole decade.

Two years ago, I was on a television programme in Ireland to talk about my novel, and Bob Geldof was one of the guests. I was extremely apprehensive about meeting him, because he had been such a hero of mine, and because he was connected to so many painful memories, I suppose, and, also, because I've met enough pop stars to know that they usually have the intelligence quotient of a piece of toast. But he was absolutely great. He had the air of a survivor. He seemed like a man who had come through.

In the green room after the show, he introduced me to his sister Cleo, and to his father. (He described his father as 'the real Bob Geldof'.) He was very polite to everybody, he made real efforts to include people in the conversation. We chatted for a while about nothing at all, his eyes flitting around the room as he talked, his hands running through his straggly hair. When the time came to go I asked him if he wanted to come out for a jar, but he said no. He was going out for a meal with his family. So we shook hands and he got his stuff together and sloped from the room with his father and his sister, a guitar case under his arm. It was like watching a part of your past walk out the door.

I never got the chance to tell him what was on my mind that night. There were too many people around, and, anyway, I suppose I hadn't really found the words I was looking for. But when I think about it now, what I wanted to say was actually very simple. It was this: I didn't have the worst childhood in Ireland by any means. I had some things that other kids could only have dreamed about. I had them because people who loved me worked hard and made sacrifices to ensure that I would, and for those blessings I am grateful and always will be. But there were bad things, too. There were dark days. I don't say it to blame or to hate, just to acknowledge that there were very dark days. Just to tell that truth. We in

Ireland need to tell the truths of our past if we are to build up the decent and compassionate and merciful home that all our children deserve to live in. This country could be an absolutely wonderful place. For me, it wasn't always. And Bob Geldof helped me through. When I was a scared kid, who felt that there was little point to life, his music and his example were second only to the love of my father and my stepmother and my brother and sisters in keeping me going through all the terror and misery. It helped me survive. It helped me sit out the dark days, and wait for the better times to come. They did come. They often do. And I don't care whether nobody likes the music now. Tastes change, and times change, and so they should. Besides, a hell of a lot of people didn't like it then. But *I* did. Big time. His music embodied a world-view with which I felt I had some connection. It opened my eyes to things that had never occurred to me before. Like the greatest pop music, it was fun, unpredictable, alive, iconoclastic, intelligent, witty, danceable, tender when it wanted to be, tough as nails when it had to be. It just made me feel better. It healed. And it made me think I could make it, if *he* could. A foolish and adolescent belief, if ever there was one. But in a world where I had to grow up too fast, at least Bob Geldof and his band allowed me to be foolish and adolescent just once in a while.

I'm grateful indeed, for that little, or that much. I'm very grateful for that.